Fodors POCK[ ] S0-AJJ-071

amsterdam

Portions of this book appear in *Fodor's The Netherlands*

fodor's travel publications
new york • toronto • london • sydney • auckland
www.fodors.com

contents

On the Road with Fodor's   v

Don't Forget to Write vi

📖 introducing amsterdam   2

☞ perfect days and nights   28

✗ eating out   34

🛍 shopping   62

🪧 here and there   78

🍴 side trips   112

🍸 nightlife   128

🎭 the arts   140

🏨 where to stay   150

💡 practical information   174

📄 index   210

maps

the netherlands *vii*
amsterdam dining 38–39
exploring amsterdam 82–83
side trips from amsterdam 114
amsterdam lodging 154–155

Your checklist for a perfect journey

WAY AHEAD
- Devise a trip budget.
- Write down the five things you want most from this trip. Keep this list handy before and during your trip.
- Make plane or train reservations. Book lodging and rental cars.
- Arrange for pet care.
- Check your passport. Apply for a new one if necessary.
- Photocopy important documents and store in a safe place.

A MONTH BEFORE
- Make restaurant reservations and buy theater and concert tickets. Visit fodors.com for links to local events.
- Familiarize yourself with the local language or lingo.

TWO WEEKS BEFORE
- Replenish your supply of medications.
- Create your itinerary.
- Enjoy a book or movie set in your destination to get you in the mood.
- Develop a packing list. Shop for missing essentials. Repair and launder or dry-clean your clothes.

A WEEK BEFORE
- Stop newspaper deliveries. Pay bills.
- Acquire traveler's checks.
- Stock up on film.
- Label your luggage.
- Finalize your packing list— take less than you think you need.
- Create a toiletries kit filled with travel-size essentials.
- Get lots of sleep. Don't get sick before your trip.

A DAY BEFORE
- Drink plenty of water.
- Check your travel documents.
- Get packing!

DURING YOUR TRIP
- Keep a journal/scrapbook.
- Spend time with locals.
- Take time to explore. Don't plan too much.

EVERY TRIP IS A SIGNIFICANT TRIP. Acutely aware of that fact, we've pulled out all stops in preparing Fodor's Pocket Amsterdam. To guide you in putting together your Amsterdam experience, we've created multiday itineraries and regional tours. And to direct you to the places that are truly worth your time and money, we've rallied the team of endearingly picky know-it-alls we're pleased to call our writers. Having seen all corners of Amsterdam, they're real experts. If you knew them, you'd poll them for tips yourself.

Barbara S. Krulik is trained as an art historian and museologist. She has served as deputy director of the National Academy of Design and director of the Graduate School of Figurative Art, both in New York; organized exhibitions in England, France, Italy, Mexico, the Netherlands, and the Nordic countries; and lectured in museum management at the Reinwardt Academy in Amsterdam. Barbara lives in Amsterdam and writes on 20th-century and contemporary art and international museums.

Andrew May moved to Amsterdam almost a decade ago, after completing his post-graduate studies in historic Durham in northeast England. The Netherlands has opened up many new vistas: Andrew started out writing about classical music but soon branched into other areas, including travel. After a stint as a news reporter in the Dutch political and diplomatic capital, The Hague, he is again working freelance. As a translator from Dutch and French to English, he is gradually adding to a bookshelf of work about art, architecture —which some call "frozen music"— and urban planning.

Olivia Mollet is a native Belgian who has been living in New York City on and off for about six years. Restless, she has been known to disappear and travel whenever the city gets too small. Amsterdam was one of her first urban loves.

Don't Forget to Write

Keeping a travel guide fresh and up-to-date is a big job. So we love your feedback—positive and negative—and follow up on all suggestions. Contact the *Pocket Amsterdam* editor at editors@fodors.com or c/o Fodor's, 280 Park Avenue, New York, New York 10017. And have a wonderful trip!

Karen Cure

Editorial Director

North Sea

Schiermonnikoog

Ameland

Delfzijl

Terschelling

Groningen

Dokkum

Winschoten

Vlieland

Leeuwarden

Harlingen

Drachten

Assen

Bolsward

Texel

Sneek

Emmen

Hoogeveen

Den Helder

IJsselmeer

Meppel

Enkhuizen

Zwolle

Almelo

Alkmaar

Lelystad

Hoorn

Deventer

Hengelo

Purmerend

Apeldoorn

Enschede

Zaanstad

Amsterdam

Haarlem

Bussum

Amersfoort

Winterswijk

Hilversum

Arnhem

Doetinchem

Leiden

Utrecht

Oude Rijn

Neder Rijn

Rhine

Den Haag
(The Hague)

Lek

Tiel

Nijmegen

GERMANY

Delft

Rotterdam

Waal

Oss

Maas

's-Hertogenbosch

Dordrecht

Veghel

Haringvliet

Overflakkee

Goeree

Steenbergen

Breda

Tilburg

Eindhoven

Schouwen
Duiveland

Weert

Tholen

Goes

Bergen op Zoom

Walcheren

Beveland

Middelburg

Westerschelde

Roermond

Breskens

Terneuzen

Antwerp

Maastricht

Sittard

Aachen

Vaals

BELGIUM

Liège

KEY

- - - - Ferry

0   40 miles

Brussels

0   60 km

amsterdam

Whether you're in the mood for strolling along the canals, bicycling on cobblestone streets, eating aromatic Indonesian food, visiting a contemporary art museum, or quietly smoking a joint, Amsterdam offers it all. Praised for its tolerance throughout the centuries, it is no wonder that Amsterdam has evolved into a destination beloved by a diverse yet loyal group of visitors, each of whom finds his or her particular fancy in its accommodating streets and venues.

In This Chapter

THE MAKING OF AMSTERDAM 4 • The City Grows 5 • The Reformation 7 • The Golden Age 9 • The Decline 9 • The Depression and World War II 10 • Post World War II 11 • PORTRAITS 12 • Cityscapes 12 • Voc, the United East India Company 14 • The Jewish Community 17 • Dutch Art 18 • Sensual Pleasures 25

By Olivia Mollet

introducing
amsterdam

ONCE A BUSTLING TRADING PORT, Amsterdam has a vibrant core that is unlike any other Western European city. A small town with a cosmopolitan veneer, this city allows you to be whoever you would like to be and guides you to unexpected discoveries at every turn. Today the city has two personalities: a cultural 17th-century city built on canals and an important international business center. Its multilingual workforce, its prime central location, and lax tax laws have combined to draw business giants from around the globe. Established multinationals as varied as IBM and Sony as well as newer, technology-oriented dot.coms have taken advantage of the many resources the city has to offer. Even so, it requires only a little imagination and a gentle dose of moonlight to replace the traffic, telephone booths, construction, and souvenir shops with the romance of the canals.

An additional draw is the depth of cultural heritage to be found in its great art museums. Amsterdam's museums are filled with some of the best art in the Western world. There are the home-grown Old Masters in the galleries and art museums, as well as works by artists such as Georg Breitner, who roamed Amsterdam with his friend Vincent van Gogh and produced atmospheric scenes of the city at night and in winter. But don't judge Amsterdam art solely on its history; there is also a wealth of contemporary art. Long an inspiration for generations of artists, the attractive canals and gabled houses are popular subjects for today's Sunday painters. You can find them displaying their latest work along the water.

The city's pragmatic, liberal attitudes explain its famous Walletjes, or Red Light District, where prostitutes display their wares in the windows facing the city's oldest church (Oude Kerk). While urban misconception often portrays the Netherlands as condoning indiscriminate drug trade, in reality the Netherlands, more than many other countries, distinguishes between hard and soft drugs. It is possible to smoke a joint in a designated coffee shop since it allows "soft drugs" in small doses. It's also easy to join the locals for a drink or a cold beer on a terrace or in one of the famous brown cafés, where years of nicotine have stained the walls.

You can skim the surface of the museums and get a glimpse of the canals in two to three days, but to really savor the city's charm, a week is recommended. The city is best in the spring when the parks and window boxes are filled with flowers (yes, tulips abound), and you can get a clear view of the gables between the branches of trees not yet in full leaf. Winters can be icy, with biting winds, but one of the compensations of frozen canals is ice-skating. Afterward, warm yourself with some hearty *erwtensoep* (pea soup) from stands on the ice.

THE MAKING OF AMSTERDAM

Poet H. Marsman writes in "Herinnering aan Holland" ("Thinking of Holland") of wide rivers in a flat lowland: "the voice of water and its endless disasters / is feared and heard" (translation by Olivia Mollet). As the poem painfully but accurately illustrates, most of the Netherlands territory is swampy marshland. The Dutch have been conquering water as far back as Roman times when the Belgae, the Batavi, and the Frisian tribes occupied the area now known as the Netherlands.

While the first two tribes were eventually incorporated into the greater Roman Empire, the northernmost Frisians held on to their independence, and as a result, the Rhine served as the Empire's most northern border. To this day, the Frisians are known for speaking their own language and asserting their fierce individuality within the unified country. As the people tamed more and more of the water and dammed parts of the river IJ, more land became habitable and soon the area around what is now known as Amsterdam began to attract fishermen for its easy access to lucrative fishing waters, both in the IJ and the Zuiderzee. In 1240, the river Amstel was dammed to control the flow of water and "Aemstelledamme," or what is now known as Amsterdam, was born. Two sluices at the edge of the city still control the water level today. The city's official birthday, however, is October 27, 1275, when Count Floris V granted the people of Amsterdam toll privileges on travel and trade, thus allowing them to sail through the many locks and bridges of Holland without paying. Soon after, Amsterdam received full city stature with the right to self govern and tax its inhabitants.

THE CITY GROWS

Thanks to trade, the city grew rapidly. In 1323 Amsterdam was granted the sole right to import beer from Hamburg, which was then the largest brewing town in Europe. Because the water was so infected and germ-ridden, most people drank beer, and thus merchants began to get rich. Another invention that helped advance trade was the ability to preserve herring more efficiently, which allowed merchant ships to stay at sea for longer periods of time. When the herring then decided to move its spawning ground south, from the Baltic to the North Sea, it seemed that the roads—or the seas—were paved with gold. At the time, maritime trade in the North and Baltic seas was dominated by the Hanseatic League. Instead of joining the league, the Dutch merchants had no qualms about breaking in on the league's trade routes as well as developing new ones of

Nothing Exists but God

Benedict (Baruch) de Spinoza was born in Amsterdam in 1632, the son of Portuguese Jews fleeing persecution. The young Spinoza showed intellectual promise, and since it was his father's wish for him to be a rabbi, he studied the Talmud and Jewish medieval philosophies from an early age. As he grew older, under the tutelage of the gentile Frances Van den Enden, he was influenced by the philosophies of Descartes and Hobbes. Through the free inquiry he was encouraged to pursue, he soon developed his own unconventional views, and the Dutch Jewish community, fearing renewed persecution, excommunicated Spinoza in 1656 on the grounds of unorthodox speculation and atheism (as he later developed his philosophy, he came to believe that only one substance exists: God is all, but there is no creator God and no separation between God and the world or man).

After renouncing his father's inheritance, Spinoza was destitute and supported himself by grinding optical lenses and giving lessons on Cartesian philosophy, but he remained fiercely independent and never stopped studying, writing, or developing his own philosophical ideas. The intellectual community highly praised Principles in Cartesian Philosophy (1663), the only work he published during his lifetime under his own name. In 1670, he anonymously published the Theologico-Political Treatise, which was banned because of its advocacy of tolerance in a time of religious fervor. In 1673, he declined a teaching position at the University of Heidelberg in Germany for fear of losing his intellectual freedom in a more rigid academic setting.

Spinoza finished the cornerstone of his philosophical thought, Ethics, in 1675, but refrained from publishing it in his lifetime due to fear of censorship after rumors circulated in Amsterdam that the book argued that there was no God. His friends finally published the long-overdue Ethics after his death in 1677, thus securing his place among the great philosophers of the 17th century.

their own, and soon Amsterdam was considered fierce competition.

During medieval times, Amsterdam had remained relatively small, with dwellings mostly along the Amstel. In 1300, Amsterdam had only one church, the Oude Kerk, and two streets, the contemporary Warmoesstraat and Nieuwendijk, but it was growing. In 1452, however, a great fire razed the city and most of its wooden buildings. It was soon rebuilt with stricter regulations, and the use of mortar and brick was adopted as a safeguard. New churches as well as monasteries, chapels, and inns were added to handle the influx of pilgrims who had begun to flock to the scene of the Miracle of the Host. Legend has it that on the Tuesday before Palm Sunday in 1345, a dying man vomited up the eucharistic bread after his last communion. The vomit was quickly cast into the fire, but the host refused to burn and was later imbued with healing powers. A shrine was built to commemorate this miracle and the host became an object of worship to many. Today it is still honored during the Stille Ommegang (Silent Procession), which takes place every year on the Sunday closest to March 15. When the host allegedly cured ailing Maximilian I, Emperor of Austria, he returned the favor by granting to the city the use of his royal insignia in its coat of arms. By the mid-15th century, Amsterdam had become one of the strongest trade forces around.

THE REFORMATION

In the 16th century, separation of church and state was virtually nonexistent. Europe was firmly in the grip of the Roman Catholic Church. In 1517, when Martin Luther nailed his "95 Theses"— condemning superstition and indulgent practices within the Church—to the door of a Catholic Chapel in Wittenberg, Germany, Protestantism and its ideas for the reformation of the Roman Church spread through Europe. The Church responded fiercely, and the infamous Inquisition took its toll throughout

Europe, killing those—such as Lutherans, Jews, and intellectuals—considered heretics.

During this time of religious fervor and upheaval, Amsterdam stayed characteristically tolerant, holding its trade interests at heart. The religious struggles quickly pervaded life even here, however, and while Calvin's austere doctrines appealed to the newer wealthy merchants, Catholicism maintained its firm roots within the aristocracy and landowning classes. The Netherlands was then ruled by the fanatically Catholic Spanish King Philip II, who was known as a cruel despot. Even the Dutch Catholics could not condone the monarch's zeal, and Calvinism became integral to the natives' struggle for independence.

Intent on defeating the Reformation throughout his entire empire, Philip II introduced the Inquisition to the Netherlands in the summer of 1556, despite a counter petition signed by an inter-religious alliance of the key nobles of the city. This act marked the beginning of the long Dutch war of independence against Spain. Fanatical Calvinists organized themselves in bands of brigands nicknamed *geuzen* (beggars) and began terrorizing the land, killing priests and nuns and destroying religious artifacts in churches. In 1578, the *watergeuzen,* similar bands operating on the canals and led by Willem the Silent (he earned his name when he refused to engage in religious discussions), of the House of Orange, captured Amsterdam after a long siege and signaled the so-called Alteration. With the final backing of Amsterdam, the seven northern provinces signed the Union of Utrecht and became the Seven United Provinces, thus rejecting Spanish rule. The Dutch Republic, also referred to as Holland (the dominant province within the republic), held as its core the freedom of religious beliefs, the 16th-century equivalent of a "don't ask, don't tell policy," where one was allowed to *be* a Catholic but not to worship openly. Again, Amsterdam looked the other way when clandestine churches began opening their doors.

THE GOLDEN AGE

Amsterdam was now about to enter the 17th century, its most prosperous era. When trade rival Antwerp was recaptured by the Spanish (1589), many Protestants and Jews fled north to this historically tolerant city. They brought along information about trade routes, introduced the new diamond industry, and made Amsterdam a tobacco center. The city continued to grow and assert its place in the world economy. By 1650, the population had shot past 200,000. Fortunately, city planners had begun building the city's canal system as early as 1613 and by 1662 the familiar half-moon shape was completed. The arts flourished as a result of the intellectual influx to the city and the newly rich commissioned portraits from Rembrandt and Hals for their beautiful houses along the recently dug canals.

Meanwhile, by 1600, Amsterdam dominated the maritime trade. The Verenigde Oostindische Compagnie (VOC, or United East India Company) was founded in 1602 and held a trade monopoly from the Cape of Good Hope to Cape Horn. The Dutch ran plantations and established posts in America—New Amsterdam being the most famous example—and Africa. The Dutch were traders first, however, and since they did not have the population to sustain most of their colonies, they were not able to adopt the long term colonizing strategies employed by most other European countries. At the beginning of the 18th century, the ports of London and Hamburg became powerful rivals, and while Amsterdam remained the wealthiest city in Europe, it lost some of its enthusiasm to conquer the world.

THE DECLINE

In 1648, the war with Spain officially ended. After a period of independence with the Republic, Napoléon and his revolutionary French troops invaded Amsterdam in 1794, putting an end to their hard-fought freedom. In 1806, he appointed his brother, Louis Napoléon, as king of the

Netherlands. The king Louis set up palace in the old Stadhuis (Town Hall), but reigned without insight. The French rule was short lived and after Napoléon's defeat at Leipzig in 1813, the French departed peacefully. The Dutch proclaimed themselves a constitutional monarchy under the House of Orange with William I (Willem Frederik to the Dutch, son of William V)—they reset the counter and started numbering their kings afresh.

The first half of the 19th century proved calm except for Belgium's declaration of independence in 1830 and its secession from the Low Countries. Amsterdam woke from its torpor as the railway system began to develop and the country took to equipping itself for modern trade. The building of the Suez Canal in 1869, which facilitated travel to Asia, allowed the city to take an active part in the industrial revolution. Amsterdam's port expanded, and in 1889 the building of the city's Centraal Station, the main railway station, cut off Amsterdam's open waterfront. Population grew tremendously between 1850 and 1900, and a sudden housing problem ensued. Life in the city became harsh as the city began to outgrow itself.

THE DEPRESSION AND WORLD WAR II

Amsterdam remained neutral during World War I, and the city flourished once again in the 1920s. The Wall Street crash of 1929 rang in the beginning of the Depression, and the densely populated Netherlands was hit hard. Unemployment reached a previously unseen high of 25% and, ironically in retrospect, many poor families fled to Germany where more jobs were available. The Netherlands was unable to remain neutral in World War II, and in May 1940 German troops marched through the streets of Amsterdam. After 400 years, the country found itself in the midst of a war again. Queen Wilhelmina and her parliament fled to England and five hard years followed. After the severe winter of 1944–45, later dubbed the Hunger Winter, Amsterdam was finally liberated by the success of the Allies.

Living on the Canals

While strolling along the canals of Amsterdam, you'll notice abundant colorful riverboats moored upon their waters. In Amsterdam proper, about 2,400 families use "houseboats" as their primary residence. These boats have all the comforts of a regular, landlocked house but add a certain mystique to day-to-day living. Houseboats began appearing after World War II as an answer to a citywide housing shortage combined with a surplus of old cargo ships. Often well renovated, some of these floating houses are truly luxurious, and many serve as permanent residences. Most are connected to the city's water and electrical systems, and some are even equipped with gas heating. Their residents are taxed just like property owners; recently, the Amsterdam city council limited the number of boats allowed to moor within city limits, thereby increasing the price and desirability of these floating homes. To see what life in such a home is like, visit the **Amsterdamse Woonbootmuseum** (Prinsengracht, opposite number 296, tel. 020/427–0750), Tuesday–Sunday 10–5.

POST WORLD WAR II

The war had certainly taken its toll on the Netherlands. Only one in sixteen of its Jews had survived, and many Dutch soldiers were killed at the Eastern front. The country found itself licking its wounds. With the help of the Marshall Plan, the economy was jumpstarted and the country began its recovery. In 1948, Juliana was crowned Queen and citizens celebrated for the first time since the liberation. In the 1960s, Amsterdam became a center of radical politics and a blossoming youth culture invaded the streets. The Provos, a small, radical group, began staging actions throughout the city and, although they disbanded in 1967, their ideas were taken over by the Kabouters (or Green

Gnomes), who successfully won several seats in municipal council. While Amsterdam long remained famous for its political and social activity, free love, and drug culture, these traits were tempered. The '70s and '80s were turbulent, with various protests such as those against the underground metro, squatters' movements, and the first influx of non-European immigrants. The growing economy of the '90s brought a new kind of prosperity to the city, and like many other Western cities, Amsterdam experienced an urban renewal. Even though Amsterdam has been hailed as the new financial center of Europe, it has retained its characteristically independent and spirited edge.

PORTRAITS

CITYSCAPES

Amsterdam is situated on the southern shore of the IJsselmeer lake, formerly the Zuiderzee, 3.3 meters (10 feet) below sea level, protected from the water by an intricate system of dams and locks. As early as 1613, city planners began working on what would later become the famous crescent shape of the Amsterdam city-center, carving canals and damming parts of the marshland. It is that early well-thought-out plan that gives contemporary Amsterdam its alluring islands, 150 canals, and 400 stone bridges and allows the visitor to roam the waterfront for hours. Starting from the contemporary Centraal Station, the main train station, narrow streets and canals fan out and are traversed by a network of concentric semicircular canals. One of the most important intact historical city centers in the world, Amsterdam's center is almost small enough to be a village. Once you've worked out which way you're facing the unique ring of *grachten* (canals)— from the center outward: Singel, Herengracht, Keizersgracht, Prinsengracht, and Singelgracht—you should be able to orient yourself easily. On foot is the best way to view Amsterdam. Get a walking tour map from the VVV (Vereniging voor Vreemdelingen Verkeer—Society for Foreigners Traffic), the official tourist information center (☞ Practical Information) and follow the colored markers throughout the city.

The Amstel river, from which Amsterdam took its name, flows through the old city cutting it in half with its Oude Zijde (Old Side) on the east and its Nieuwe Zijde (New Side) on the west. The Dam Square, or just the Dam, is the city's largest square, and major roads radiate from it. But it is difficult to speak of one true center and there are many other squares and locations that compete for that title. There's the Leidseplein, which harbors much of the city's nightlife; the Stationsplein, in front of the station where you can catch buses, trams, and trains that will take you almost anywhere; the Nieuwmarkt square on the frontier of the Red Light District; the Waterlooplein, which was the center of the old Jewish Quarter and is now the home of a large flea market; and the Museumplein whose stately buildings house some of the best art collections in the world.

With the exception of the Royal Palace on the Dam, Amsterdam is not known for its churches and pompous palaces. Instead you're more likely to encounter monumental mansions built by the wealthy merchants during prosperous times. The best examples can be seen on the Golden Bend along the Herengracht between the Leidsestraat and the Vijzelstraat. Most of these buildings now belong to financial and other private institutions, but you can experience the lush interiors by visiting the Goethe Institut.

One of the liveliest neighborhoods in the city is the Jordaan. Originally built to accommodate the working class, the contemporary streets exude a blend of real life that you might miss in the other parts of the city. The pubs, offbeat shops, and little art galleries are all inviting, and as you ramble from one open-air market to another it's easy to get pleasantly lost.

Beyond the canal belt, be sure to take a walk in the Museum Quarter, which encompasses the Rijksmuseum, built by Pierre Cuypers (1827–1921), the same architect who designed the Centraal Station; the Van Gogh Museum; the Stedelijk Museum; the Concertgebouw (Concert Building); and of course, the Vondelpark, named after the poet and playwright Joost van den Vondel (1587–1679).

It is the varied neighborhoods and the canals that make the cityscape so wonderful for visitors. Even if you are visiting for a short time, be sure to stand by a canal with your back to a gabled house to contemplate and absorb the richness of this amazing city.

VOC, THE UNITED EAST INDIA COMPANY

The founding of the most powerful trade organization in Western Europe can be traced back to a voyage organized by Cornelius Houtman. After Philip II of Spain conquered Portugal and closed ports to the Dutch, it became clear that Amsterdam should become involved in sending a fleet of its own eastward. In 1595, Houtman set off with four ships on an exploratory journey. Despite the facts that only half of the original crew sailed back in 1597 and investors in the enterprise hardly broke even, the spirit of adventure was contagious and a second voyage was swiftly organized. This one managed to produce a profit, and the first trading company was founded. The Compagnie van Verre (Far Away Company) did not exist on its own for very long, however, and soon competition threatened to kill all profit.

In 1602, investors from each of the major cities in the Republic of the Seven Provinces united the existing companies and the VOC was born. It was to be the most powerful trade organization in Western Europe for nearly two centuries. Originally organized to mount safer, more cost-effective exploratory voyages and trading ventures into the East Indies, it was soon granted a monopoly on trade in the East and operated with a great degree of autonomy, including the authority to negotiate with local rulers on behalf of the Dutch Republic. At its peak the company owned 150 vessels protected by 40 fighting ships and 100,000 soldiers, sailing from the Cape of Good Hope to Cape Horn. Great wealth flowed back to Amsterdam and the city flourished. Canals were built and impressive houses rose along what is now known as the Golden Bend on the Herengracht.

Following the success of the VOC, the West Indische Compagnie (WIC, or West India Company) was organized in 1624. This was a smaller venture that held the trade monopoly between Africa and the Americas. Since trade in the Atlantic tended to be less risky as a result of shorter, less dangerous voyages, the rate of return was not as great and the company's expenditures often exceeded its income. It also suffered more competition from Spain and Portugal. Even so, it was lucrative enough to continue and accomplished several impressive feats, the most noteworthy of which is still recognized as the purchase of Manhattan island and the establishment of New Amsterdam.

Working for either company entailed a fair amount of risk and often meant being away from the Netherlands for months at a time. Consequently, the VOC and WIC recruited most of their employees among the poorer citizens of Dutch society. The workers were often underpaid, and since there was no official governmental supervision to reduce any abuse of power, exploitation of the workforce ran high and personal enrichment seemed easy for both the unscrupulous deckhand and the savvy investor. Multatuli denounced some of the practices in the Eastern Colonies, but his cries went unheard. Penalties were rarely enforced and great personal fortunes were amassed during those times, allowing Amsterdam to become one of the wealthiest port cities in Europe.

Multatuli

Eduard Douwes Dekker (1820–87), a.k.a. Multatuli (from the Latin, meaning "I have suffered greatly") was the son of an Amsterdam sea captain. A restless youth and a rather poor student, he joined the work force and at 18 accompanied his father to the Dutch Indies (Indonesia) and joined the Dutch Civil Service. At the time the Indies attracted a like-minded collection of misfits and adventurers.

While he liked the Indies and his career advanced steadily through many appointments, his strong sense of justice, coupled with his independent nature and a bad temper, made for an uneasy life in the civil service. As assistant resident to the district of Lebak in West Java, he wrote reports on the exploitation of the native population. Instead of the expected government action, his reports were ignored and he was told he was to be transferred. Outraged, he resigned and returned to Europe, where he tried in vain to see justice prevail.

After years of poverty and wandering, in 1860 he wrote and published the now notorious Max Havelaar, or the Coffee Auctions of the Dutch Trading Company, denouncing and exposing the colonial landowners' narrow minds and inhumane practices. This work shocked Dutch society, but even its commercial success failed to bring about concrete social change. In many ways Dekker was ahead of his time, and this is the first book to juxtapose an everyday colloquial style with a more formal literary form. Emotional outbursts and dry official documents sit side by side, and this intriguing composition garnered him a small circle of admirers. After his death, the fame he courted caught up with him, however, and Dutch intellectuals and progressive thinkers respect him greatly. His name has become synonymous with the pairing of a critical mind and tolerance of minorities. The new Multatuli Museum (Korsjespoortsteeg 20, 020/638–1938), honoring his beliefs and work and continuing his legacy, is open Tuesday 10–5 and weekends noon–5.

THE JEWISH COMMUNITY

Among its many nicknames Amsterdam includes "Jerusalem of the West." As early as the 16th century, Amsterdam's religious tolerance attracted Jews fleeing persecution in other European countries. The flood of Sephardic refugees resulting from religious intolerance in Spain and Portugal helped establish the first real Jewish center around the current Nieuwmarkt neighborhood. While the refugees brought inside information on the opposition's trading routes and colonies, the city's trade guilds refused to accept Jews and they could only find work in fields that did not present direct competition with the local population. Many became physicians, worked in apothecaries, and involved themselves in new trades associated with cotton and the diamond industry. Most, however, worked as laborers or small traders and lived on the margins of society. In Amsterdam, as nowhere else in Europe, they could practice their religion and were not forced to live in ghettos. They were even allowed to buy property, and eventually a bustling Jewish quarter grew.

In the 17th century, Ashkenazi Jews began fleeing the pogroms in Central and Eastern Europe, again finding refuge in Amsterdam. The two groups did not always get along, however, as the settled Sephardim resented the increased competition imposed by their often poorer brethren. Separate synagogues were built, a total of five in the 17th and 18th centuries, and the antagonism helped turn the Jewish center into a lively place.

During the French occupation in the early 19th century, the remaining restrictions on Jews were abolished and the community thrived. Real poverty still existed, and the Jewish quarter was one of the worst slums in the city. A middle class, however, began to emerge from this burgeoning scene of economic, social, and political emancipation. Many middle-class Jews chose to move away to the Plataanlaan, creating a suburb of their own.

It is estimated that before World War II about 90,000 Jews lived in Amsterdam. Only about 5,500 of those who remained throughout the war survived. Many fled the country and some became *onderduikers* (hideaways) in the city itself. Anne Frank is probably the most famous example, and today the Anne Frank House has exhibitions not only on the Holocaust, but on racial tolerance in contemporary Amsterdam as well.

The Holocaust stripped the Jewish quarter of its life, and the once-thriving area lay empty and derelict for a long time. Its dark shadows stood as a daily reminder of past horrors. In 1955, many of the buildings were sold to the city, but recovery still took decades. The old Portuguese synagogue was restored to its former glory in the '50s and now holds private weekly services. In 1987, the new Jewish Historical Museum opened a restored Ashkenazi Synagogue Complex, which houses a large collection of memorabilia, photographs, and artwork. Today the market at Waterlooplein, where the Jewish community once thrived, hosts the famous flea market and is as lively as it was in the 17th century. The Jewish community itself exists largely beneath the surface of Amsterdam, many of its constituents placing Dutch identity before Judaism.

DUTCH ART

Amsterdam has always been an international arts center. During the Golden Age of the 17th century, an estimated 20 million paintings were executed and every native seemed to have an oil painting tacked on the wall. Today, in addition to the approximately 150 art galleries that trade in everything from authentic Picassos to native hopefuls, Amsterdam has more than its share of art museums. Every June, Amsterdam hosts a month-long art fair and overnight the city seems to grow stalls selling much more than just the predictable pottery and watercolors. During this celebration, artists open their studios to the public and openings are the place not only to see art, but to be seen.

At the Anne Frank House

Anne Frank was born in Germany in 1929; when she was four her family moved to the Netherlands to escape growing anti-Jewish sentiment. Otto Frank operated a pectin business and decided to stay in his adopted country when the war finally reached the Netherlands in 1940. In 1942, three weeks after Anne's thirteenth birthday, the family went into hiding in the annex of Otto's business in the center of Amsterdam. The van Pelsen family, including their son Peter (van Daan in Anne's journal), along with the dentist Fritz Pfeffer (Dussel) soon joined them in their cramped quarters. Four trusted employees provided them with food and supplies. In her diary, Anne chronicles the day-to-day life in the house: her longing for a best friend, her crush on Peter, her frustration with her mother, her love for her father, and her annoyance with the petty dentist, Dussel. In August 1944, the Franks were betrayed and the Gestapo invaded their hideaway. All the members of the annex were transported to camps, where Anne and her sister Margot died of Typhoid fever in Bergen Belsen a few months before the liberation. Otto Frank was the only survivor of the annex. Miep Gies, one of the friends who helped with the hiding, found Anne's diary after the raid and kept it through the war. It was first published in 1947, and has been translated into more than fifty languages, selling over thirteen million copies worldwide. Anne has become the national celebrity she always dreamed of being.

In 1957, the Anne Frank Foundation turned the house into a museum (☞ Anne Frankhuis in Here and There), memorializing the persecution of Jews during World War II and mounting exhibitions on the racial issues in the Netherlands. As you pass through the bookcase and climb the narrow stairs to the achterhuis (annex) with the rest of the tour group, imagine yourself trying to be as quiet as the onderduikers (people in hiding) had to be.

Leading up to the Golden Age

To begin, it is important to make the distinction between Flemish and Dutch painting. In the late 16th century, the Netherlands was divided into a Flemish, predominantly Roman Catholic South, still under Spanish rule, and an independent alliance of seven Dutch Protestant northern provinces. Until then, most of the painters hailed from the southern cities of Ghent, Antwerp, and Bruges, and their subject matter was mostly biblical and allegorical. A few of the most influential include Jan van Eyck (1385–1441), who founded the Flemish School and perfected the technique of oil painting, and Rogier van der Weyden (1399–1464), who swept the canvas clean and focused on the personalities of his subjects, injecting an emotional intensity into his work and straying from the typical devotional pictures that were crammed with detail and symbolism and showed static groups of bodies. Two other notables were Hieronymus Bosch (1450–1516), whose meticulously detailed, macabre allegorical paintings can take hours to decipher, and Pieter Breugel the Elder (1525–69), whose scenes depicting peasant life in Flemish landscapes are an amalgam of color and texture.

In the northern provinces, around Haarlem, a different style of painting began to surface. Jan Mostaert (1475–1555) and Lucas van der Leyden (1489–1553) were on the cusp of this new movement, which brought a kind of realism into previously static and religious paintings. In Utrecht, meanwhile, followers of the Italian master Caravaggio made a complete break with mannerist painting. The chiaroscuro technique used light and shadow to play out dramatic contrasts and created realism as had never been seen on canvas before. Gerrit van Honthorst (1590–1656) is probably the most well known Dutch representative of this particular style.

The Golden Age

Out of these two disparate schools flowed the Golden Age of Dutch painting. Hals, Rembrandt, and Vermeer were all influenced by such diversity of technique. During the height of the Golden Age, paintings were mass-produced and artists specialized in different genre paintings to keep up with the demands of the market. Religious paintings and portraits remained highly popular, but maritime, city, landscapes, and other genre paintings found an outlet as well.

Frans Hals (1581–1666) is considered one of the most influential portraitists of the time. In his works he breaks with the static tradition and his naturalistic portraits capture the emotional expression of his subjects while also giving the impression of an informal, relaxed scene. His psychological portraits, however, are not generally considered as perceptive as those of his most famous contemporary. Rembrandt van Rijn (1606–69) is regarded as the most versatile artist of the 17th century and his fame is uncontested. He began his career painting commissioned portraits for wealthy merchants but soon grew bored of pleasing the increasingly political and fickle rich. His quick temper and his interest in darker subjects soon made him unpopular in those more elite circles. "The Night Watch" (1642), his major group portrait, was considered artistically innovative but failed to please his audience, and he soon found himself at the margins of "good" society; still, he continued to work. Some of his most impressive work dates from that later period in his life. Jan Vermeer (1632–72) is the third in this triumvirate of artists and is a different case altogether. He only produced 35 known paintings during his career, but these exquisite portraits of simple domestic life make him the most precious genre painter of his time. A rather reticent man, he lived his whole life in Delft and died poor.

Around the middle of the century, baroque influences began to permeate Dutch painting. Artists such as Jacob van Ruysdael, Albert Cuyp, and Meindert Hobbema started producing works that were lighter and more playful in tone. Probably the most famous recorder of riotous scenes was the tavern keeper Jan Steen (1625–79). His lively, sometimes lewd domestic scenes are imbued with humor and satire; "a Jan Steen household" suggests a scene of disorder. Steen's canvases are still a joy to see today, even if some of the nuances are lost on us.

The 18th Century

With the deaths of Hals, Rembrandt, and Vermeer and the French invasion, the Golden Age was gone for good. Following French models, painting became over-refined and stylized, falling away from its earlier innovations. Fortunately not everyone followed that school, and some painters used this period to inject more humor into established styles; Cornelis Troost (1697–1750) became famous for his delicately composed satires. It is interesting that painters such as Gerard de Lairesse (1640–1711) and Jacob de Wit (1695–1754) were masters at painting and decorating not only grand new canal mansions but public buildings as well. With the resurgence of the Catholic churches, de Wit also made a fortune painting lavish interiors.

The 19th Century

The 19th century moved toward a more documentary style of painting. The use of allegories disappeared and landscapists such as A. G. Bilders (1838–65) and Johan Barthold Jongkind (1819–91) became popular. George Breitner's (1857–1923) almost photographic renditions of Amsterdam were a welcome exception and became a precursor to French Impressionism and the Hague School. The greatest Dutch painter of the 19th century is undoubtedly Vincent van Gogh (1853–90). During his short but troubled life, he produced an array of masterworks. He did not begin painting until 1881, and his first paintings often depicted dark peasant scenes (the most famous being "The Potato Eaters," 1885) and many self-portraits. Since he never received much recognition during his lifetime, van Gogh supported himself by painting copies of famous paintings. During the last four years of his life, which he spent in France, he produced his most colorful and arresting works. In 1890, however, he committed suicide after having struggled with depression and mental health problems for years (he cut off an ear earlier in life). To this day, his powerful legacy continues to move art lovers around the world.

The 20th Century

The 20th century brought new confusions to the art scene. Unsure what style to adopt, many artists attempted to reinvent themselves. Piet Mondriaan (1872–1944) is a beautiful example of someone who evolved with his century. Early in his career Mondriaan painted in the tradition of the Hague School. Bucolic landscapes, cows, and windmills belonged to his repertoire. Then, in 1909, at the age of 41, he painted "The Red Tree," noted for its explosion of expressionism. Mondriaan once said, or so the story goes, that when he found his true personality he would drop the second a in his name. "The Red Tree" must have been a step in this direction, because he signed the canvas "Mondrian." (Dutch museums do not acknowledge that name change, preferring the original.) After flirting with Cubism, he developed a style of his own called neo-plasticism. Using only the primary colors of yellow, red, and blue set against neutral white, gray, and black, he created stylized studies in form and color. In 1917, together with his friend Theo van Doesberg (1883–1931), he published an arts magazine called *De Stijl (The Style)* as a forum for a design movement attempting to harmonize all the arts through purified abstraction. Although the movement lasted only 15 years, its impact was felt around the world and across the arts. In 1940, Mondriaan moved to New York City to escape the war.

The most vibrant movement that emerged after World War II was the experimental CoBrA (made up of artists from Copenhagen, Brussels, and Amsterdam), which was cofounded by Karel Appel

Royalty

The Netherlands, unlike most European countries, began as a united republic and was able to resist royalty until the French occupation in 1806 when Napoléon took power. In 1814, after the fall of Louis Bonaparte and another taste of monarchy, the country crowned William (Willem) of Orange king and proclaimed itself a constitutional monarchy. The House of Orange has been in power ever since. Today the Netherlands is ruled by Queen Beatrix, who succeeded to the throne in 1980. She is the fourth successive female monarch and is popular with her constituents. Admired for her openness and accessibility, she nevertheless maintains the sense of decorum expected of a monarch. Though she was groomed to be queen from early in life and under close public scrutiny, there were protests and rumblings when in 1966 she decided to marry the German Prince Claus van Amsburg. The union produced three sons, Willem-Alexander, the future heir, Johan Friso, and Constantijn. At the time of writing, the three are still single and much expectation surrounds Willem-Alexander's choice of spouse. While the role of monarch may have changed over the centuries from that of executive leader to that of figurehead, much is still expected from them. A popular anecdote tells of the Queen's three boys playing in the backyard with the two youngest exclaiming: "Don't hurt Willem-Alexander, or else we have to be king."

On Koninginnedag (Queen's Day), every April 30, the country celebrates its queen and her birth. One of the most beloved national holidays, Queen's Day was traditionally celebrated on the monarch's birthday, but when Beatrix ascended to the throne she chose to keep the former date in honor of her mother Juliana. On the eve of the 30th, streets close and a citywide street fair takes over. Musicians play and food vendors appear out of nowhere, changing the appearance of the city overnight. It's a great time to visit and experience some essential Dutch traditions.

(1921–) and Constant (nee Constant Nieuwenhuis, 1920–). With bright colors and abstract shapes, their paintings had a childlike quality. They searched for what they called a *volwassen kinderstijl* (grown-up child style), and their canvasses often provoked the rote exclamation: "My child could do that!" It was an extremely vital movement, and the artists involved continue to have influence in their respective countries.

SENSUAL PLEASURES

Sex is a big business in Amsterdam and attracts tourists from all over the world. The history of prostitution in Amsterdam, with its successful harbor, is almost as long as the history of the city. Men who were seeking companionship and comfort have been regular visitors since the Middle Ages. In the 16th century, the city's sheriff and his enforcement officials actually ran the brothels. When prostitution was outlawed, these government officials required significant raises in their salaries due to the loss of income. In the 17th century, window prostitutes were working out of their own homes. Others solicited on the streets or in taverns along the Zeedijk, but prostitution was limited to certain sections of the city. "Honest" labor for women was poorly paid, and, therefore, many women—particularly seamen's wives—supplemented their earnings with prostitution.

In the 18th century, affluent men made contacts with prostitutes at elite gentlemen's clubs offering musical ensembles and gambling and followed them back to their impoverished rooms or brothels. Because their poverty was distasteful to the gentlemen, the club owners eventually provided the prostitutes with elegant rooms in which to entertain their clients and even imported women from Germany, Denmark, and France to supplement the local talent (throughout the centuries, foreign women in the sex trade were often virtually enslaved). With the Napoleonic domination of the Netherlands, regulations for controlling venereal diseases were instituted for prostitutes.

Prostitutes were registered, checked regularly, and removed from service if found to be diseased. The customers, of course, were free to spread diseases as it was considered necessary for men to satisfy their sexual desires. The 19th century saw a dramatic rise in the urban poor and a razing of slum areas. Newly built dwellings were too expensive for craftsmen and artisans to maintain, so people started renting rooms to prostitutes and students to supplement their income. The often-privileged students, prostitutes, and artists coming together in the neighborhood stimulated a carefree and fun atmosphere that still dominates in today's Red Light District. Prostitution in Amsterdam has been appreciatively and informatively portrayed in John Irving's book *A Widow for One Year*.

Dutch pragmatism is evident in the city government's approach to the unsavory aspects of life: The goal is to control and maintain public order and safety through tolerance of existing activities. There are three official locations for window prostitution: the infamous and central Red Light District; along part of the Spuistraat on the Nieuwe Zijde; and on the Ruysdaelkade on the periphery of de Pijp. As of October 1, 2000, the permit/license system introduced in the 1990s, primarily to prevent the spread of sexually transmitted diseases by targeting the prostitutes with information and help, was extended to brothels. The women, now, have legal recourse should the brothel not meet the standards the license demands.

The Red Light District is active day and night. Most of the women are scantily dressed and dance or bounce their breasts in windows and doors surrounded with red and blue fluorescent light to highlight their costumes. Prostitutes come in all sizes, shapes, and nationalities and a rainbow of color. The narrowness of the streets, with windows on both sides, has an "in your face" boldness and the new visitor will certainly feel confronted. When visiting the Red Light District, your first stop should be the **Prostitute Information Center,** or PIC, which is also Dutch slang for penis (Enge Kerksteeg 3, tel. 020/420–7328). Founded and staffed by former prostitutes, the center provides information to prostitutes, customers, and tourists on the new laws, codes of behavior, and the neighborhood in general. For those that feel more comfortable in groups, PIC recommends tours organized by Lindbergh Excursions (26 Damrak, tel. 020/622–2766).

Come rain or shine, Amsterdam offers you myriad possibilities: a glass-covered boat to ferry you between museums in the rain, walking or cycling along the canals, or sunning yourself in the Vondelpark. Canal-side restaurants and lively bars and clubs can satisfy your desires for a romantic night or a hot all-nighter.

In This Chapter

The Perfect Fair-Weather Day 29 • The Perfect Foul-Weather Day 30 • The Perfect Romantic Night 31 • The Perfect All-Nighter 32

By Andrew May

perfect days and nights

AMSTERDAM HAS SOMETHING FOR EVERYONE, and something for every occasion, from the sophisticated to the casually informal, from the classic to the trendy, in weather good or grim. Here are some choice selections and ideas to send you off in the right direction.

THE PERFECT FAIR-WEATHER DAY

The crystal-clear light of a summer's day in Amsterdam makes a splendid backdrop for the city's varied streetscapes and gables. Through the ages this unique brightness has inspired the creative efforts of Dutch artists and brought many more from other lands to live and work in Amsterdam. On such a day, a good starting point in the morning is the Nieuwmarkt, where you can take a terrace seat and watch Amsterdam as it slowly awakens. From here, continue to the Waterlooplein wander around the flea market, famous for its new and second-hand clothes, ethnic jewelry and wares, and piles of bric-a-brac. If you have children in tow, then Artis zoo is close by, as well as the Joods Historisch Museum (Jewish Historical Museum). If you have less time, the Hortus Botanicus gardens and its tropical greenhouses are a lusciously verdant environment.

A short walk from the Amstel river along one of the stately canals of the *grachtengordel* (canal ring or girdle) will bring you to the Spiegelstraat cross-street, and to the left stands the imposing facade of the Rijksmuseum. Head under its arches to the Museumplein square, where you can promenade under the trees or bask on the lawns. Stifling weather is not the time to spend hours perusing the massive collections of the Rijksmuseum, but the smaller and more easily digested Van Gogh Museum and Stedelijk Museum of Modern Art are also ranged around the Museumplein.

If museum-hopping sounds too much like hard work, head to the Vondelpark, where locals will be lapping up the sun alongside its cooling waterways and lakes, or will be cycling and skating in shorts.

Many restaurants sprout terraces along canals and squares as soon as there is even a hint of spring, and demand for an outdoor seat is high. For dinner try the Land van Walem and its gardens—though you'll certainly have to book in advance—the terrace of Lorreinen under the shadow of the Noorderkerk church close to the Prinsengracht, or the waterside terrace of Het Gasthuys.

THE PERFECT FOUL-WEATHER DAY

With umbrellas and mackintoshes at the ready, there is no reason to have your stay in Amsterdam dampened by the weather. The maritime climate of northwestern Europe is not always clement, and grey skies and rain feature regularly in spring, autumn, and winter. A museum-filled capital like Amsterdam is ideal for filling your day with indoor activities.

Start out at the Anne Frankhuis (Anne Frank House), to discover how the Nazi occupation affected the local population, Jew and Gentile, during World War II. From here you can travel by glass-covered Museumboot or Circle Tram 20 to the Rijksmuseum, where even an exploratory tour of the myriad galleries of Dutch masterpieces and applied arts takes a couple of hours. The Van

Gogh Museum and the Stedelijk Museum of Modern Art are only a short dash across the Museumplein square. The museum cafés serve sandwiches and snacks for a lunchtime break without venturing out into the rain showers.

If you want to make for the shopping malls, there is covered shopping at the Magna Plaza and the Kalvertoren. However, if you are in this part of town, make sure to pass through the Begijnhof courtyard on the way to the adjoining Amsterdams Historisch Museum, to gain some insight into life in the city in ages past.

A potent *genever* (the local gin), sipped in an old-style *bruine café* (brown café), is a warming aperitif that will give you a flush for the evening. Traditional Dutch food is ideal for a cold winter's night, so an *eetcafé* (a casual restaurant/bar) is a good idea for dinner. At restaurants expensive and moderate, Amsterdam's chefs are expert in the preparation of seasonal game, and as winter closes in they create dishes that are a great antidote to a day under oppressive clouds.

THE PERFECT ROMANTIC NIGHT

A view of a canal or lapping waves while dining can't be beat for romance, so make sure to reserve a table by the window in advance. Waterside restaurants include Pier 10 and the Wilhelmina-Dok, the latter including an enchanting trip across the IJ river by ferry. Equally intimate are the small Kint Co. and the art deco interior of De Belhamel in the city. If you can flash the cash, then head to the glamorous surrounds of the restaurants La Rive at the Amstel Hotel or Breitner. Most of Amsterdam's mid- to upper-price restaurants have a hushed, civilized atmosphere, and you will find sufficient privacy amidst the madding crowd, though beware of the trendier joints noted for people-watching, where you may be subjected to glaring designer lighting.

After dinner take a hand-in-hand stroll along the canals and across bridges. The intimacy of a walk down one of the streets of the grachtengordel horseshoe of 17th-century canals or along the expansive Amstel River and across its beautiful bridges is always memorable.

A world-class ballet or opera performance might be your choice for a sophisticated romantic date; if so, the sweeping staircases of the Muziektheater make the ideal venue. If holding hands in the cinema is more your style, then head to the stunning Tuschinski theater, an art deco masterpiece, for mainstream movies. Ask for a slightly more expensive box—the bonus is a glass of champagne at the interval. Head to the smaller Kriterion for art-house fare.

The most romantic hotels? The Pulitzer's winding corridors and beamed rooms, converted from 17th-century canal-side houses, or the personal service at Blake's and Seven one Seven are an alternative to all-out five-star treatment in the Amstel Inter-Continental Hotel, the Grand Sofitel Demeure Amsterdam, or Hotel de l'Europe. In the softer price range, try the Atlas Hotel or Hotel de Filosoof near the green spaces of the Vondelpark.

THE PERFECT ALL-NIGHTER

So you want to hit Amsterdam with a bang? Start out at a bar such as Bep, Seymour Likely, or Getto for early cocktails with the in-crowd, and check out what the locals consider the hot spots for that evening; it changes all the time, after all. Then head to an *eetcafé* such as Het Gasthuys for a traditional Dutch dinner, Japan Inn for sushi or yakitori, or a quick and delicious Thai restaurant such as Song Kwae, for a reasonably priced dinner. If you are so inclined, then a trip to a calm coffee shop such as De Tweede Kamer might be in order. Just be careful not to get stuck there all night or lose your bearings.

Jazz lovers can find a handful of traditional jazz and blues bars near the Leidseplein, such as Alto or something more esoteric at the Bimhuis. For those interested in mainstream pop and dance, leading venues such as De Melkweg or Paradiso often host international bands, ranging from Britpop to R&B. After the gig, these venues host club nights that go on into the small hours and offer light meals and snacks.

If you want to really shake your thang, things start to warm up around the Rembrandtplein around midnight. The large Escape nightclub is a current house and dance hot spot, the iT more extravagant—it's mixed Thursday to Sunday, gay-only on Saturdays. For the latest in esoteric house sounds try the Mazzo, while the canal-side Odeon has three dance and bar spaces with a mix of music that includes rock and blues.

"You can eat in any language" is the city's proud claim, so when Dutch restaurants are closed, Indonesian, Chinese, and Turkish restaurants are often open. A specialty not to be missed is Indonesian food, with a plethora of restaurants where you can savor its delights for a price from expensive to budget.

In This Chapter

EAST OF THE AMSTEL 37 • Eclectic 37 • French 37 • Mediterranean 40 • Vegetarian 40 • GRACHTENGORDEL: THE CANAL RING 41 • American Casual 41 • Asian 41 • Continental 42 • Eclectic 45 • English 45 • French 45 • Indonesian 47 • Italian 47 • Turkish 48 • JORDAAN 48 • Continental 48 • Indian 49 • Indonesian 49 • Italian 51 • LEIDSEPLEIN 51 • Continental 51 • French 51 • Japanese 52 • Seafood 52 • MUSEUM QUARTER AND SOUTH AMSTERDAM 52 • Contemporary 52 • Continental 53 • French 54 • Indonesian 54 • OUDEZIJDS AND DE WALLEN 55 • Chinese 55 • Continental 56 • French 58 • Thai 59 • REMBRANDTPLEIN 59 • Tex-Mex 59 • STATION AND DOCKLANDS 60 • Continental 60 • Mediterranean 61

By Andrew May

eating out

AMONG AMSTERDAM'S MORE THAN 700 RESTAURANTS you'll find everything from international fast-food joints to chandeliered, waterfront dining rooms frequented by the royal family. In between are small, chef-owned establishments on the canals and their side streets, restaurants that have stood the test of time on the basis of service, ambience, and consistency. Finer city restaurants combine good local ingredients with the more subtle art of haute cuisine.

Prices

If you're used to New York, California, or London prices, then expect to pay less for the same quality in Amsterdam. At the haute cuisine end of the scale, the Netherlands has only recently started to gain international recognition, some of it long overdue. As a result, you can enjoy the upper echelons of the market without breaking the bank. If you are on a budget, your choices are definitely not limited, and though you may have to sacrifice glamor, you won't have to skimp on quality.

There are excellent *eetcafés*, casual eating houses that often double as bars for locals and serve main courses for between Fl 20 (€9.10) and Fl 30 (€13.60). The blue-and-white tourist menu sign in a restaurant guarantees an economical (Fl 25 or €11.35), yet imaginative, set menu created by the head chef. For traditionalists the NEDERLANDS DIS SOUP TUREEN sign is a promise of regional recipes and seasonal ingredients. Many of the interesting ethnic restaurants offer excellent food for a reasonable price and are open for extended hours as well.

CATEGORY	COST*
$$$$	over Fl 85 (€40)
$$$	Fl 60–Fl 85 (€30–€40)
$$	Fl 35–Fl 60 (€15–€30)
$	under Fl 35 (€15)

*per person for three- or four-course meal, including service and taxes and excluding drinks

How and When

There is a very particular lunch culture in the Netherlands. At lunchtime, follow the Dutch to a charming café and choose from a selection of *broodjes* rolls filled with cheese, cold cuts of meat, and salad. Many restaurants do not open till evening and, if open at all (noon–2), usually serve a limited menu of lighter fare. The few establishments that do offer a full lunchtime menu, a norm in the top-notch hotel restaurants, are noted in the reviews below.

Even cosmopolitan Amsterdammers dine early, often even starting at 6 PM. This leaves more space for visitors who prefer a late, leisurely dinner, but makes it tricky to dine after 10 PM, because most kitchens close by this time.

Because the Dutch dine early and Amsterdammers like to eat out often, restaurants are busiest 6–9 PM on any night of the week. For these periods, be sure to make a reservation, because the locals can fill the restaurants whether it is high or low season. Reservations are always advisable in classier restaurants, especially on weekends, and in some less expensive restaurants; in the reviews, we note only when reservations are essential (because you won't get a table without one) or not accepted.

Although it would not be the done thing to turn anyone away from a restaurant in Amsterdam because of being underdressed, in the $$$ and $$$$ price categories, a jacket is advisable. Even if you are on vacation, you might feel uncomfortable sitting in a restaurant in sneakers and casual sportswear, surrounded by people in business suits. Where a dress code is specified, this is not a hard-and-fast rule, but a strong suggestion.

Throughout the city and in every class of restaurant, the menus are often translated into English, so don't be shy to ask for a version you can read. Otherwise, those who serve you will have a sufficient level of proficiency in English to help you through. Many restaurants have three- or four-course menu options and most allow you to make your own selection from the full à la carte menu.

EAST OF THE AMSTEL
Eclectic

$$ **PLANCIUS.** This place took off quickly after being launched in late 1999. Serving breakfast and lunch during the day, it metamorphoses into a fashionable restaurant with superb food in early evening. Tables are packed tight, but the atmosphere is convivial enough to make you feel comfortable. The menu is adventurous, mixing and matching everything from the Pacific to the Indian Ocean for European tastes. A delicious starter is the tasty north-African salad with tabbouleh, chickpeas, and sausage. As a main course, try the mushroom risotto topped with seared fillet of lamb. *Plantage Kerklaan 61a, tel. 020/330–9469. AE, DC, MC, V.*

French

$$$$ **LA RIVE.** This world-class restaurant is fit for royalty. The French ★ cuisine, with an awe-inspiring "truffle menu" of dishes prepared with exotic (and expensive) ingredients, can be tailored to meet your every whim. Epicureans should inquire about the "chef's table": with a group of six you can sit at a table alongside the open kitchen and watch chefs prepare and describe each of your courses. Otherwise turn your attention to one of the city's most

amsterdam dining

Al's Plaice, 6

Balraj, 2

Beddington's, 52

Bird, 18

Blauw aan
de wal, 24

Bodega
Keyzer, 50

Brasserie van
Baerle, 51

Breitner, 39

Café
Americain, 44

Café de Reiger, 9

Caffe Esprit, 31

Christophe, 10

D' Theeboom, 15

D' Vijff
Vlieghen, 29

De Belhamel, 4

De Kersentuin, 49

De Kooning
van Siam, 13

De Oesterbar, 43

De Poort, 16

De Silveren
Spieghel, 5

Dim Sum
Court, 19

Dynasty, 36

Eerste Klas, 7

Excelsior, 38

The Goodies, 28

Hemelse
Modder, 20

Het Gasthuys, 32

Humphreys, 11

In de Waag, 26

Japan Inn, 46

Kam Yin, 12

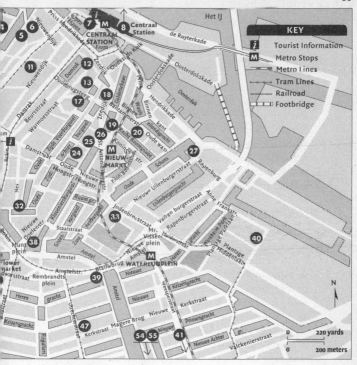

Het IJ

Centraal Station

KEY

i	Tourist Information
M	Metro Stops
	Metro Lines
	Tram Lines
	Railroad
	Footbridge

CENTRAAL STATION

0 220 yards

0 200 meters

N

Kantijl en de Tijger, 30

Kint & Co., 27

La Rive, 54

La Vallade, 41

Land van Walem, 42

Le Garage, 53

L'Indochine, 34

Lonny's, 14

Lorreinen, 3

Lucius, 23

Pianeta Terra, 35

Plancius, 40

Rose's Cantina, 37

Sama Sebo, 48

Sluizer, 47

Song Kwae, 25

Soup en zo, 33

't Swarte Schaep, 45

Tibet Restaurant, 17

Toscanini, 1

Turquoise, 22

Van Puffelen, 21

VandeMarkt, 55

Wilhelmina-Dok, 8

elegant views over the broad river Amstel, and still a rarity in this country, enjoy a no-smoking section. *Amstel Inter-Continental Hotel, Professor Tulpplein 1, tel. 020/622–6060. Jacket and tie. AE, DC, MC, V.*

$$ LA VALLADE. For an authentic taste of French atmosphere and a close imitation of French home cooking, take Tram 9 to this outlying restaurant on the Ringdijk, the city's perimeter dike. There is a new four-course menu each evening for just Fl 49 (€22.25). Start with a mushroom bouillon, followed by an entrée of *confit de canard* (preserved duck) and sauerkraut. The meal includes a cheeseboard with a choice of local and French varieties and, for dessert, a sticky apricot tart with almonds. *Ringdijk 23, tel. 020/665–2025. No credit cards. No lunch.*

Mediterranean

$$$ VANDEMARKT. "From the market" (the three-course, three-
★ choice menu changes daily) evolved from a catering operation. The three proprietors created a stylish, modern interior: the walls are a patchwork of color blocks, and you eat at pine tables with contemporary seating. Starters might include succulent gurnard baked in a Parma ham parcel on a bed of bitter radicchio salad. As an in-between course, try an aromatic and creamy lobster bisque with prawn wonton parcels. Half a wild duck with a sauce of sage is a flavorful main course, followed by ripe figs poached in Marsala wine and ice-cream. Service is swish, and there is an excellent wine cellar, making this a hot spot well worth discovering. *Schollenbrugstraat 8–9, tel. 020/468–6958. Reservations essential. AE, DC, MC, V. Closed Sun. No lunch.*

Vegetarian

$ SOUP EN ZO. The combination of growing health awareness and the need for speed (at least between 10 AM and 7:30 PM daily) is hitting Amsterdam, too, and this soup bar has a selection of at least four tasty soups, largely using organic ingredients, and served with delicious bread. There are also salads, and exotic fruit juices imported from Brazil as frozen fruit pulp. *Jodenbreestraat 94a, tel. 020/422–2243. No credit cards.*

GRACHTENGORDEL: THE CANAL RING
American Casual

$ CAFFE ESPRIT. Clean-cut, small, and popular, this restaurant has tall windows that overlook the busy Spui square. The menu is contemporary American, with choices such as Surf Burger garnished with avocado and bacon or Yankee Doodle Sandwich (crisp roll with pastrami, mustard, mayonnaise, and grilled bell peppers). There are salads, pastas, pizzas, standard sandwiches, and a children's menu. *Spui 10, tel. 020/622–1967. Reservations not accepted. No credit cards.*

Asian

$$$ DYNASTY. At this trendy, interesting spot, the decor is a fanciful mating of Asian and art deco. Although it's not required, you'll feel much more comfortable in a jacket. Chef K. Y. Lee's menu is as fascinating as the decor: the medley of Asian cuisines includes authentically prepared, classic Chinese dishes, such as Three Meats in Harmony, and selections from the cuisines of Thailand, Malaysia, and Vietnam, such as succulent duck and lobster on a bed of watercress. There are two fixed-price menus. *Reguliersdwarsstraat 30, tel. 020/626–8400. AE, DC, MC, V. Closed Tues. No lunch.*

$$$ L'INDOCHINE. Opened in early 2000, this is one of the city's first
★ ventures into authentic Vietnamese food amidst a stylish ambience. The chef's skillful preparation of the freshest ingredients, many specially flown in, has made it an immediate success. Sample the healthy, mint-flavored Vietnamese spring rolls in translucent rice paper or the more meaty seared prawn and beef skewers to start, followed by lightly fried fish with vegetables in a subtly spiced sauce. There are also some classic dishes from the world of Thai cuisine.

The maître d', from California, ensures attentive service, and you can choose from a truly international wine list. *Beulingstraat 9, tel. 020/627–5755. Reservations essential. AE, DC, MC, V. Closed Mon. No lunch.*

Continental

$$$ **D' VIJFF VLIEGHEN.** Dining in a traditional canal-house environment is part of the Amsterdam experience, though you are more likely to find yourself seated among closely packed tables of Swedes and Japanese than among Dutch diners. Still, the "Five Flies" is a charming spot that in the 1950s and 1960s was frequented by the likes of Walt Disney and Orson Welles. Set in five adjoining houses that date from 1627, the restaurant incorporates a series of small, timbered dining rooms, each well adorned with mementos and bric-a-brac. The kitchen, long a bastion of traditional Dutch meat-and-potatoes cooking, is now drawing on fresh local ingredients in such dishes as suckling pig cutlets coated in pastry, and grilled halibut with a mussel ragout. *Spuistraat 294–302, tel. 020/624–8369. Jacket and tie. AE, DC, MC, V. No lunch.*

$$–$$$ **DE BELHAMEL.** A stunning art deco interior and a fine view down the Herengracht set the tone for a well-prepared and attentively served dinner in a French style. In winter, the emphasis is on hearty game dishes such as venison with a red-wine and shallot sauce. In summer, you can sample lighter fare and enjoy the view from an outside table under the trees along the canal. *Brouwersgracht 60, tel. 020/622–1095. AE, MC, V. No lunch.*

$$–$$$ **LUCIUS.** The plain setting and the simple service belie the fact that this is one of the best fish restaurants in town. On the exclusively marine menu, your choices range from grilled lobster to more adventurous creations such as sea bass with buckwheat noodles and mushrooms. You can also opt to have any fish available cooked to your taste. The wine list includes a good selection from California and even a Dutch wine from Apostlehoeve

Dutch Brews

With brands such as Heineken and Grolsch available all round the world, you can be sure that the Dutch know their beers. Although most breweries have moved outside Amsterdam, a cloud of malt and hop vapors occasionally envelops the city in its rich aroma.

The Dutch are especially fond of their **pils**, a light golden lager usually served with a large head. Locals claim their pils tastes better if sipped through the foam, so asking for a top-up may offend. There are stronger, more aromatic beers on the market, usually referred to as bokbier, but they do not resemble bitter or real ales. They have a higher sugar and alcohol content and a darker, reddish-brown color. They are usually seasonal beers, made with warming spices in the winter. In the summer, witte bier (white beer), is a popular and refreshing terrace drink, though it is most likely to have come from a Belgian brewery. This zesty beer with a clouded yellow appearance is served cool with a twist of lemon.

The indigenous liquor of the Netherlands is **jenever**, a potent gin. It is not as bitter as English gin—which in fact originated as a mishap in trying to copy the Dutch recipe—and is usually drunk neat from small, tall glasses. It comes in myriad varieties, from jonge (young gin), with a rough edge, to the more sophisticated oude (mature gin), usually based on a single grain, for example rye, and matured in vats for years. The locals might knock back their gin borrel (in one gulp), but beware. When served accompanying a beer it is known as a **kopstoot** ("headbang"). The name should be taken as a warning to the uninitiated to sip more daintily. There are also sweetened and fruit-flavored gin variants, with currant or lemon juice, for those with a sweeter tooth. Try out Dutch liquors at a proeflokaal or proeverij, an old-fashioned "tasting-house." An after-work phenomenon, most tasting-houses close by early evening.

in Limburg province, the country's only vineyard. *Spuistraat 247, tel. 020/624–1831. Reservations essential. AE, DC, MC, V. Closed Sun. No lunch.*

$$ SLUIZER. Sluizer is really two side-by-side restaurants with a bistrolike atmosphere—one serves only meat, the other only fish. Both are simply decorated and unpretentious; both are known for good food that is prepared without a lot of fanfare or creativity; both are reasonably priced; and, not surprisingly, both are crowded every night. *Utrechtsestraat 43–45, tel. 020/622–6376 (meat) or 020/626–3557 (fish). AE, DC, MC, V. No lunch Sat.–Sun.*

$$ VAN PUFFELEN. This traditional restaurant and *proeverij* (tasting house) is on a quiet section of the Prinsengracht, with a terrace if weather permits. On one side is the proeverij, with a large selection of traditional Dutch jenever (☞ Dutch Brews box, *above*) for you to sample. The bustling popular restaurant has classic late-19th-century fittings and fills up with locals every night of the week. If it's too noisy, you can escape to the more secluded and intimate mezzanine floor. Starters include goat cheese salad; the meat main course or daily special might be braised duck's breast with passion-fruit sauce. Red meat tends to be done rare, so let them know if you prefer medium to well-done. Service is alert, and there is an excellent and reasonably priced wine list. *Prinsengracht 375–377, tel. 020/624–6270. Reservations essential. AE, DC, MC, V.*

$ HUMPHREYS. This formula restaurant has branches in 10 different cities in the Netherlands and, in Amsterdam, enjoys a cavernous space that is full of character, with brick walls and exposed beams. There is seating for no fewer than 200 people, and it is usually full. Start with a soup of the day such as pumpkin, followed by an entrée of rib of lamb and vegetables, and a dessert of cinnamon ice cream with a compote of stewed berries. Young and old, in large groups and intimate couples, are attracted by the prix-fixe dinner. *Nieuwezijds Kolk 23, tel. 020/422–1234. AE, MC, V. No lunch.*

Eclectic

$$–$$$ **LAND VAN WALEM.** At this popular all-day *grand café*, elegant breakfast and brunch options are served on chic *ciabatta*, flat and crunchy Italian bread. At dinnertime, the chefs prepare a menu of up-to-the-minute fusion cooking. Start with a filo pastry parcel of Cypriot goat cheese with ginger and olives, followed by Japanese salad with marinated duck and chicken with crispy greens and buckwheat noodles, or grilled ribeye with Cajun spices. In the summer, you can relax in the formal garden or on the canal-side terrace, and late at night the guest DJs spin hip lounge tunes for neophytes. *Keizersgracht 449, tel. 020/625–3544. AE, MC, V.*

English

$ **AL'S PLAICE.** British tourists and locals have been flocking here for the last year for good ol' British fish 'n' chips. Choose from cod, haddock, or plaice, deep-fried in crispy batter, with fries cooked to a soft consistency. Al also offers a traditional selection of imported steak and kidney pie, pasties, fried chicken, and other frittered fare. It can be wrapped up to go or you can eat in at Formica tables, with a selection of the day's British tabloids for amusement. *Nieuwendijk 10, tel. 020/427–4192. No credit cards. Closed Tues. No lunch Mon.*

French

$$$$ **CHRISTOPHE.** After Algerian-born Frenchman Jean-Christophe Royer opened his *eettempel* (eating temple) on a small canal between the Keizersgracht and Prinsengracht in the 1980s, he and his French kitchen staff quickly became recognized for their fine French cuisine with Arabic and African influences. The ever-changing menu may include entrées such as ragout of lobster with cocoa beans, pimentos, and coriander or sweetbreads of veal in a sauce of *vin jaune* (a deep golden-colored wine from a grape from one very small area in the Jura) with white cabbage and chanterelles. There is also a selection of vegetarian dishes. The atmosphere is welcoming and the service personalized. *Leliegracht 46, tel. 020/625–0807. Reservations essential. Jacket required. AE, DC, MC, V. Closed Sun. and Mon., 1st week in Jan. and 2 weeks in July–Aug. No lunch.*

$$$$ DE SILVEREN SPIEGHEL. This intimate restaurant is in two delightfully crooked houses from 1614 designed by then-city architect Hendrik de Keyser. The candlelit, beamed interior is a romantic setting. The cuisine is French-influenced, but uses the best of local ingredients, styling itself as "New Dutch." Ingredients include succulent lamb from the small island of Texel, and the honey of Amsterdam's Vondelpark. There are also expertly prepared fish plates, such as turbot on a bed of beetroot and nettle leaves. Lunch is available by appointment only (phone a day ahead). *Kattengat 4–6, tel. 020/624–6589. Reservations essential. AE, MC, V. Closed Sun. No lunch.*

$$$–$$$$ BREITNER. ★ This beautiful, formal dining room is decorated in cool pastel shades and modern artworks, and has wonderful views of the lights on the Amstel river and the Muziektheater–Stadhuis (Music Theater–City Hall complex). The French-inspired menu goes to town with luxury products such as foie gras. Start with a baked quail with goose liver and bacon, followed by an entrée of skate with Indonesian-style vegetables or smoked rib of beef with a sauce of whole-grain mustard and marinated vegetables. Service is impeccable, and most patrons dress smartly to match. *Amstel 212, tel. 020/627–7879. Reservations essential. AE, DC, MC, V. Closed Sun.–Mon. No lunch Sat.*

$$–$$$ D' THEEBOOM. Located just behind the Dam, the ground floor of this historic canal-side warehouse has been converted into a stylish, formal restaurant. The menu here offers you a royal choice of mouthwatering and original French haute cuisine for an honest price. The seasonal menu might include a delicious parcel of vegetables flavored with a selection of mushrooms, followed by carefully prepared red mullet with a saffron sauce. The wine list befits the sophisticated tastes of the French chef–proprietor, who will be most pleased to advise. This is one of the few city restaurants where you can linger over a long lunch during the week. *Singel 210, tel. 020/623–8420. AE, DC, MC, V. No lunch Sat.–Mon.*

Indonesian

$$ KANTIJL EN DE TIJGER. ★ This lively Indonesian restaurant is a favorite with the locals and close to the bars on the Spui. The menu is based on three different *rijsttafel* (rice table), with an abundance of meat, fish, and vegetable dishes varying in flavor from coconut-milk sweetness to peppery hot. Alternatively, you can select separate dishes to create your own feast. *Spuistraat 291/293, tel. 020/620–0994. AE, DC, MC, V. No lunch.*

Italian

$$$ PIANETA TERRA. After many years as an old-school French restaurant, this place has changed hands and improved standards, with a kitchen and menu focused more on the Italian, but incorporating other southern European influences. To start, try a carpaccio of swordfish with pecorino cheese and an orange salad, then an appetizing home-made organic pasta such as gnocchi with butter and sage. Follow with octopus and mussels prepared in a *tagine*, a traditional Moroccan clay pot, and served on a bed of rucola. The restaurant makes all its own pasta and bread using organic products. For the truly health- and environment-conscious there is a three-course set menu that uses only organic ingredients. Fittings of marble slabs provide soft light across the multiple levels of the dining room, making it an intimate setting. *Beulingstraat 7, tel. 020/626–1912. Reservations essential. AE, DC, MC, V. No lunch.*

$–$$ THE GOODIES. ★ Fresh homemade pastas, healthy salads, and tasty meat and fish are the secret of this spaghetteria's success. You will be seated at tightly packed wooden tables and benches, and there is a small no-smoking section. During the day the restaurant is a popular café serving filling sandwiches on wedges of Italian farmer's bread, plus salads and deliciously thick fruit shakes. *Huidenstraat 9, tel. 020/625–6122. Reservations essential. AE, MC, V.*

Turkish

$$ TURQUOISE. The groups of Turkish city residents who frequent this cozy, long-established restaurant vouch for the quality and authenticity of the food. It is also set on one of the charming *Negen Straatjes* (nine streets) between the main ring of canals. Lamb is the meat of choice and is prepared in countless ways, either skewered on a kebab, roasted, or minced and formed into patties and served with potatoes or aromatic rice. There are also chicken dishes. For a starter try one of the deliciously herbed salads or oven-roasted prawns with a sauce of fresh tomatoes and peppers. There is a good selection of Turkish wines, rarely found in other restaurants, including a delicious, fruity rosé. Service is friendly and attentive, and the dining room is decorated with beautiful and ornate artwork from Turkey. *Wolvenstraat 22–24, tel. 020/624–2026. AE, DC, MC, V.*

JORDAAN
Continental

$$ CAFÉ DE REIGER. This neighborhood café-restaurant is always
★ packed in the evening with noisy drinkers and diners. At lunchtime there is a menu of sandwiches and warm snacks. The place has a long history, witness the tile tableaus and the early 20th-century fittings behind the bar. Amidst the bustle, the staff pay careful attention to their patrons and serve them wholesome food in substantial portions. The cuisine is basically Dutch, with good meat and fowl cooked in a simple fashion, but there are also some adventurous additions, such as sea bass with a sauce of fennel and spinach. All dishes are accompanied by a choice of fries or

rice and vegetables or salad. *Nieuwe Leliestraat 34, tel. 020/624–7426. Reservations essential. AE, MC, V.*

$$ LORREINEN. This is a romantic place to eat, and offers well-prepared food at an excellent price. The restaurant has little nooks and corners where you can hide away, and in the summer there is a terrace on the Noordermarkt. The menu includes some nice twists on Dutch fare, such as thick tuna steak smothered with pesto and served with polenta. In season, try the game, such as a melt-in-the-mouth steak of venison with a pear stewed in red wine and endives. *Noordermarkt 42, tel. 020/624–3689. AE, DC, MC, V. Closed Tues. No lunch.*

Indian

$–$$ BALRAJ. This may be small, but it's certainly a favorite Indian restaurant, and faithful customers have kept it thriving for more than a quarter century. Start with a familiar *bhaji*, a battered fritter of sliced onions with a yogurt and mint dressing. Each dish is prepared to order, so the spiciness and intensity of the curries can be adjusted to your tastes. As well as the hotter Madras curries, there are rich, creamy sauces, or plainer *saag* curries with spinach. A delicious accompaniment is the sweet Indian tea, richly laced with cardamom. *Haarlemmerdijk 28, tel. 020/625–1428. No credit cards. No lunch.*

Indonesian

$$–$$$ LONNY'S. Lonny Gerungan offers Indonesian cuisine at its best.
★ His family have been cooks on Bali for generations, and the recipes used for the feasts in his restaurant are those that his forefathers used for royal banquets on the island. Treat yourself to a *Selamatan Puri Gede*, a sumptuous Balinese rice table fit for royalty, with more than 15 succulently spicy dishes. The waiters wear sarongs, and the restaurant is decorated with silky fabrics and colorful parasols. *Rozengracht 46–48, tel. 020/623–8950. Reservations essential. AE, DC, MC, V. No lunch.*

Indonesian Delights

On any night of the week, large groups of Amsterdammers troop into Indonesian restaurants, tempted by the conviviality of a rijsttafel, or rice table, a feast ordered for two persons or more. The number of dishes—a dozen to a score or more—adds up to a substantial meal that requires a good appetite. Most restaurants offer three or four choices with varying emphasis on meat, fish, or vegetables. Try a jasmine tea or beer with your meal; few wines can hold their own in this sea of flavors.

If you are really ravenous, go for an appetizer of soto ajam, a clear chicken broth with rice noodles, or loempia, deep-fried rolls of bean sprouts, vegetables, and meat. After this, the waiting staff will bring a number of hotplates, warmed by candles, to the table. The ritual of describing the myriad dishes as they are placed on the table in small dishes is a ceremony in itself. Many restaurants make the effort to arrange the dishes according to their level of spiciness.

Standard dishes—working from mild to hot—include saté, a skewer of bite-size morsels of babi (pork) or ajam (chicken), drenched in a rich peanut sauce. Gado gado is a mix of cold, cooked vegetables, also in peanut sauce; atjar ketimon is cucumber in vinegar. Seroendeng, a mix of fried coconut and peanuts, or Sayur lodeh, vegetables cooked in coconut milk, can help take the bite out of an accidental overexposure to peppery spiciness. Daging is meat, often beef, stewed lovingly in a subtle mix of no fewer than eleven spices. Bali is the name for dishes made with sambal, a red chili-based sauce with a bite, which may be used for meats and fish such as mackerel. There's a pot of sambal on the table.

Pisang goring, fried bananas, are usually included in the feast, if you have room for dessert.

Italian

$$-$$$ **TOSCANINI.** This cavernous, noisy Italian restaurant is a perennial
★ favorite with local professionals. The food is superb, and all
prepared to order, which can involve a wait if the place is as busy
as usual. In addition to such familiar favorites as a varied plate
of antipasti, which is scrumptious here, you'll find pasta with
game sauce, subtle fresh fish dishes, such as trout with fresh
basil, and other delights. *Lindengracht 75, tel. 020/623–2813.
Reservations essential. AE, DC, MC, V. Closed Sun. No lunch.*

LEIDSEPLEIN
Continental

$$$ **CAFÉ AMERICAIN.** Though thousands of buildings in Amsterdam
are designated as historic monuments, the one that houses this
restaurant is the only structure whose interior, an art nouveau
treasure designed by Kromhout, is also protected. Opened in 1902
and said to have been the venue for Mata Hari's wedding reception,
the Café Americain is a hybrid restaurant–café serving everything
from light snacks to full dinners. To one side are formal tables
draped with white linens, where traditional entrées such as
medallions of beef with béarnaise sauce are served; to the other
side are tiny bare-top tables, perfect for a quick coffee and pastry.
There is a well-stocked buffet complete with hot dishes, salads,
and desserts. *American Hotel, Leidsekade 97, tel. 020/624–5322.
Reservations not accepted. AE, DC, MC, V.*

French

$$$$ **'T SWARTE SCHAEP.** This cozy upstairs restaurant overlooking the
★ noisy Leidseplein is named for a legendary black sheep that
roamed the area in the 17th century. It's a study in traditional Dutch
decor, with copper pots hanging from the wooden beams and
heavily framed paintings on the walls. Together with this Old
Holland atmosphere, the excellent French cuisine sometimes
attracts members of the Dutch royal family during incognito visits

to the capital. The menu includes luxury foie gras starters, chateaubriand with béarnaise sauce, and lobster mousse with asparagus salad. Dinner orders are accepted until 11 PM—late for Amsterdam. *Korte Leidsedwarsstraat 24, tel. 020/622–3021. Reservations essential. AE, DC, MC, V.*

Japanese

$$ JAPAN INN. This lively Japanese restaurant is a refreshing contrast to the many tourist-trap outlets around the Leidseplein. You can choose one of various menus or order single portions to create your own dinner. There are fish and meat yakitori on wooden skewers, seared over an open fire and served with a sweet sauce, as well as sushi and sashimi, all served with miso soup and salad. *Leidsekruisstraat 4, tel. 020/620–4989. AE, DC, MC, V. No lunch.*

Seafood

$$–$$$ DE OESTERBAR. The Oyster Bar is a local institution. It's the first place to think of when you hanker for a half-dozen small and flavorful oysters fresh from the Oosterschelde in the south of the Netherlands or the simply prepared catch of the day. Choices are straightforward: grilled, baked, or fried fish served with tartar sauce, potatoes, and salad. Live lobster is also available in season. The no-nonsense room on the ground floor has a small bar at the back, with white tile walls incorporating nautical murals and a long row of eerily lighted fish tanks along one side. In the upstairs dining room, the mood is oddly bordellolike, with elaborately patterned wallpaper and an assortment of innocuous paintings on the walls. *Leidseplein 10, tel. 020/623–2988. Reservations essential. AE, DC, MC, V.*

MUSEUM QUARTER AND SOUTH AMSTERDAM
Contemporary

$$$–$$$$ BEDDINGTON'S. Near the Concertgebouw and the art museums, Beddington's sits at the junction between the business district and the city's most prestigious modern residential neighborhoods. The decor is ultra-minimal, designed by artist Boris Sipek. The English chef, Jean Beddington, takes an imaginative multicultural approach in the kitchen, mixing Japanese and other East Asian flavors and concepts with those from England, Spain, and the West Indies. Main courses you might encounter here include bisque of clams and lobster and perfectly balanced spring lamb with thyme. *Roelof Hartstraat 6–8, tel. 020/676–5201. Reservations essential. Jacket required. AE, DC, MC, V. Closed Sun. No lunch.*

$$$–$$$$ LE GARAGE. On April 1, 1990, a backstreet garage near the Concertgebouw began a new lease on life. Oil stains and engine parts had given way to mirrored walls, plush seating, and clinking cutlery, designed by maverick Dutch architect Cees Dam. Chef Joop Braakhekke, who is famed in the Netherlands as the zany presenter of a TV cooking show, comes up with superb New Dutch cuisine, including a few old family recipes, such as eel stewed with raisins, barley, and herbs, or breast of duck with date chutney. Media stars, politicians, and leading lights in the Dutch art world eat here, making this a hot spot for spotters of celebrities "world-famous in the Netherlands." *Ruysdaelstraat 54, tel. 020/679–7176. Reservations essential. Jacket and tie. AE, DC, MC, V. No lunch Sat. and Sun.*

Continental

$$ BODEGA KEYZER. After what's closing in on nine decades spent serving musicians, concertgoers, and residents of the neighborhoods surrounding the art museums and Concertgebouw, this half restaurant, half café-bodega has evolved into something as familiar and comfortable as an old shoe. You can come at almost any hour for a simple drink or a full meal. The interior is paneled with dark wood, the lights are dim, and Oriental rugs cover the tables. The menu is equally traditional—among the meat and fish selections are tournedos, schnitzel, and sole meunière— though it may also include a more adventurous *ris de veau* (veal sweetbreads) with orange and green pepper sauce or fricassee of veal with nut-basil sauce. *Van Baerlestraat 96, tel. 020/671–1441. AE, DC, MC, V.*

$$ BRASSERIE VAN BAERLE. Begun as a neighborhood lunch and Sunday brunch restaurant, this bright, appealing spot with an uncomplicated European modern decor now even draws late diners who come in following performances at the nearby Concertgebouw. The chef's creativity is the main attraction. Imaginative dishes include spicy Asian salads and heavier fare, such as duck in truffle sauce. There is outdoor dining in good weather. *Van Baerlestraat 158, tel. 020/679–1532. AE, DC, MC, V. Closed Sat.*

French

$$$ DE KERSENTUIN. The name of this cheerful, high-ceiling restaurant, which means "cherry orchard," signals the color scheme that extends from the dinnerware to the decor. It is a good place for a leisurely meal. Although there are large windows overlooking a residential street, the focal point is the kitchen, visible behind glass panels. As you dine, you can watch chef Guus Vredenburg and his staff prepare French dishes with a Far Eastern twist. Start with a rich terrine of duck liver, and try entrées such as perch flavored with coconut and spicy Thai sauce or suckling pig glazed in honey and soy sauce, served with a ginger sauce. *Dijsselhofplantsoen 7, tel. 020/664–2121. Reservations essential. Jacket and tie. AE, DC, MC, V. Closed Sun. No lunch Sat.*

Indonesian

$$ SAMA SEBO. Come to this small, busy, and relaxed neighborhood Indonesian restaurant near the Rijksmuseum and Museumplein for a rijsttafel, a feast with myriad small dishes. There are simpler dishes such as *bami goreng* (spicy fried rice with vegetables), or a lunch of *nasi goreng* (spicy fried noodles with vegetables). The colors are muted tans and browns with rush mats covering the walls.

When things are busy, the restaurant can be cramped. P. C. Hoofstraat 27, tel. 020/662–8146. AE, DC, MC, V. Closed Sun.

OUDEZIJDS AND DE WALLEN
Chinese

$ DIM SUM COURT. If you're ravenous, then this unpretentious buffet restaurant is ideal. You pay your Fl 15 (€16.80) and then you can eat as much as you want for the next hour. The eatery was set up by the city's leading *dim sum* producer, so there is always a rolling selection of five or six pot-stickers steaming away in bamboo baskets. In addition there are tasty fried rice, noodles and vegetable dishes, and crispy chicken and pork. You can order a pot of jasmine tea, or buy beverages from the vending machine, and serve yourself to your belly's content, while staff focus on keeping all the fresh selections available. This restaurant is open till 11 PM Monday–Wednesday and till midnight Thursday–Sunday. Zeedijk 109, tel. 020/638–1466. Reservations not accepted. No credit cards.

$ KAM YIN. The food of the small country of Surinam on the northern coast of South America is a favorite economical meal in Amsterdam, which is home to many people from the former Dutch colony. Surinam's cuisine is a multicultural mix of influences from South America, India, and China. Try the traditional *roti*, a flat-bread pancake, and a light meat curry with potatoes and green beans. Another filling main course is *pom*, a tasty mix of chicken and root vegetables served with rice. The menu here includes Chinese standards. The restaurant is basic but clean, has a convivial, noisy atmosphere, and is open daily noon–midnight. There is also a takeaway section, where service is quick, and a delivery service for a supplement of Fl 2.50 (€1.15). Warmoesstraat 6–8, tel. 020/625–3115. No credit cards.

$ TIBET RESTAURANT. For a budget or late-night meal that offers something different, this restaurant (open daily 1:30 PM–1:30 AM) has a whole range of Tibetan specialties in addition to standard

Chinese Szechuan fare. The walls and niches are occupied by icons and painted fabrics from Tibet. The big selection of pork dishes is especially tasty, prepared in spicy Tibetan "folk-style" chunks or as milder "family-style" forked shreds. There are also well-filled soups with Tibetan *momo* (dumplings). *Lange Niezel 24,* tel. 020/624–1137. MC, V.

Continental

$$$ **BLAUW AAN DE WAL.** "Blue on the quay" is a surprise, hidden down a small alleyway on the edges of the Red Light District. You will find yourself in a different world, set in a beautiful courtyard formerly belonging to the Bethanienklooster monastery that backs onto it. Inside, the proprietors have turned on the style, with a small lounge area for waiting guests and about five tables. Upstairs is a no-smoking dining room with original wooden floorboards, smart table linen, and a view into the kitchen on the upper of the two levels. The menu takes an inspired approach to local ingredients. After a delicious garlic soup or a goat-cheese terrine with asparagus shoots, savor the melt-in-the-mouth cod with a sauce of chorizo and fennel, or rabbit in an autumnal red wine and shallot sauce. *Oude Zijds Achterburgwal 99,* tel. *020/330– 2257. AE, MC, V. Closed Sunday. No lunch.*

$$–$$$ **DE POORT.** The De Poort brasserie has preserved its simple Dutch charm and character. It is part of the Die Port van Cleve hotel complex, which reopened in 1999 after extensive renovation. The food is traditional Dutch, renowned for its succulent steaks and homey Dutch standards. Start with a plate full of tasty smoked salmon or "Grandmother's" Dutch pea soup with bacon. For a main course, try sole with a creamy remoulade sauce and vegetables, or one of the steaks, offered with eight different accompaniments. *Nieuwezijds Voorburgwal 176–180,* tel. *020/622– 6429. AE, DC, MC, V.*

Local Food: From Land and Sea

For many a century, meat and two vegetables was the basis of cooking in the Dutch home, and there are still remnants of this tradition. The best feature of traditional Dutch fare is that it is simple but filling, and often ideal for warming the insides on cold, damp evenings.

Standard dishes include hutspot, a mashed hotchpotch of potatoes, carrots, and onions. The variant stamppot contains mashed potatoes and greens, and chunks of cured sausage. A favorite winter meal is erwtensoep, a thick pea soup with pieces of smoked sausage or pig's knuckle for flavor, a nourishing dish often associated with the ice-skating season.

To a nation of seafarers, fish is also an important food. Strolling around town, you are bound to notice the fish stalls at strategic spots. Raw haring, the common herring, is a favorite snack—something like "Dutch sushi." The delicacy is not quite raw, but cured in vats of salt water. It is most succulent at the start of the fishing season, from late May to early June, when nieuwe haring, fresh from the sea, can be found on the menus of the most chic restaurants. At the dock-side fish auction top chefs will bid unheard of prices to get the first catch. At fish stalls, in a celebratory mood, the delicacy is washed down with a tot of jenever, Dutch gin. Throughout the rest of the year, the salted herring is eaten with chopped onions and pickled gherkins, and sometimes in a bread roll.

If you can't stomach the idea of raw herring, reckoned to be a sure cure for a hangover, try Noordzee garnalen, or North Sea shrimps, which are a smaller, browner, and tastier relative of the pink Norwegian shrimp. Other cured fish include gerookte heilbot, thin slivers of smoked halibut, and paling, freshwater eel from the IJsselmeer lake, which is a costly delicacy and rich in fat.

$–$$ HET GASTHUYS. In this bustling eetcafé near the university you'll be served handsome portions of traditional Dutch home cooking, choice cuts of meat with simple sauces, the most delicious fries in town, and piles of mixed salad. Sit at the bar or take a table high up in the rafters at the back. In summer you can watch the passing boats from the enchanting canal-side terrace. During the day you can order broodjes and other snacks. *Grimburgwal 7, tel. 020/ 624–8230. No credit cards.*

French

$$$$ EXCELSIOR. The Excelsior's view over the Amstel River, to the
★ Muntplein on one side and the Music Theater on the other, is the best in Amsterdam. The dining room is a gracious, chandeliered hall with plenty of room for diners, waiters, dessert trolleys, preparation carts, towering palms, tall candelabra, and a grand piano. The approach is traditional French with a twist: you might choose a lobster bisque or an adventurous dish such as grilled turbot with shrimp and parmesan risotto. For dessert, try the delicious lemon tart or poached figs. There are five fixed-price menus. *Hotel de l'Europe, Nieuwe Doelenstraat 2–8, tel. 020/531– 1777. Jacket and tie. AE, DC, MC, V. No lunch Sat.*

$$$ IN DE WAAG. The lofty, beamed interior below the Theatrum Anatomicum has been converted into a grand café and restaurant. The reading table harbors computer terminals with free Internet access. Open from 10 AM, you can enjoy sandwiches and a selection of snacks and salads during the day. Dinnertime brings a seasonal selection of hearty Burgundian cuisine to be savored by candlelight. Entrées include baked fillet of salmon with mussels and a creamy sorrel sauce or charcoal-grilled beef with green pepper sauce and a gratin of Emmmental cheese. The long wooden tables make this an ideal location for larger groups to eat. *Nieuwmarkt 4, tel. 020/422–8641. AE, DC, MC, V.*

Thai

$$$ DE KOONING VAN SIAM. This Thai restaurant, which is favored by the city's Thai residents, sits smack in the middle of the Red Light District, but don't let that keep you away. Although the beams and wall panels are still visible in this old canal house, there is nothing Old Dutch about the furniture or the wall decorations. Main course selections might include hotly spiced stir-fried beef with onion and chili peppers or a milder chicken and Chinese vegetables with coconut, curry, and basil. *Oude Zijds Voorburgwal 42, tel. 020/623–7293. AE, DC, MC, V. No lunch. Closed Feb.*

$$ BIRD. After many years of success operating a miniscule Thai snackbar and eatery, Bird's proprietors expanded into a 100-seat restaurant on the opposite side of the street, and with the extra kitchen space, they also have a more comprehensive menu of Thai food prepared fresh to order. The interior is filled with chunky wooden furniture imported from Thailand and other regional decoration. The restaurant bustles every night. After a delicious coconut and chicken soup with lemongrass to start, try a fruity curry with mixed seafood on a bed of aromatic rice. *Zeedijk 72–74, tel. 020/620–1442. AE, DC, MC, V.*

$ SONG KWAE. The traditional offerings in and around Amsterdam's Chinatown, centered on the Nieuwmarkt and along the Zeedijk, have now been complemented by a surge of Thai restaurants. This buzzing joint offers speedy service and quality food for a budget price and is always packed. Alongside the traditional red and green Thai curries and the stir-fry options, there are specialities such as green papaya salad with crab and *potek,* a searingly spicy mix of meats and fish. *Kloveniersburgwal 14, tel. 020/624–2568. AE, DC, MC, V.*

REMBRANDTPLEIN
Tex-Mex

$$ ROSE'S CANTINA. A long-time favorite of the sparkling set, this restaurant serves up spicy Tex-Mex food and lethal cocktails. The noise level can be lethal, too. Pop in for a full meal or sundowner. Tex-Mex connoisseurs will not find the food brilliant, but it suffices. In summer you can sit in the gardens facing the backs of the stately mansions on the Herengracht. *Reguliersdwarsstraat 38, tel. 020/625–9797. AE, DC, MC, V. No lunch.*

STATION AND DOCKLANDS
Continental

\$\$–\$\$\$ **EERSTE KLAS.** Amsterdam's best-kept secret is in the most obvious of places: the former first-class waiting lounge on Platform 2b of the central train station. Classic dark-wood paneling, turn-of-the-century frescoes, and soft interior lighting create the perfect hideaway from the city's hustle and bustle. The cafe opens at 9 AM daily and serves a variety of sandwiches, omelets, and salads. From noon to 10 PM, the brasserie-like menu offers a grand choice of ten meat dishes and ten fish dishes as a main course. Savor a tender fillet of mull on a bed of beetroot to start, followed by half a guinea fowl or a breast of duck and crisp, steamed vegetables. Ingredients are local, but accompanying sauces are in the classic French tradition. Staff are highly professional but friendly, and will happily advise you on the international wine selection. *Stationsplein 15, Spoor 2b, tel. 020/625–0131. AE, DC, MC, V.*

\$\$–\$\$\$ **HEMELSE MODDER.** This bright, stylish restaurant is on one of the city's broadest canals and has a long-standing reputation for quality at a great price. Patrons select from fixed-price formulas with three to five courses, costing Fl 50–Fl 62.50 (€22.70–€28.35). Main course choices also take vegetarians into account, with delicious dishes such as an envelope of mushrooms and ricotta cheese with a Gorgonzola soufflé. Meat-eaters can savor entrées such as pork tenderloin baked in a bacon wrap with a rosemary and cider sauce. For a supplement of Fl 12.50 (€5.65) you can tuck into the mountainous *grand dessert*, with tasters of at least four different sweets, including the "heavenly mud" mousse of dark and white chocolate that gives the restaurant its name. *Oude Waal 9, tel. 020/624–3203. AE, DC, MC, V. Closed Mon. No lunch.*

$$–$$$ **WILHELMINA-DOK.** Getting to this restaurant involves a trip
★ across the Noordzeekanaal (North Sea Canal) behind Centraal
Station. On two levels, the restaurant buzzes with the excitement
of the unique view back across the IJ river to Amsterdam's recently
redeveloped docklands. And the food is good: start with a fish soup
on a tomato base, royally filled with chunks of sea fish and
shellfish. The changing daily menu offers main courses such as
seared tuna on a bed of Mediterranean vegetables. There is a
heavily laden sweets trolley with a selection of tarts and pies, or
opt for a rich chocolate soufflé. The establishment also serves
sandwiches and soups during the day. *Noordwal 1, Amsterdam-
Noord, tel. 020/632–3701. Ferry service every 10 minutes to IJplein in
Amsterdam-Noord from Steiger 8 (Pier 8). Turn right off the ferry, follow
the banks of the canal, and you will stumble across the restaurant in less
than five minutes. You can also take the restaurant's own boat from Steiger
9 (Pier 9), making sure to call in advance. No credit cards. Closed Jan.*

Mediterranean

$$$ **KINT & CO.** This small, family-run restaurant is worth the short
walk through one of the city center's best hidden but most
charming residential neighborhoods. The interior is like a well-
loved living room, with simple furniture, and there are canal
views. The menu changes every day, depending on the chef's finds
at the markets, and you can watch her in the open kitchen as she
produces simple but scrumptious surprises inspired by
Mediterranean cuisine. There are entrées such as partridge roasted
with folksy lentils and pulses, and desserts such as light pancakes
filled with mascarpone and apples stewed in Calvados. *Peperstraat
10, tel. 020/627–0280. Reservations essential. No credit cards. Closed
Tues. and Wed. No lunch.*

Amsterdam is a city that is filled with whimsical and unique shops offering exclusive items in all price ranges, appealing to travelers of all ages. Wander through the city, looking out for small specialty stores that are entertaining and unusual. Go ahead: go on in and just look around. The Dutch are notorious window shoppers and bargain hunters, so "when in Rome, do as the Romans do." The temptations, however, will be enormous.

In This Chapter

AREAS 64 • DEPARTMENT STORES 64 • MALLS 66 • MARKETS 67 • SPECIALTY SHOPS 68 • Antiques 68 • Beer 68 • Ceramics and Crystal 69 • Chocolate 69 • Clothes 69 • Collectibles 71 • Diamonds 72 • Duty-Free 72 • Gifts and Souvenirs 72 • Housewares 74 • Jewelry 75 • Leather Goods 76 • Millinery 76 • Music 76 • Shoes 77 • Tobacco 77

By Barbara Krulik

shopping

THE VARIETY OF GOODS AVAILABLE HERE and the convenience of a shopping district that snakes through the city in a continuous parade of boutiques and department stores are the major joys of shopping in Amsterdam. Be sure to visit the year-round outdoor flea market at Waterlooplein, a holdover from the pushcart days in the Jewish Quarter.

Antiques always have been a staple item of shopping in Amsterdam, and the array of goods available at any time is broad. There are more than 150 antiques shops scattered throughout the central canal area. The greatest concentration of those offering fine antiques and specialty items is in the Spiegel Quarter. Nieuwe Spiegelstraat and its continuation, Spiegelgracht, constitute the main thoroughfare of the quarter, with shops on both sides of the street and canal for five blocks, from the Golden Bend of the Herengracht nearly to the Rijksmuseum. Shops on Rozengracht and Prinsengracht, near the Westerkerk, offer country Dutch furniture and household items; you'll also find antiques and curio shops along the side streets in that part of the city.

When and How

Shopping hours in the Netherlands are regulated by law: One night a week is reserved for late shopping. In Amsterdam, department stores and many other shops are closed Monday morning but open Thursday evening. Increasingly, following an easing of legislation governing shopping hours, you'll find main branches of major stores in the center of the city open on Sunday afternoon.

AREAS

The **Dam Square** is home to two of Amsterdam's main department stores. Popular shopping streets radiate from the square, offering something for nearly all tastes and wallets.

Kalverstraat, the city's main pedestrians-only shopping street, is where Amsterdam does its day-to-day shopping. **Leidsestraat** offers a range and variety of shopping similar to Kalverstraat's, but with more of an eye to the tourist trade. **Nieuwendijk** is a busy pedestrian mall, good for bargain hunters.

In the **Grachtengordel,** the shops along the *negen straatjes,* nine charming, tiny streets that radiate from behind the Royal Palace, often have highly specialized merchandise. In the Museumkwartier (Museum Quarter), the posh and prestigious **P. C. Hooftstraat,** generally known as the P. C. (pronounced "pay-say"), is home to chic designer boutiques (such as Edgar Vos, Kookai, Leeser, Max Mara, Gianni Versace Boutique, and Mexx Image Shop); this is where diplomats and politicians buy their glad rags. **Van Baerlestraat,** leading to the Concertgebouw, is lined with bookstores specializing in art, music, and language and clothing shops that are smart—but somewhat more conservative than those on the adjoining P. C. Hooftstraat.

In the **Jordaan** neighborhood, generation after generation of experimental designers have set up shop to show their imaginative creations. Antiques and used-clothing shops are also in this part of town. **Rokin** is the place to go for high-price trendy fashion, jewelry, and accessories. **Utrechtsestraat** offers a variety of opportunities for the up-to-date home shopper, with stores specializing in kitchen, interior, and design objects.

DEPARTMENT STORES

C&A (Damrak 79, tel. 020/626–3132) offers discount clothing. **De Bijenkorf** (Dam 1, tel. 020/621–8080) is the city's best-known department store and the stomping ground of its

Foodies Full-City Tour

This full-day walking-tour takes you from the quiet and elegant oud zuid (old south) along the Ceintuurbaan to the bustling heart of the city. Start at de Waterwinkel for designer waters to drink along the way and head east to the intersection of the Ferdinand Bolstraat, where you can visit the tea and coffee specialist Simon Lévelt's Koffie-en Theehandel N.V.

Make a left to the Albert Cuypstraat and the open-air market Albert Cuypmarkt, with stalls selling flowers, fruits, vegetables, cheese, and household items. Try some decidedly Dutch street food: Nieuwe haring, herring cured in brine but considered raw, served with onions and pickles, or a paling (smoked eel) sandwich. Stop into the Gallerie Casbah for exotically decorated glazed dishes or a handmade tagine, a conical shaped ceramic oven for making Moroccan stews and couscous. De Pittenkoning on the Albert Cuypstraat has fine cookware.

On the van Woustraat, take Tram 4 (Direction Centraal Station) to the Muntplein or walk across the Frederiksplein to the Utrechtsestraat, follow the Utrechtsestraat past the Rembrandtplein to the Muntplein, cross the bridge onto the Nieuwe Doelenstraat, and bear to the right over the bridge to the Staalstraat for chocolates at Puccini Bomboni. Double back along the Staalstraat and make a right onto the Kloveniersburgwal to fill your spice cabinets with spices from Jacob Hooy & Co. At the end of the Kloveniersburgwal on the Nieuwmarkt, browse in the organic farmers market. With De Waag directly in front of you and the Kloveniersburgwal behind, make a left onto the Barndesteg in the Red Light District. Take the first left onto the Oudezijds Achter burgwal for three blocks to the intersection of the Oude Doelenstraat/Oude Hoogstraat, where you can pick up tablecloths, place mats or napkins of natural fibers at Capsicum Natuurstoffen. Finish your day at De Bierkoning by walking along the Oude Doelenstraat/Damstraat over Dam Square to the left side of the Royal Palace. Proost, cheers!

monied middle classes. **Hennes & Mauritz** (Kalverstraat 114-118, tel. 020/520–6090), better known as H & M, is a great place for high style at discount prices. The gracious and conservative **Maison de Bonneterie en Pander** (Rokin 140–142, tel. 020/626–2162), all crystal chandeliers and silently gliding shop assistants, stocks a selection of elegant clothing and household items.

The Amsterdam branch of England's **Marks & Spencer** (Kalverstraat 66–72, tel. 020/620–0006) is a good bet for inexpensive clothing and expensive food. **Metz & Co.** (Keizersgracht 455, tel. 020/624–8810) stocks textiles and household goods from Liberty of London and Sheridan as well as a range of breathtaking designer articles from all over the world; above the top-floor café is a "cupola" designed by the modernist Dutch architect Gerrit Reitveld where you can get the best bird's-eye view of the city.

Peek & Cloppenburg (Dam 20, tel. 020/622–8837) specializes in durable, middle-of-the-road clothing. **Vroom & Dreesmann** (Kalverstraat 203, tel. 020/622–0171), Amsterdam's third smartest department store, after De Bijenkorf and Maison de Bonneterie, sells good-quality clothing, home accessories, and temptations from its terrific bakery and candy counter.

MALLS

The imposing **Kalvertoren** (Kalverstraat, near Munt, Singel 456) offers covered shopping and a rooftop restaurant with magnificent city views. The **Magna Plaza** (Nieuwezijds Voorburgwal 182), inside the glorious old post office behind the Royal Palace, is the place for A-to-Z shopping in a huge variety of stores. **Max Euweplein** is a small shopping plaza/square surrounding a summer café and adjacent to the Amsterdam Casino. The square is approachable from either the Weteringschans near the Leidseplein or from the corner of the Hobbemastraat and Stadhouderskade.

MARKETS

A favorite with locals is the **Albert Cuypmarkt** (Albert Cuypstraat between Ferdinand Bolstraat and Van Woustraat). The market, four streets to the south of the Heineken Museum, boasts stalls with fresh fish, cheese, poultry, flowers, and a vast selection of hardware and household articles, clothes, bedding, and sundries of all kinds. It's open Monday through Saturday, 10–5.

The **Bloemenmarkt** (Along Singel canal, between Koningsplein and Muntplein) is another must-see market, where flowers and plants are sold from permanently moored barges. The market is open Monday through Saturday, 9:30–6; some flower stalls are open Sunday. Stalls at the **Boekenmarkt** (Spui square opposite Begijnhof) offer antiquarian and used books on every subject and in every language imaginable, Friday, 10–6.

On Saturday, the **Noordermarkt and Nieuwmarkt** (The former winds around Noorderkerk and along Lindengracht; the latter is at northern end of Kloveniersburgwal) host the **organic farmers' markets,** with stalls selling essential oils and other New Age fare alongside the oats, pulses, and vegetables.

The **Postzegelmarkt** (Along Nieuwezijds Voorburgwal) stamp market is held on Wednesday and Saturday from 1 to 4. **Sunday art markets** are held in good weather from April to October on Thorbeckeplein, and from April through November at Spui.

Few markets compare with Amsterdam's **Waterlooplein** flea market, which surrounds the perimeter of the Stopera (Muziektheater/Town Hall complex) building. It is a descendant of the haphazard pushcart trade that gave this part of the city its distinct and lively character in the early part of the century. You're unlikely to find anything of value here, but it's a good spot to look for the secondhand clothing young Amsterdammers favor, and it is a gadget lover's paradise. The flea market is open Monday through Saturday, 9:30–5.

68

SPECIALTY SHOPS
Antiques

You'll find several dealers under one roof in the **Amsterdam Antiques Gallery** (Nieuwe Spiegelstraat 34, tel. 020/625–3371). For a broad selection of high quality 19th-century prints and books, visit **Antiquariaat Kok** (Oude Hoogstraat 14-18, tel. 020/623–1191), in a marvelous building from the 1920s. The internationally known auction house **Christie's Amsterdam** (Cornelis Schuytstraat 57, tel. 020/575–5255) hosts sales of works of art, objects d'art, and collectables. **De Haas** (Kerkstraat 155, tel. 020/626–5952) specializes in small art nouveau and art deco objects from the end of the 19th and beginning of the 20th century. The indoor flea market **De Rommelmarkt** (Looiersgracht 38, tel. 020/627–4762), is a warren of stalls selling everything from art deco lamps to defunct electrical equipment.

Galerie Frans Leidelmeyer (Nieuwe Spiegelstraat 58, tel. 020/625–4627) is a good source of top-quality art deco and Jugendstil artifacts. For a broad range of vintage and antique furniture, curios, jewelry, clothing, and household items, try **Kunst- & Antiekmarkt De Looier** (Elandsgracht 109, tel. 020/624–9038), housing more than 50 dealers.

Competitor of Christie's, **Sotheby's Amsterdam** (De Boelelaan 30, tel. 020/550–2200) also offers sales in fine arts, antiques and collectables. **Tangram** (Herenstraat 9, tel. 020/624–4286) deals in the art deco and Jugendstil items that are so popular in the Netherlands. A specialist in art deco and modernist furnishings is **Vredespijp** (1e van der Helststraat 5-11, tel. 020/676-4855).

Beer

Beer aficionados will be amazed by the selections of beer from around the world at **Bert's Bierhuis** (2e Hugo de Grootstraat 3, tel. 020/684–3127). **De Bierkoning** (Paleisstraat 125, tel. 020/625–2336) stocks a worldwide selection of beer.

Ceramics and Crystal

You'll find a unique, comprehensive selection of glassware at **Breekbaar** (Weteringschans 209, tel. 020/ 626–1260). **Focke & Meltzer** (P. C. Hooftstraat 65–67, tel. 020/664–2311; Hotel Okura Shopping Arcade, tel. 020/678 7111) is Amsterdam's primary source for authenticated Delft and Makkumware and fine crystal. For superb antique glass and tiles from before 1800, visit **Frides Lamëris** (Nieuwe Spiegelstraat 55, tel. 020/626–4066).

For 19th-century glass and crystal, **A Glass of Beauty** (Rusland 27, tel. 020/626–8107) is the place to shop. **Ingeborg Ravenstijn** (Nieuwe Spiegelstraat 37, tel. 020/625–7720) has a full line of fine glass, silver and silver plate, and Continental decorative items. At **'t Winkeltje** (Prinsengracht 228, tel. 020/ 625–1352) you'll find a charming jumble of hotel porcelain, glass, and other household collectibles.

Chocolate

For the convenience of choco-holics, **Bonbon Jeannette** (Stationsplein 15, tel. 020/421-5194) has homemade bonbons in Centraal Station's central hall. Amsterdam's best handmade chocolates come from **Puccini Bomboni** (Singel 184, tel. 020/ 427–8341; Staalstraat 17, tel. 020/626–5474). Here, exotic combinations of chocolate and herbs (such as thyme and pepper) and spices are a specialty.

Clothes

MEN'S

For high-style apparel and designer togs, head to **Dik** (P. C. Hooftstraat 35, tel. 020/662–4328). The **English Hatter** (Heiligeweg 40, tel. 020/623–4781) has tweed jackets, deerstalkers, and many other trappings of the English country gentleman. **Gaudi** (P. C. Hooftstraat 116, tel. 020/679–9319) is a mecca for the trendy and label conscious. For European menswear, **Hugo Boss** has four lines available in Amsterdam.

Grachtengordel: Head to Toes Male and Female

The girdle of canals, or grachtengordel, that fan out from the center of the city are the starting point of this shopping tour. Bordered by the Raadhuisstraat and the Liedsestraat, the nine little streets that intersect the canals are referred to as the negen straatjes and host a concentration of specialty and fashion shops. Begin on the Gasthuismolensteeg at BrillenmuseumBrillenwinkel for a pair of glasses of either vintage or new design footware from Antonia Shoes. Follow the Gasthuismolensteeg until it continues as the Hartenstraat and consider a wallet or handbag at Hester van Eeghen. Turn left on the Keizersgracht to de Witte Tanden Winkel, where you can pick up a traveling toothbrush by French designer Philippe Stark. At the corner of the Liedsestraat, visit one of the designer boutiques at Metz & Co. for a glamorous new suit or dress and then take this street towards the heart of the city. On the corner of the Herengracht, top off your new look with a hat from Hoeden M/V.

The sportswear line is available at **Boss Sport** (P. C. Hooftstraat 112, tel. 020/379–5050). Hugo Boss's high-end and trendy design lines for men are available at **Hugo** (P. C. Hooftstraat 49, tel. 020/470–2297).

McGregor and Clan Shop (P. C. Hooftstraat 113, tel. 020/662–7425) has a distinctly Scottish air, with chunky knitwear and the odd flash of tartan. **Meddens** (Heiligeweg 11–17, tel. 020/624–0461) stocks a good range of fairly conservative men's casual and formal wear. **Mulberry Company** (P. C. Hooftstraat 46, tel. 020/673–8086) sells stylish fashions from England. **Oger** (P. C. Hooftstraat 75-81, tel. 020/676–8695) puts suits on the backs of leading Dutch politicians and TV personalities.

Hip and casual threads are found at the three locations of **Sissy-Boy** (Van Baerlestraat 12, tel. 020/672–0247; Kalverstraat 199, tel. 020/626–0088; Liedsestraat 15, tel. 020/623–8949). **Society Shop** (Van Baerlestraat 20, tel. 020/664–9281) stocks good basics for businessmen.

WOMEN'S

Boetiek Pauw (Van Baerlestraat 66 and 72, tel. 020/662–6253), which also operates men's and children's shops, is part of a chain that stands out for the quality of both design and craftsmanship of its clothing. The international fashion house **Esprit** (Spui 1c, tel. 020/626–3624) has a large branch in central Amsterdam. The Dutch minichain **Cora Kemperman** (Liedsestraat 72, tel. 020/625–1284) offers architecturally designed clothes that are ageless and elegant. The colorful and funky women's and children's clothing shop **Oilily The Exclusive Store** (P. C. Hooftstraat 131-133, tel. 020/672–3361; Singel 456, in the Kalvertoren, tel. 020/422–8713) is now an international chain; their flagship stores are in Amsterdam.

For a funky look go to **Sjerpetine** (1e van der Helststraat 33, tel. 020/664–1362). The shop is aesthetically organized in a rainbow of color and patterns. **Claudia Sträter** (Beethovenstraat 9, tel. 020/673–6605; Kalverstraat 179–181, tel. 020/622–0559) is part of a Dutch minichain that sells simply styled, well-made clothes for all occasions.

Collectibles

Couzijn Simon (Prinsengracht 578, tel. 020/624–7691) specializes in molting teddies and vintage toys. **Galerie Animation Art** (Berenstraat 39, tel. 020/627–7600) offers original Disney and other cartoon sketches. One special shop—**Latei** (Zeedijk 143, tel. 020/625–7485)—is also a café where all that you sit on and drink from are for purchase, in addition to Italian olive oil.

The selection of antique advertising posters at **Quadra Original Posters** (Herengracht 384-389, tel. 020/626–9472) is top quality. **A Space Oddity** (Princengracht 204, tel. 020/427–4036) combs the world for robots, toys, and memorabilia from TV and film classics. Collectors of medical and pharmaceutical antiques can find a broad selection of instruments based upon medical specialty at **Thom en Lenny Nelis Antiques** (Keizersgracht 541, tel. 020/623–1546).

Diamonds

The **Amsterdam Diamond Center** (Rokin 1–5, tel. 020/624–5787) houses several diamond sellers. **Coster Diamonds** (Paulus Potterstraat 2–4, tel. 020/676–2222) not only sells jewelry and loose diamonds but gives free demonstrations of diamond cutting. You can see a replica of the most famous diamond cut in the factory—the Koh-I-Noor, one of the prize gems of the British crown jewels. **Van Moppes Diamonds** (Albert Cuypstraat 2–6, tel. 020/676–1242) has an extensive diamond showroom and offers a glimpse of the process of diamond cutting and polishing.

Duty-Free

If you don't have time to shop in Amsterdam, save your guilders for the airport, as **Amsterdam Airport Shopping Centre** (Amsterdam Schiphol Airport, tel. 020/601–2497) is bigger, better, and cheaper than almost any other airport duty-free shopping area in the world. The airport's departure hall looks more like a shopping mall than a transportation facility, and auxiliary shops for the most popular items (electronics, liquor, perfume, delicatessen, chocolates) are found in every wing of the terminal. The arrival hall, although not duty free, has a terrific selection of shops, including a grocery store, cafés, gift shops, a satellite of Metz & Co., and the wonderful World of Wings, with models of every imaginable aircraft.

Gifts and Souvenirs

BrillenmuseumBrillenwinkel (Gasthuismolensteeg 7, tel. 020/421–2414) displays a collection of eyeglasses from antique to

Going Dutch

While warm and cozy houses with overstuffed chairs, lace curtains, and carpeted floors prevail in most of Holland, modernist architects and furniture designers are popular with the urban population. Amsterdam has a concentration of international design firms and shops with great contemporary furniture and accessories for the home. In shops around the city, modern European and American classics from Stark and the Eames are interspersed with Dutch designs from the Bauhaus-inspired W. H. Gispen of the 1920s to contemporaries such as Martin Visser, Benno Premsela, Piet Hein Eek, and Henk Stallinga. In the 1990s, Dutch designers represented by Droog Design (Dry Design)—more a "mentality" than a "style"—achieved international fame (and shows at museums in North America and Europe) with whimsical items such as wobble vases, soft sinks, and lamps made of recycled milk bottles.

The Dutch are "environmentally correct" and this has entered into the design consciousness, too. Objects are made from all sorts of recycled materials: wastepaper baskets are made from billboard advertisements thereby giving new meaning to "waste paper." A plethora of old bicycle inner tires has inspired some clothing and accessory designers to come up with kinky designs in black rubber. Plastic film canisters become string lights that resemble mini-lanterns, and old-fashioned milk bottles become whimsical floor lamps.

There is a place at the **Vormgevingsinstituut** (Netherlands Design Institute; Keizersgracht 609, tel. 020/551–6500) for all aspects of design, from city planning to architecture, fashion, interior, and graphics. Founded in 1993, the organization's mission is to increase the quality of design and to stimulate interest in well designed products. It initiates exhibitions (staged in its palatial home), conducts research into emerging topics specifically related to the design industry (such as a project that investigated design issues for the elderly), and sponsors a magazine, library, lecture series, and workshops.

contemporary in a shop that evokes the atmosphere of the 17th century (the upstairs galleries actually have museum status); open Wednesday–Saturday. The delightful **de Beestenwinkel** (Staalstraat 11, tel. 020/623–1805) has nothing but animal toys in every price range. At **de Condomerie** (Warmoestraat 141, tel. 020/ 627–4174) the discrete, well-informed staff promotes healthy sexual practice in this shop that specializes in condoms.

More than 100 varieties of bottled water are available at **de Waterwinkel** (Roelof Hartstraat 10, tel. 020/675–5932). The store's interior design is as crystal clear as its waters. If you're concerned about your dental health, **de Witte Tanden Winkel** (Runstraat 5, tel. 020/623–3443) offers everything you could need. The **Greenpeace Infoshop** (Leliegracht 51, tel. 020/ 524– 9579) dispenses information on the activities of the internationally known activists and offers cards, T-shirts, and educational materials on the environment.

Jacob Hooy & Co. (Kloveniersburgwal 12, tel. 020/624–3041) has been selling herbs, spices, and medicinal potions from the same shop beside the Nieuwmarkt since 1743. Gold-lettered wooden drawers, barrels, and bins contain not just spices and herbs but also a daunting array of *dropjes* (licorice candies that range from "double" salty to sweet and other medicinal chewy lozenges) and teas.

Olivaria (Hazenstraat 2a, tel. 020/638–3552) stocks only olive oil. A tasting table dominates the interior, which resembles a library reading room. **Simon Lévelt's Koffie-en Theehandel N.V.** (Prinsengracht 180, tel. 020/624–0823; Ferdinand Bolstraat 154, tel. 020/400–4060) offers nearly 100 different kinds of tea and more than two dozen coffees.

Housewares

Capsicum (Oude Hoogstraat 1, tel. 020/623–1016) designs and produces luxurious textiles in all-natural fibers for the home. **De Kasstoor** (Rosengracht 202-210, tel. 020/521–8112) is an interior design department store offering three floors of 20th-century design for every room in the home. Fine cookware can be found at **De Pittenkoning** (1e van der Helststraat 35, tel. 020/671–6308). The prime location for new design in every discipline is the **Frozen Fountain** (Prinsengracht 629, tel. 020/622–9375). Everything from packets of suction-cup hooks and inexpensive tea light holders to Martin Visser's minimalist sleep sofa is here. **Gallerie Casbah** (1e van der Helststraat 68, tel. 020/671–0474), in an evocative atmosphere, has handmade crafts from North Africa.

Even the Dutch equivalent of Woolworths, **Hema** (Nieuwendijk 174-176, tel. 020/623–4176), has well-designed household items at reasonable prices and a cheese and deli counter. **Homestore** (Cornelis Schuytstraat 37, tel. 020/379–0408) has exotic accessories like Asian basketwork and Peruvian pillows. Inexpensive kitchen and interior items in brilliant colors and patterns at **Kitsch Kitchen** (1e Bloemdwarsstraat 21, tel. 020/622–8261) come from Latin America and Asia. With fantastic views of the harbor, **Pakhuis** (Oostelijke Handelskade 15-17, tel. 020/421–1033) is an old warehouse with over thirty design boutiques under one roof. If your time is short, the **Stedelijk Museum** (Paulus Potterstraat 13, tel. 020/573–2911, ext. 632) has a splendid collection of design items on the balcony above the book shop.

Jewelry

The international leader in contemporary jewelry design is **Hans Appenzeller** (Grimburgwal 1, tel. 020/626–8218). **Bonebakker** (Rokin 88/90, tel. 020/623–2294) is one of the city's oldest and finest jewelers and carries an exceptionally fine range of watches and silverware. **Galerie RA** (Vijzelstraat 80, tel. 020/626–5100) boasts wearable art by Dutch jewelry designers. **Premsela & Hamburger** (Rokin 98, tel. 020/624–9688; closed Saturday) has sold fine antique silver and jewelry since 1823. The century-old **Schaap and Citroen** (Heiligeweg 36, tel. 020/626–6691) has an affordable range of jewelry and watches.

Leather Goods

Hester van Eeghen (Hartenstraat 1, tel. 020/626–9212) designs gorgeous and pricy leather briefcases, handbags, billfolds, and wallets in brilliant colors. A small selection of leather items is available at the **Stedelijk Museum** (Paulus Potterstraat 13 tel. 020/573–2911 x632).

Millinery

The well-stocked **Hoeden M/V** (422 Herengracht, tel. 020/626–3038), in a canal house, carries Borsalino hats for men and women as well as Dutch and international designer hats. For handmade hats by Dutch designers, the **Madhatter** (Van der Helstplein 4, tel. 020/664–7748) has offerings from inexpensive rain hats to custom-made brides' millenery.

Music

Near the Concertgebouw, **Broekmans & Van Poppel** (Van Baerlestraat 92-94, tel. 020/675–1653) specializes in recordings, sheet music, and accessories for classical and antiquarian music. There's an antiques-store atmosphere at **Datzzit Verzamel—Muziek en Filmwinkel** (Prinsengracht 306, tel. 020/622-1195). The merchandise includes music on 78s, vinyl, and CD as well as film memorabilia. Hip hop enthusiasts have **Fat Beats Amsterdam** (Singel 10, tel. 020/423–0886).

The well-informed staff at **Kuijper Klassiek** (Ferdinand Bolstraat 6, tel. 020/679–4634) offers hard-to-find recordings. **Sounds of the Fifties** (Prinsengracht 669, tel. 020/623–9745) offers vintage recordings, nostalgia, and the owner's vast knowledge, kept on the tip of his tongue. The vast **South Miami Plaza** (Albert Cuypstraat 182, tel. 020/662–2817) has just about every music category, including the Dutch answer to country music, *smartlap*; listening booths are available, too.

Shoes

Antonia Shoes offers three stores of hip footwear from top European designers for men (Gasthuismolensteeg 16, tel. 020/320–9443) and women (Gasthuismolensteeg 12, tel. 020/627–2433) and a special store for slippers only (Gasthuismolensteeg 6 tel. 020/626–3884). **Bally Shoes** (Leidsestraat 8-10, tel. 020/622–2888) is a byword for good taste in women's shoes.

Dr. Adams (P. C. Hooftstraat 90, tel. 020/662–3835 and Liedsestraat 25, tel. 020/626–4460; Oude Dolenstraat 5-7, tel. 020/622–3734) sells chunkier, more adventurous styles of shoes for men and women. **Shoebaloo** (Koningsplein 7, tel. 020/626–7993) is the place for 8-inch heels, mock leopard-skin boots, and other outrageous footwear. **Smit Bally** (Leidsestraat 41, tel. 020/624–8862) sells classically smart shoes for men.

Tobacco

Davidoff (Van Baerlestraat 84, tel. 020/671–1042) stocks fine cigars and other smokers' requisites. One of the best places in the world to buy cigars and other smoking materials is **Hajenius** (Rokin 92, tel. 020/623–7494), in business since 1826. A visit to **Smokiana** (Prinsengracht 488, tel. 020/421–1779) is a special treat for pipe smokers.

Amsterdam is a gem of a city for the tourist. It is small and densely packed with fine buildings, many dating from the city's Golden Age between the 16th and 18th centuries. The city's seedier side, however, is just as much a factor in making it the tourist attraction it is today.

In This Chapter

CITY OF THE ARTS: FROM THE DAM TO THE GOLDEN BEND 80 • A Good Walk 80 • What to See 84 • HISTORIC AMSTERDAM: FROM THE JEWISH QUARTER TO REMBRANDT'S HOUSE 92 • A Good Walk 92 • What to See 94 • THE CANALS: CITY OF BRIDGES 104 • A Good Walk 104 • What to See 106

By Andrew May

here and there

AMSTERDAM HAS A TREASURE TROVE OF ART MUSEUMS, a cultural life extraordinarily rich for a city with far fewer than one million inhabitants, and a reputation for a seedier side. The city's key sights can be covered in two or three days, but a week or more is needed to savor its relaxed tempo as you people-watch from a café terrace or wander at leisure through its charming neighborhoods and browse in the unique shops. You can easily see most of the city on foot, but there are also rental bikes, a superb tram system, and canal boats.

Amsterdam is laid out in orderly concentric rings of canals around the old center. The main canals, constructed in the 17th century, form a horseshoe around the center, known as the *grachtengordel* (canal ring or girdle), and are crosscut by a network of access roads and alleylike connecting streets. A walk from the center (Centraal Station) directly down to the southern edge takes you through the heart of town to the museum district. To the east of the center of town lie the Old Town and the former Jewish Quarter; to the west you'll find the charming Jordaan.

Numbers in the text correspond to numbers in the margin and on the Exploring Amsterdam map.

CITY OF THE ARTS:
FROM THE DAM TO THE GOLDEN BEND

Amsterdam's 17th-century Golden Age left behind it a tide-mark of magnificent buildings and some of the greatest paintings in western art. Amsterdam's wealth of art—from Golden Age painters through Van Gogh up to the present day—is concentrated in the area around the recently re-landscaped Museumplein. The perimeter of this open plain is defined by the Stedelijk Museum of Modern Art, the Van Gogh Museum, the Rijksmuseum, and the Concertgebouw concert hall. There are water features, lawns, and an unusual upturned grass bank known disparagingly as the *ezelsoor* ("donkey's ear"). This open, landscaped square also serves as the transition point between the central canal area and the modern residential sections of the city. On the way from the site of the original dam to the museum quarter, you encounter some of the grand mansions built over the ages by Amsterdam's prosperous merchants.

A Good Walk

Begin where Amsterdam began, at the seething hub of the **Dam** ①. On the south side, where Kalverstraat and Rokin meet the square, is **Madame Tussaud Scenerama** ②, a branch of the famous wax museum. For a taste of ancient cultures, take a turn in the **Allard Pierson Museum** ③ farther down Rokin, on the left. From the Dam, follow the busy pedestrian shopping street, Kalverstraat, south to the entrance to the **Amsterdams Historisch Museum** ④ (or get there through the Enge Kapelsteeg alley if you have visited the Allard Pierson Museum). Here you can get an enjoyable, easily digestible lesson on the city's past.

Passing through the painting gallery of the Historisch Museum brings you to the entrance of the **Begijnhof** ⑤, a blissfully peaceful courtyard. Behind the Begijnhof you come to an open square, the Spui, lined with popular sidewalk cafés, and to the

Singel, the innermost of Amsterdam's concentric canals. Cut through the canals by way of the romantic Heisteeg alley and its continuation, the Wijde Heisteeg, turning left down the Herengracht to the corner of Leidsegracht. This is part of the prestigious **Gouden Bocht** ⑥, the grandest stretch of canal in town.

Continue down the Herengracht to the Vijzelstraat and turn right to the next canal, the Keizersgracht. Cross the Keizersgracht and turn left to find the **Museum van Loon** ⑦, an atmospheric canal house, still occupied by the family that has owned it for centuries but open to the public. Turn back down Keizersgracht until you reach Nieuwe Spiegelstraat; take another right and walk toward Museumplein. Rising up in front of you is the redbrick, neo-Gothic splendor of the **Rijksmuseum** ⑧, housing the world's greatest collection of Dutch art. When you leave the Rijksmuseum, walk through the covered gallery under the building. Directly ahead is Museumplein itself; to your right is Paulus Potterstraat (look for the diamond factory on the far corner), where you'll find the **Van Gogh Museum** ⑨, which contains a unique collection of that tortured artist's work.

Continuing along Paulus Potterstraat, at the corner of Van Baerlestraat, you reach the **Stedelijk Museum** ⑩, where you can see modern art from Picasso to the present. Just around the corner, facing the back of the Rijksmuseum across Museumplein, is the magnificent 19th-century concert hall, the **Concertgebouw** ⑪. A short walk back up along Van Baerlestraat will bring you to the **Vondelpark** ⑫—acre after acre of parkland alive with people in summer.

TIMING

To see only the buildings, allow about an hour. Expand your allotment depending on your interest in the museums en route. At minimum, each deserves 60–90 minutes. At the Rijksmuseum allow at least that just to see the main Dutch

Westerstraat
Anjeliersstraat
Tuinstraat 38
Egelantiersstraat

Rombout Hogerbeetsstraat
Frederik Hendrikstraat
Nassau Kade
Marnixkade
Singelgracht
Lijnbaansgracht
Van Oldenb. Straat

Prinsenstr. Herenstr.
Prinsengracht
Keizersgracht
Herengracht
Spuistr.

39

Eglantiersgracht
Nieuwe Leliestraat
gracht
Bloem
gracht
Bloemstraat

37
36
35

Lelliegracht
Singel

34
33
1
2

Hugo De Grootstr.

Raadhuisstraat
Reestraat
Hartenstraat

Daqe

Rozengracht
Rozenstraat
Laurierstraat

De Clercq-straat
Nassau
Marnixstraat
Lijnbaans
Singel gracht

gracht
Laurier
Elandsstraat
Elandsgracht

Prinsengracht
Keizersgracht
Herengracht
Singel

Berenstraat
Wolvenstraat·

4
Kalverstraat

Da Costastraat
Da Costa

Kade

Løøiersgracht

Woonbootmuseum
Runstraat   Huidenstraat

5
Spui

Kinkerstraat

6

Singel
Reguliersdv.

J. van Lennepstraat

gracht

J. van Lennep Kanaal

gracht

Constantijn Huygensstraat

Lange Leidsedwarsstraat
Leidse
Leidsestraat

Kerkstraat
Nieuwe Spiegelstr.

Helmersstraat
Overtoom

_i_

11
8

10   9

12

Lijnbaans
Prinsengracht

Vondelstraat

Allard Pierson
Museum, 3

Amsterdams
Historisch
Museum, 4

Anne
Frankhuis, 37

Artis, 20

Begijnhof, 5

Beurs van
Berlage, 42

Brouwers-
gracht, 39

Centraal
Station, 40

Concert-
gebouw, 11

Dam, 1

Damrak, 41

Gouden Bocht, 6

Het Koninklijk
Paleis te
Amsterdam, 33

Hollandsche
Schouwburg, 19

Hortus
Botanicus, 17

Joods Historisch
Museum, 15

Jordaan, 38

Madame Tussaud
Scenerama, 2

Montelbaan-
storen, 25

Museum
Amstelkring, 31

Museum het
Rembrandt-
huis, 22

Museum van
Loon, 7

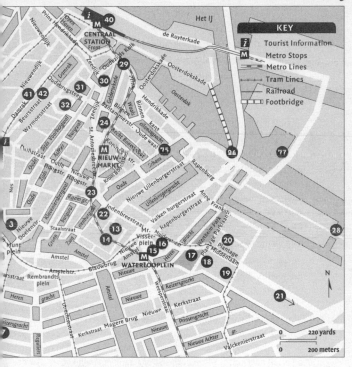

KEY

i Tourist Information

M Metro Stops

Metro Lines

Tram Lines

Railroad

Footbridge

Het IJ

de Ruyterkade

CENTRAAL STATION Front

Prins Hendrikkade

Nieuwebrug

Nieuwendijk

Open Haven

Oosterdoksstraat

Oosterdokskade

Oosterdok

Hendrikkade

Binnen kant

eilandsgracht

Oude waal

Nieuwendijk

Damrak

Beursstraat

Warmoesstraat

Oudebrugsteeg

Geldersekade

St. Antoniesbreestraat

Zeedijk

Oudezijds Kolk

Warmoesstraat

St. Jacobstraat

Oude Hoogstr.

Nieuwe Hoogstr.

Koningsstr.

NIEUWE MARKT

Nieuwe Uilenburgerstraat

Uilenburgergracht

Rapenburg

Anne Frankstr.

Valkenburgerstraat

Mr. Visserplein

Nieuwe Amstel

Heren

Jodenbreestraat

Mr. Kapenburgwrstraat

's-Gravelandseveer

Wertheim Park

Plantage Parklaan

Plantage Middenlaan

Staalstraat

Raamgr.

Kloveniersburgwal

Groenburgwal

Zwanenburgwal

WATERLOOPLEIN

Blauwbrug

Nieuwe

Nieuwe

Keizersgracht

Kerkstraat

Prinsengracht

Nieuwe

Magere Brug

Kerkstraat

Nieuwe Achter gr.

Valckenierstraat

Amstel

Amstelstr.

Rembrandtsplein

Munt plein

Nieuwe Doelenstr.

Oude Doelenstr.

Nes

Kalverstr.

Singel

Herengracht

Keizersgracht

Regulier

N

0   220 yards

0   200 meters

Museumwerf 't Kromhout, 28

Muziektheater/ Stadhuis, 14

Nederlands Scheepvaartmuseum, 27

Nederlands Theatermuseum, 35

Nemo Science & Technology Center, 26

Nieuwe Kerk, 34

Nieuwmarkt, 24

Oude Kerk, 32

Portugees Israelitische Synagoge, 16

Rijksmuseum, 8

Schreierstoren, 29

Stedelijk Museum, 10

Tropenmuseum, 21

Van Gogh Museum, 9

Verzetsmuseum, 18

Vondelpark, 12

Waterlooplein, 13

Westerkerk, 36

Zeedijk, 30

Zuiderkerk, 23

paintings. You could easily pass most of the day there if you want to investigate the entire collection.

The best time to visit the Vondelpark is in the late afternoon or evening, especially in summer, as this is when the entertainment starts. In the busy season (July–September), lines at the Van Gogh Museum are long, so it's best to go early or allow for an extra 15 minutes' waiting time.

What to See

❸ ALLARD PIERSON MUSEUM. The fascinating archaeological collection of the University of Amsterdam is housed here, tracing the early development of Western civilization (from the Egyptians to the Romans) and of the Near Eastern cultures (Anatolia, Persia, Palestine) in a series of well-documented, interestingly presented displays. *Oude Turfmarkt 127, tel. 020/525–2556. Fl 9.50 (€4.30). Tues.–Fri. 10–5, weekends and holidays 1–5.*

★ **❹ AMSTERDAMS HISTORISCH MUSEUM** (Amsterdam Historical Museum). Housed in a former orphanage, this museum traces the history of Amsterdam, from its beginnings in the 13th century as a marketplace for farmers and fishermen through the glorious period during the 17th century when Amsterdam was the richest, most powerful trading city in the world. A tall, skylighted gallery is filled with the guild paintings that document that period of power. In one of the building's tower rooms you can have a go on an old church carillon. *Kalverstraat 92/Nieuwezijds Voorburgwal 357, tel. 020/523–1822. Fl 12 (€5.45). Weekdays 10–5, weekends 11–5. Closed Dec. 25, Jan. 1, Apr. 30. www.ahm.nl*

★ **❺ BEGIJNHOF** (Beguine Court). Here, serenity reigns just a block from the screeching of trams stopping next to the bustling **Spui** square (☞ Need a Break, *below*). The Begijnhof is the courtyard of a residential hideaway, built in the 14th century as a conventlike residence for unmarried or widowed laywomen. It's typical of many found throughout the Netherlands. The court is on a square where you'll also find No. 34, the oldest house in Amsterdam and

A Breath of Fresh Air: The Amsterdamse Bos

The largest of Amsterdam's many parks is the Amsterdamse Bos, or Amsterdam Woods, covering a total area of 895 hectares (2,210 acres) to the south of the city. An extraordinary piece of engineering, all this was dug, laid out, planted, or constructed from 1934 onward, providing work for 20,000 unemployed people during the Depression. Perhaps even more remarkable is that much of it lies up to 4 m (13 ft) below sea level. This woodland habitat harbors no fewer than 150 tree varieties, but it also has open fields, a boating lake, the Bosbaan rowing course with stadium, and a goat farm. With 137 km (85 mi) of footpaths and 51 km (32 mi) of bicycle paths traversing 50 bridges—many designed in the early 20th-century Amsterdam School style with characteristic redbrick and sculpted stone detailing—it is an easy escape from the city for adults and ideal for children.

To get here by bike, cycle through the Vondelpark to its southern tip, then take a left onto the Amstelveenseweg and follow it until you reach the Van Nijenrodeweg. Turn right into the Amsterdamse Bos, and you will find yourself at the stadium end of the Bosbaan rowing course. Buses 170, 171, and 172 take passengers from the Leidseplein to the Van Nijenrodeweg, where you can rent bikes from June to August. Maps and signposting are plentiful throughout the park.

At the **Grote Vijver** (Big Pond) you can hire kayaks, pedalos, and rowing boats from April through September. The **Bosmuseum** (Koenenkade 56, tel. 020/676–2152) has displays about natural history and the management of the woods, and is open from 10 AM to 5 PM daily for free. If you didn't pack your own lunch, the neighboring **Boerderij Meerzicht** (Koenenkade 56, tel. 020/679–2744) is a café-restaurant serving sandwiches and traditional Dutch pancakes with a selection of savory and sweet toppings.

one of only two remaining wooden houses in the city center. After a series of disastrous fires, laws were passed in the 15th century forbidding the construction of buildings made entirely from timber. The small **Engelse Kerk** (English Church) in one corner of the square dates from 1400 and was used by the Pilgrim Fathers during their brief stay in Amsterdam in the early 17th century. *Begijnhof 29, tel. 020/623–3565. Free. Weekdays 11–4.*

NEED A BREAK? The Spui is at the end of the alley that passes out of the Begijnhof. The open square has benches and is surrounded by bars and eateries that are a good place to take a break. At **Caffe Esprit** (Spui 10, tel. 020/622–1967), attached to the international clothing store of the same name, you can choose from an American-style lunchtime menu. **Broodje van Kootje** (Spui 28, tel. 020/623–7451) is the home of the classic Amsterdam *broodje* (sandwich), good for a quick bite. More exclusive is the **Lanskroon** bakery and tearoom down the small Heisteeg alleyway to the Singel canal (Singel 385, tel. 020/623–7743), where you can enjoy savory pastries and delicious *vlaai* (fruit pies) in a smoke-free environment.

⑪ **CONCERTGEBOUW** (Concert Building). The Netherlands' premier concert hall, the world-famous Concertgebouw, has been filled since the turn of the century with the music of the Royal Concertgebouw Orchestra, as well as visiting international artists. There are two concert halls in the building, Grote (large) and Kleine (small). The larger hall is one of the most acoustically perfect anywhere. You will recognize the building at once (it is topped with a lyre); enter through the glass extension along the side. There are no tours of the building, so you will need to buy a ticket to a concert to see beyond the broad lobby, or, if you arrive before 12:30 on a Wednesday in September–June, you can attend a free lunchtime concert. *Concertgebouwplein 2–6, tel. 020/675–4411 24-hr concert schedule and hot line or 020/671–8345 box office.*

① **DAM** (Dam Square). The Dam, the official center of town, traces its roots to the 12th century, when wanderers from central Europe came floating in their canoes down the Amstel River and stopped to build a dam. Soon this muddy mound became the focal point of the small settlement of Amstelledamme and the location of the local weigh house. The Dam is still the official center of town. Once, ships could sail right up to the weigh house, along the Damrak. But in the 19th century the Damrak was filled in to form the street leading to Centraal Station, and King Louis Napoléon had the weigh house demolished in 1808 because it spoiled the view from his bedroom window in the palace across the way. The monument in the center of the square was erected in 1956 to commemorate the liberation of the Netherlands at the end of World War II. *Follow Damrak south from Centraal Station; Raadhuisstraat leads from Dam to intersect main canals.*

⑥ **GOUDEN BOCHT** (Golden Bend). This stretch of the Herengracht, from the Leidsegracht to the Vijzelstraat, contains some of Amsterdam's most opulent 18th-century architecture. Construction of the main ring of canals, the Prinsengracht (Princes' Canal), the Keizersgracht (Emperors' Canal), and the Herengracht (Gentlemen's Canal), began during the Golden Age. In true Dutch egalitarian style, the most prestigious of the three was the Herengracht. Built by wealthy merchants, the houses are wide, with elaborate gables and cornices, richly decorated facades, and heavy, centrally placed doors—an imposing architecture that suits the bank headquarters of today as well as it did the grandees of yore. The most notable are numbers 475 (designed by Hans Jacob Husly in 1703); 485 (Jean Coulon, 1739); 493 and 527, both in the Louis XVI style (1770); and 284 (Van Brienen House, 1728), another ornate Louis XVI facade.

② **MADAME TUSSAUD SCENERAMA.** A branch of the world-famous wax museum, this Madame Tussaud's—at Dam Square above the P. C. Hooftstraat department store—includes a life-size, 3-D rendering of a painting by Vermeer—a remarkable vision or a kitschy delight, depending on your sensibility. Alongside the familiar stars, there are waxen statues of Dutch royalty and historic figures such as Rembrandt. *Dam 20, tel. 020/622–9949. Fl 19.50 (€8.85). Sept.–June, daily 10–5:30; July–Aug., daily 9:30–5:30.*

★ ⑦ **MUSEUM VAN LOON.** The city's best look at life in the canal houses, the Museum van Loon still serves as a residence for a descendant of one of Amsterdam's powerful families. Today, however, it is also open to the public, still brimming with 18th-century furnishings and portraits of the Van Loon family. *Keizersgracht 672, tel. 020/624–5255. Fl 7.50 (€3.40). Fri.–Mon. 11–5. www.musvloon.nl*

★ ⑧ **RIJKSMUSEUM** (State Museum). The Netherlands' greatest museum celebrated its second centenary as the national art collection in 2000. When architect P. J. H. Cuypers came up with the museum's extravagant design in the late 1880s, it shocked Calvinist Holland. Cuypers was persuaded to tone down some of the more ostentatious elements of his neo-Renaissance decoration and to curb the excesses of his soaring neo-Gothic lines—but, while the building was being constructed, he managed to visit the site and reinstate some of his ideas. The result is a magnificent, turreted building that glitters with gold leaf.

The Rijksmuseum has more than 150 rooms displaying paintings, sculpture, and objects from both the West and Asia, dating from the 9th through the 19th centuries. The primary collection is of 15th- to 17th-century paintings, mostly Dutch (the Rijksmuseum has the largest concentration of these masters in the world). There are also extensive holdings of drawings and prints from the 15th to the 20th centuries and room after room of antique furniture, silverware, and exquisite porcelain, including Delftware. The 17th-century doll's houses—made as showpieces for wealthy merchant families—are especially worth seeing.

If your time is limited, then head directly for the Gallery of Honor on the upper floor, in which hangs Rembrandt's *The Night Watch*,

Bureau de change

Cambio

外国為替

In this city, you can find money on almost any street.

NO-FEE FOREIGN EXCHANGE

The Chase Manhattan Bank has over 80 convenient
locations near New York City destinations such as:

        Times Square
        Rockefeller Center
        Empire State Building
        2 World Trade Center
        United Nations Plaza

Exchange any of 75 foreign currencies

CHASE

THE RIGHT RELATIONSHIP IS EVERYTHING.

as well as a selection of other well-known Rembrandt paintings, and works by Vermeer, Frans Hals, and other great Golden Age artists. A clockwise progression through the rooms of the adjoining East Wing takes you past works by some of the greatest Dutch painters of the 15th to the 17th centuries— meticulous still lifes, jolly tavern scenes, and rich portraits full of character.

The museum has allotted Fl 345 million (about $150 million) towards the biggest renovation in the building's 115-year history. Much of the building will be closed from 2003 through 2006, though highlights of the collection will remain on exhibit in the South Wing. *Stadhouderskade 42, tel. 020/674–7000. Fl 15 (€6.80). Daily 10–5. Closed Jan. 1. www.rijksmuseum.nl*

🔟 **STEDELIJK MUSEUM** (Municipal Museum of Modern Art). Hot and happening modern art has one of its most respected homes here at the Stedelijk. Works by such trendy contemporary artists as Jeff Koons are displayed alongside a collection of paintings and sculptures by the granddaddies of modernism: Chagall, Cézanne, Picasso, Monet, and others. Major movements that are well documented here are CoBrA (Appel, Corneille), American pop art (Johns, Oldenburg, Liechtenstein), American action painting (Willem de Kooning, Pollock), and neorealism (Niki de Saint-Phalle, Tinguely). *Paulus Potterstraat 13, tel. 020/573–2911. Fl 9 (€4.10). Daily 11–5. Jan. 1. www.stedelijk.nl*

★ 9️⃣ **VAN GOGH MUSEUM.** Based on a design by Gerrit Rietveld and opened in 1973, this museum venerates the short but prolific career of the 19th-century Dutch painter Vincent van Gogh. The collection of 200 paintings and 500 drawings by the artist ranges from a dramatic *Sunflowers* to ear-less self-portraits. The permanent collection also includes other important 19th-century artists. The year 1999 marked the 200th anniversary of Van Gogh's birth and the reopening of the museum with a new extension designed by Japanese architect Kisho Kurokawa. The new annex to the modernized Rietveld building is a freestanding, multistory, oval structure, built in a bold combination of titanium and gray-brown stone and connected to the main galleries by an underground walkway. It provides space for temporary exhibitions, allowing more room to show the works of Van Gogh himself. *Paulus Potterstraat 7, tel. 020/570–5200. Fl 12.50 (€5.65). Daily 10–6. Closed Jan. 1. www.vangoghmuseum.nl*

⑫ VONDELPARK. First laid out in 1865 on 25 acres, the park soon expanded to cover some 120 acres and was renamed after Joost van den Vondel, the "Dutch Shakespeare." Landscaped in the informal English style, the park is an irregular patchwork of copses, ponds, and fields linked by winding pathways. In good weather the park buzzes with activity. People come to roller skate and play tennis. Dutch families string up flags between the branches and party under the trees. Lovers stroll through the fragrant formal *Rozentuin* (rose garden). Children sit transfixed by colorful acrobatics in the outdoor theater. Later, the clowns give way to jazz bands and cabaret artists who play well into the night, and the Vondelpark takes on the atmosphere of a giant outdoor café. From June to August free outdoor concerts and plays are performed at the open-air theater from Wednesday through Sunday.

Over the years a range of sculptural and architectural delights have made their appearance in the park. There's an elegant 19th-century bandstand, and the famous **Round Blue Teahouse,** a rare beauty of functionalist architecture, built beside the lake in 1937. Picasso himself donated a sculpture to commemorate the park's centenary in 1965. An elegant 19th-century entertainment pavilion has been converted into the **Nederlands Filmmuseum** (Netherlands Film Museum). Although there is no permanent exhibition, the museum has shows every day in its two cinemas, drawing on material from all over the world as well as from its substantial archive (which includes such gems as hand-tinted silent movies). On summer Saturdays, there are free outdoor screenings. *Stadhouderskade. Filmmuseum, Vondelpark 3, tel. 020/589–1400.*

Amsterdam on Wheels

As soon as you step out of the train and leave Centraal Station, you are confronted by bikes in all states of disrepair, piled against railings, standing precariously against each other, or in ramshackle heaps. Why not rent a bike yourself? It can make all the difference to your stay in the city and offer you an insider's perspective on this compact city. Taking the necessary care to watch for other traffic and pedestrians, you can get around on two wheels at a pace that still allows you to take in your surroundings.

Most rental bikes are fitted with pedal brakes, rather than hand brakes. To stop, you pedal backwards, which can take a while to grow accustomed to. Rental bikes are usually one-speed, but this is sufficient for the flat city. Because Amsterdammers got on their bikes as soon as they were weaned, cycling lessons are anathema. If you are out of practice, wheel your bike to the Vondelpark, the city's "green lung," and start out on the grass for a soft landing without scrapes. Make sure you lock the frame of your bike to something fixed, such as a bike-rack or railing, even when leaving it unattended for the shortest time.

Nowadays the Vondelpark is also the place for a leisurely in-line skate, though there are also the hip-and-trendy practicing their pirouettes. During the summer you can rent skates and protective knee, elbow, and wrist pads from a booth at the southern end of the park. For the inexperienced it is certainly worth having a lesson with a friendly instructor, which only adds a little to the overall rental costs. Weather permitting, you can join the **Friday Night Skate** (www.fridaynightskate.nl), an initiative copied from the massively popular event in Paris. Here in Amsterdam, hundreds of skaters tour the streets of the city with guides and qualified first-aid officers on hand for any unlucky bumps. Join them at 8 PM outside the Nederlands Filmmuseum (Netherlands Film Museum, Vondelpark 3) at the northeastern end of the Vondelpark.

HISTORIC AMSTERDAM: FROM THE JEWISH QUARTER TO REMBRANDT'S HOUSE

From the time in the 16th century when the diamond cutters of Antwerp first arrived to find refuge from the Spanish Inquisition, the area east of the Zwanenburgwal has traditionally been Amsterdam's Jewish Quarter. During the 16th and 17th centuries, Jewish refugees from Spain, Portugal, and Eastern Europe also found a haven in Amsterdam. By 1938, 10% of Amsterdam's population was Jewish, but this thriving community was decimated by the Nazi occupation.

The area to the north and northeast of the Jewish Quarter is the oldest part of Amsterdam. This is the site of Amsterdam's original harbor and the core of the Old Town, an area steeped in the history and romance of exotic trade and exploration, much of it conducted under the auspices of the wealthy Verenigde Oostindische Compagnie (VOC, or United East India Company).

A Good Walk

Start at what was once the heart of Amsterdam's Jewish Quarter, **Waterlooplein** ⑬. Today the square is dominated by the imposing modern **Muziektheater/Stadhuis** ⑭, which is surrounded by a large and lively flea market. East of Waterlooplein, on Jonas Daniël Meijerplein, is the **Joods Historisch Museum** ⑮, skillfully converted out of a number of old synagogues. Just to the east of that, on the corner of Mr. Visserplein and Jonas Daniël Meijerplein is the stately **Portugees Israelitische Synagoge** ⑯. Its interior is simple but awe-inspiring because of its vast size and floods of natural light.

The varied flora cultivated in the greenhouses of the **Hortus Botanicus** ⑰ is just across the canal. Then you might want to make a short diversion to the **Verzetsmuseum** ⑱, which explains the Dutch resistance to the occupying forces, passive and active, during the Second World War. Returning to the main road, the **Hollandsche Schouwburg** ⑲ is a haunting Holocaust memorial. But for something more light-hearted, especially if you have children in tow, proceed to the **Artis** ⑳ zoo (which was attractively laid out in parklike surroundings in the 19th century and has a well-stocked aquarium). Time permitting, take Tram 9 or 14 farther east along Plantage Middenlaan, to the **Tropenmuseum** ㉑, which has riveting displays on tropical cultures and a special children's section.

Alternatively, you can walk from the synagogue up Jodenbreestraat, where—in the second house from the corner by the Zwanenburgwal—you'll find the **Museum het Rembrandthuis** ㉒, the mansion where Rembrandt lived at the height of his prosperity, which now houses a large collection of his etchings. Cross the bridge to St. Antoniesbreestraat and follow it to the **Zuiderkerk** ㉓, whose rather Asian spire is the neighborhood's chief landmark. Take St. Antoniesbreestraat north to **Nieuwmarkt** ㉔. Take Koningsstraat to the Kromboomssloot and turn left, then right at Rechtboomssloot (both pretty, leafy canals) and follow it through this homey neighborhood, the oldest in Amsterdam, to Montelbaanstraat; turn left and cut through to the broad Oude Waal canal. Follow it right to the **Montelbaanstoren** ㉕, a tower that dates back to the 16th century. Up Kalkmarkt from the tower is Prins Hendrikkade, which runs along the eastern docks.

Following Prins Hendrikkade east you enter the modern world with a bang at the **Nemo Science & Technology Center** ㉖. A little farther on is the **Nederlands Scheepvaartmuseum** ㉗ where there is a fascinating replica of an old Dutch East India ship. Across the bridge on Hoogte Kadijk is the **Museumwerf 't Kromhout** ㉘, where wooden sailing boats are still restored and repaired. If, on the other hand, you go west along Prins Hendrikkade to Gelderskade, you can see the **Schreierstoren** ㉙, where legend has it that women used to stand weeping and waiting for their men to return from sea.

Follow Oudezijds Kolk, beside the Schreierstoren, south to the **Zeedijk** ㉚, in the 1980s the seedy haunt of drug dealers but now lined with restaurants, cafés, and galleries that form the heart of Chinatown. From Zeedijk, take Oudezijds Voorburgwal south to **Museum Amstelkring** ㉛, a tiny but atmospheric canal house that has a church hidden in its attic. Continue south on Oudezijds Voorburgwal through part of the Red Light District to the **Oude Kerk** ㉜, Amsterdam's oldest church, which grew up haphazardly from the 14th to the 16th centuries. From here you can continue south on Oudezijds Voorburgwal through more of the Red Light District to Damstraat and the Dam.

TIMING

To see only the buildings along the main route, block out an hour and a half. Detours to Artis and the Tropenmuseum will need an extra 30 minutes' traveling time; and to the Netherlands Scheepvaartsmuseum and Museumwerf 't Kromhout, another 45 minutes. Museums along this route need at least a 30-minute visit, and the Museum Amstelkring and the Tropenmuseum deserve a little longer.

Note that the flea market does not operate on Sunday and that the children's section of the Tropenmuseum has very specific visiting times.

SAFETY

Originally the haunt of sailors on leave, and from the 1970s through most of the rest of the century taken over by drug addicts, the Zeedijk has now been considerably cleaned up and transformed into the focal point of Amsterdam's Chinatown. Nonetheless, it is still advisable to take care when visiting this area and the Red Light District. Don't carry too many valuables and avoid the district late at night.

What to See

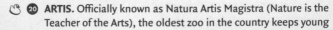

🌥 ⑳ **ARTIS.** Officially known as Natura Artis Magistra (Nature is the Teacher of the Arts), the oldest zoo in the country keeps young travelers entertained. Built in the mid-19th century, Artis is a 37-acre park that is home to a natural history museum, a zoo with an aviary, an aquarium, and a planetarium. A special Artis Express canal boat from the central railway station makes getting here fun. *Plantage Kerklaan 40, tel. 020/523–3400. Fl 26.5 (€12.05). Zoo, daily 9–5; planetarium, Mon. 12:30–5, Tues.–Sun. 9–5.*

⑲ **HOLLANDSCHE SCHOUWBURG** (Holland Theater). This former theater was requisitioned by the Nazis during World War II when they rounded up Jewish citizens; they were assembled here before being packed into trains. It is now a memorial to the estimated 60,000 to 80,000 Jews who were sent to Nazi concentration camps, and almost certain death. It is managed by the Jewish Historical Museum (☞ Joods Historisch Museum, *below*). The 6,700 plaques with family names are a reminder of the total 104,000 Jews deported from the Netherlands to concentration and death camps. *Plantage Middenlaan 24. tel. 020/626–9945. Free. Daily 11–4. Closed Yom Kippur.*

⑰ **HORTUS BOTANICUS.** The botanical garden was established at the present location in 1682, having started as a medicinal collection for doctors and pharmacists in 1638. In the 17th and 18th centuries, many plants were brought back to the Netherlands by seafaring explorers. Outside, there are attractive beds of indigenous European plants. The Palm House has a unique collection of cycad palms, a species that is becoming ever rarer in the wild. The imposing modern glasshouse from 1993 has three climate zones: subtropical, desert, and tropical. The latter imitates a South American jungle environment. In total, 8,000 plant species are represented. The classical *orangerie*, built in 1870 to protect orange trees during winter frosts, is now a café for visitors. *Plantage Middenlaan 2, tel. 020/625–9021. Fl 7.50 (€3.40). Apr.–Oct., weekdays 9–5, weekends and holidays 11–5; Nov.–Mar., weekdays 9–4, weekends and holidays 11–4. Closed Dec. 25, Jan. 1.*

⑮ JOODS HISTORISCH MUSEUM (Jewish Historical Museum). Four synagogues, dating from the 17th and 18th centuries, have been skillfully combined into one museum for documents, paintings, and objects related to the history of the Jewish people in Amsterdam and the Netherlands. Across from the entrance to the museum is a statue erected after World War II to honor a solidarity strike by Amsterdam's dock workers in protest of the deportation of Amsterdam's Jews during the war. The museum also manages the former Hollandsche Schouwburg (☞ *above*) memorial to Holocaust victims. *Jonas Daniël Meijerplein 2–4, tel. 020/626–9945. Fl 10 (€4.55). Daily 11–5. Closed Yom Kippur. www.jhm.nl*

㉕ MONTELBAANSTOREN (Montelbaans Tower). The tower dates from 1512, when it formed part of the city's defenses. Now, slightly listing, it houses offices of the City Water Board. Since 1878, this department has maintained the water levels in the canals and engineered the nightly flushing of the entire city waterway system, closing and opening the sluices to change the direction of the flow and cleanse the waters. (The canals remain murky green despite the process, due to algae.) The elegant clock tower was added early in the 17th century. *Oude Schans 2.*

㉛ MUSEUM AMSTELKRING ("Our Lord in the Attic" Museum). This appears to be just another canal house, and on the lower floors it consists of two beautiful small dwellings dating from 1661, with typical 17th- and 18th-century furnishings. The attic of this building, however, contains something unique—a small chapel that dates from the Reformation in Amsterdam, when open worship by Catholics was outlawed. The baroque altarpiece incorporates an unusual fold-out pulpit. In the uppermost galleries there are displays of religious artifacts, including chalices and robes. *Oudezijds Voorburgwal 40, tel. 020/624–6604. Fl 10 (€4.55). Mon.–Sat. 10–5, Sun. and holidays 1–5. Closed Jan. 1 and Apr. 30.*

★ **㉒ MUSEUM HET REMBRANDTHUIS** (Rembrandt's House). One of Amsterdam's most remarkable sights, this was the house that

Gables and Gable Stones

The infinite array of gables of Amsterdam's houses, historic and modern, dominates the city's picture-postcard image and is a carefully preserved asset. The lack of firm land meant that Amsterdam houses were built on narrow and deep plots, and one of the only ways to make a property distinctive was at the top, with a decorative gable.

The simplest and earliest form is the spout gable in the shape of an inverted funnel. When houses were still made of wood, this protective front could simply be nailed on. It was used later for plain canal-side warehouses, which have since been converted into trendy loft spaces. Another early form was the step gable, usually a continuation of the masonry of the facade, which rises to a pinnacle. This form was also used in Flemish architecture, as seen in the Belgian city of Bruges. The neck gable was the next development, a brick frontage in the form of a decorated oblong, hiding the angled roof behind. Bell gables are an elaboration of this, with more elaborate carved stone or decorative moldings.

Something else to keep an eye out for as you wander around Amsterdam is the gable stone. These plaster or stone tablets placed above doors or built into walls were houses' identity tags before house numbers were introduced early in the 19th century, when Louis Bonaparte was ruler of the Netherlands. The gable stones are simple reliefs, sometimes brightly painted, which usually depicted the craft or profession of the inhabitants. For example, an apothecary would have a gable stone with a gaping mouth, an apple merchant a depiction of Adam and Eve. Other examples revealed the origins of the owner, for example a relief showing the harbor of Calais. To see a whole selection of rescued gable stones, pop into the Begijnhof courtyard (☞ above). The wall nearest the Spui entrance is filled with different examples.

Rembrandt van Rijn, flush with success, bought for his family. He chose a house on what was once the main street of the Jewish Quarter because he felt that he could then experience daily and at firsthand the faces he would use in his religious paintings. He lived and worked in this redbrick house from 1639 to 1658. Rembrandt lost the house to bankruptcy when he fell from popularity following his wife's death. He came under attack by the Amsterdam burghers, who refused to accept his liaison with his housekeeper. Rooms in the historic house have been restored to the state in which Rembrandt would have known them. The ground floor was used by the artist as living quarters; the sunny upper floor was his studio, now complete with easels and brushes. The house today is a museum of Rembrandt prints and etchings and includes one of his presses. The modern wing to the left of the old house is now the main exhibition space for the extensive collection of etchings by Rembrandt and his contemporaries and additionally houses a multimedia auditorium and a shop. *Jodenbreestraat 4–6, tel. 020/520–0400. Fl 12.50 (€5.65). Mon.–Sat. 10–5, Sun. and holidays 1–5. Closed Jan. 1. www.rembrandthuis.nl*

⑱ MUSEUMWERF 'T KROMHOUT (Kromhout Wharf Museum). One of Amsterdam's oldest shipyards is still redolent of tar, wood shavings, and varnish. Although the shipyard is run as a museum, old boats are still restored here. There's a whiff of diesel in the air, too. During the first part of the 20th century, 't Kromhout produced the diesel engine used by most Dutch canal boats. Models of old engines are on display. The museum is being renovated and is set to reopen in mid 2001. *Hoogte Kadijk 147, tel. 020/627–6777. Fl 3.50 (€1.60). Weekdays 10–4.*

⑭ MUZIEKTHEATER/STADHUIS (Music Theater/Town Hall). A brick and marble complex known locally as the "Stopera" (from Stadhuis and opera), this is the cornerstone of the revival of the Jewish Quarter, which was derelict and devastated after World War II. It was completed in 1988 to a design by Dutch architect Cees Dam, and is a multifunctional accommodation for everything from opera performances to civic registry. It includes the combined opera and ballet auditorium, city hall offices, and the city's wedding chamber (Dutch marriages are a civic ceremony, with church weddings optional). Feel free to wander through the lobbies; there is interesting sculpture as well as a display that dramatically illustrates Amsterdam's position below sea level. The weekly, 1 ¼-hour backstage tours of the Muziektheater give you a chance to see the wonderful mechanics of stage productions here. *Waterlooplein 22, tel. 020/551–8054. Fl 8.50 (€3.85) for tours. Open Mon.–Fri. 9–6; backstage tours Sat. at 3 pm.*

NEED A BREAK? There are many take-out snack bars around the Rembrandtplein and Leidseplein, but for a healthy and delicious vegetarian alternative, stop off at a branch of **Maoz falafel** (Reguliersbreestraat 61, Muntplein 1, Leidsestraat 85, tel. 020/624–9290, 020/420–7435, 020/427–9720), where they serve plain and simple *falafel*. This delicious Israeli snack consists of a bread pocket filled with a fried ball of chickpeas and herbs. Condiments include *tahini*, made from crushed sesame seeds. You can top up from the varied salad bar to your stomach's content, with shredded cabbage, cucumber with dill, beetroot, and pickled eggplants, all for just Fl 6 (€2.60).

🖐 **27 NEDERLANDS SCHEEPVAARTMUSEUM** (Netherlands Maritime Museum). Once the warehouse from which trading vessels were outfitted for their journeys, with everything from cannons to hardtack, the building now incorporates room after room of displays related to the development and power of the Dutch East and West India companies, as well as the Dutch fishing industry. Moored alongside the building at the east end of Amsterdam Harbor is a replica of the VOC clipper ship **Amsterdam.** *Kattenburgerplein 1, tel. 020/523–2222. Fl 14.50 (€6.60). Tues.–Sat. 10–5, Sun. and holidays noon–5, June–Sept. also Mon. 10–5.*

🖐 **26 NEMO SCIENCE & TECHNOLOGY CENTER.** Opened in early 1997, this is already a landmark, designed by Renzo Piano, the architect of the Pompidou Centre in Paris. The building's colossal, copper-clad volume rises from the harbor waters like the hull of a ship poking up into the skyline above the entrance to the IJ Tunnel in the city's Eastern Docks. Inside is a different matter, promising a high-tech, hands-on world of historic, present-day, and futuristic technology. The disappointing reality is a series of displays that may be interesting for 5- to 8-year-olds, but with little appeal for a wider audience. Most fun is the forensics laboratory, where you can work as a sleuth, but which costs extra. Scaling the rooftop terrace, however, is worthwhile; it offers a superb panoramic view across the city. *Oosterdok 2, tel. 0900/919–1100, Fl 0.75 (€0.35) per minute. Fl 20 (€9.10). Tues.–Sun. 10–5; school holidays, daily 10– 6. Jan. 1, Apr. 30, Dec. 25. www.e-nemo.nl*

㉔ NIEUWMARKT (New Market). Dating from the 17th century— when farmers from the province of Noord-Holland began setting up stalls here—the Nieuwmarkt soon became a busy daily market. The **Waag** (Weigh House) in the center of the square was built in 1488 and functioned as a city gate until the early 17th century, when it became the weighing house. One of its towers housed a teaching hospital for the academy of surgeons of the Surgeons' Guild. It was here that Rembrandt came to watch Professor Tulp in action prior to painting *The Anatomy Lesson*. Now the building is occupied by a café–restaurant and a new media center. *Bounded by Kloveniersburgwal, Geldersekade, and Zeedijk.*

㉜ OUDE KERK (Old Church). The first construction on the site of Amsterdam's oldest church was wooden, and today's building is the result of gradual expansion and additions, mainly between 1306 and 1566. It is a pleasing hodgepodge of styles and haphazard side buildings, extensively restored from 1955 to 1979. Rembrandt's wife, Saskia, is buried here. Seminude women display their wares in the windows around the church square and along the surrounding canals—the neighborhood has doubled as a red-light district for nearly six centuries. *Oudekerksplein 23,* tel. 020/625–8284. Fl 7.50 (€3.40). Apr.–Dec., Mon.–Sat. 11–5, Sun. 1–5; Jan.–Mar., Fri.–Sun. 1–5. Closed Dec. 25, Jan. 1.

⑯ PORTUGEES ISRAELITISCHE SYNAGOGE (Portuguese Israelite Synagogue). This noted synagogue was built between 1671 and 1675 by the Sephardic Jewish community that had emigrated from Portugal during the preceding two centuries. Its spare, elegantly proportioned wood interior has remained virtually unchanged since it was built, and is still lit by candles held in two immense candelabra during services. Mr. Visserplein 3, tel. 020/624–5351. Fl 5 (€2.25). Sun.–Fri. 10–4. Closed for services on Jewish holidays.

㉙ SCHREIERSTOREN. Although today this tower houses a café-restaurant and a shop for nautical instruments, maps, and books, in the 16th century it was a lookout tower for the women whose men were fishing at sea. This gave rise to the mistaken belief that the name meant "weeper's" or "wailer's" tower. But the word "Schreier" actually comes from an old Dutch word describing the position of the tower astride two canals. A plaque on the side of the building tells you that it was from this location that Henry Hudson set sail on behalf of the United East India Company to find a shorter route to the East Indies, discovering instead Hudson's Bay in Canada and, later, New York harbor and the Hudson River. The Schreierstoren overlooks the old **Oosterdok** (Eastern Dock) of Amsterdam Harbor. Prins Hendrikkade 94–95.

㉑ TROPENMUSEUM (Museum of the Tropics). This museum honors the Netherlands' link to Indonesia and the West Indies. It is a magnificent tiered, galleried, and skylighted museum decorated in gilt and marble. Displays and dioramas portray everyday life in the world's tropical environments. Upstairs in the **Kindermuseum** (Children's Museum) children can participate directly in the life of another culture through special programs involving art, dance, song, and sometimes even cookery. Adults may visit the children's section, but only under the supervision of a child age 6–12. *Linnaeusstraat 2, tel. 020/568–8200. Fl 12.50 (€5.65). Daily 10–5; Kindermuseum activities Wed. at 1:30 and 3:15, weekends, school holidays, holidays 11, 1:30, and 3:15. www.kit.nl/ tropenmuseum*

(18) **VERZETSMUSEUM** (Museum of the Dutch Resistance). Here are displays explaining the Dutch resistance to the occupying forces, passive and active, during World War II. Occupying new accommodations since early 2000, the museum is poignantly close to the Hollandsche Schouwburg (☞ *above*), which is now a memorial to the Jews who were assembled in the theater before being sent to the concentration camps. *Plantage Kerklaan 61, tel. 020/620–2535. Fl 8 (€3.65). Tues.–Fri. 10–5, weekends noon–5. www.verzetsmuseum.org*

(13) **WATERLOOPLEIN.** (Waterloo Square). The wooden pushcarts that were used when the flea market here began (before World War II) are gone, but the Waterlooplein remains a bustling shopping arena, wrapped around two sides of the Stopera (Music Theater/Town Hall complex). A stroll past the stalls provides a colorful glimpse of Amsterdam entrepreneurship in action, day in and day out, in every sort of weather. Products range from junk and antiques to new clothes, New Age paraphernalia, and bicycle parts. *Waterlooplein. Weekdays 9–5, Sat. 8:30–5:30.*

NEED A BREAK? **Espressobar "Puccini"** (Staalstraat 21, tel. 020/620–8458) is a stylish breakfast and lunch venue, just across the water from the Waterlooplein flea market and the Muziektheater. You can get a full Continental breakfast or freshly made sandwiches with interesting fillings, while the cakes, some created in the superb *chocolaterie* next door, are mouthwatering treats. The Espressobar is open Tuesday–Saturday, 8:30–8 and Sunday 10–6.

(30) **ZEEDIJK** (Sea Dike). Once known throughout the country as the black hole of Amsterdam for its concentration of drug traffickers and users, Zeedijk is now the busy arterial street at the heart of

The Amsterdam School

The loosely grouped architects of the Amsterdam School were active at the beginning of the 20th century, working out innovative approaches to urban planning. While World War I distracted the rest of Europe, these architects and planners gave concrete form to lofty socialist principles in housing projects and monumental public buildings. The style straddles late 19th-century expressionism and the purism of de Stijl, the Dutch movement founded by Theo van Doesburg in 1917 that propounded ideas similar to the Bauhaus in Germany and the Constructivists in the Soviet Union.

An example is visible from the train from Schiphol Airport as it approaches Centraal Station. To the left is the Spaarndammer neighborhood housing development nicknamed Het Schip (the Ship; Zaanstraat, Amsterdam-West), a redbrick colossus with a tower completed in 1921 to a design by Michel de Klerk (1884–1923). Notice the wave-like undulations in the brick facade and the rhythmic placement and unusual forms of the windows.

The housing Plan-Zuid (Extension Plan for Amsterdam-South), an urban plan finalized in 1914 by H. P. Berlage (1856–1934), was designed primarily by Klerk and Pieter Kramer (1881–1961) in exuberant Amsterdam School style. The best examples include De Dageraad (the Dawn) complex (1919–23) around the P. L. Takstraat in De Pijp neighborhood, and between the Churchilllaan and Rooseveltlaan in the Rivierenbuurt neighborhood, both in southern Amsterdam. Kramer also designed hundreds of bridges in the city, with characteristic stone reliefs and decorative iron railings.

Public buildings created by architects of the Amsterdam School include the the 1916 work of Kramer, Klerk, and J. M. van der Mey (1878–1949), the Scheepvaarthuis (Shipping Office) to the east of Centraal Station at Prins Hendrikkade 108–119. Extravagantly phantasmagoric zinc detailing seems to spill down from the roof.

the city's Chinatown. The restored old buildings now house shops, restaurants, and galleries. **In 't Aepjen** (Zeedijk 1) is one of only two timbered houses left in the city, and is now a characterful café lined with beautifully painted fairground panels. The clean-up of the street was cemented by the construction of the **F. G. S. He Hwa Buddhist Temple** (Zeedijk 106–116), the only Buddhist temple and monastery in Europe, opened by Queen Beatrix in September 2000. *From Oudezijds Kolk (near Centraal Station) to Nieuwmarkt.*

㉓ ZUIDERKERK (South Church). Built between 1603 and 1611 by Hendrick de Keyser, one of the most prolific architects of the Golden Age, this church is said to have inspired the great British architect Christopher Wren. The Zuiderkerk was one of the earliest churches built in Amsterdam in the Renaissance style and was the first in the city to be built for the Dutch Reformed Church. The city planning office maintains a display here that offers a look at the future of Amsterdam. *Zandstraat. Free. Tower: June–Oct., Wed. 2–5, Thurs.–Fri. 11–2, Sat. 11–4.*

THE CANALS: CITY OF BRIDGES

One of Amsterdam's greatest pleasures is also one of its simplest—a stroll along the canals. The grand, crescent-shape waterways of the *grachtengordel* (girdle or ring of canals) are lined with splendid buildings and pretty, gabled houses. But you can also wander off the main thoroughfares, along the smaller canals that crisscross them, sampling the charms of such historic city neighborhoods as the Jordaan.

A Good Walk

Begin at the busy **Dam** ①, where the imposing **Het Koninklijk Paleis te Amsterdam** ㉝ fills the western side of the square. The richly decorated marble interiors are open to the public when the queen is not in residence. To the right of the palace looms the Gothic **Nieuwe Kerk** ㉞. Circle around behind the palace, follow the tram tracks into the wide and busy Raadhuisstraat. Once you cross the Herengracht turn right along the canal, and at the bend in the first block you will see the **Nederlands Theatermuseum** ㉟, which occupies two grandiose 17th-century houses. Return to the Raadhuisstraat and turn right, following it to the Westermarkt. The **Westerkerk** ㊱, on the right, facing the next canal, is another Amsterdam landmark, and Rembrandt's burial place. Make a right past the church and follow the Prinsengracht canal to the **Anne Frankhuis** ㊲, where you can visit the attic hideaway where Anne Frank wrote her diary.

The neighborhood to your left, across the canal, is the **Jordaan** ㊳, full of curious alleys and pretty canals, intriguing shops and cafés. At the intersection of the Prinsengracht and Brouwersgracht, turn right onto the **Brouwersgracht** ㊴, which many believe is the most beautiful canal in Amsterdam. Cross the canal and follow it to the Singel. Turn left toward the harbor, and then to the right; you will see the palatial red-brick **Centraal Station** ㊵. From Centraal Station the **Damrak** ㊶ leads past the **Beurs van Berlage** ㊷—the building that is seen as Amsterdam's first significant venture into modern architecture—and back to the Dam.

TIMING

It is difficult to say how long this walk will take as it leads you through areas that invite wandering and the exploration of side streets. At a brisk and determined pace, you can manage the route in about an hour. But you could also easily while away an afternoon in the Jordaan, or take a leisurely stroll along the Prinsengracht. Allow a minimum of half an hour each for the Royal Palace and the Anne Frank House. Waiting in line to get into the Anne Frank House can add another 10–20 minutes (get there early to beat the midday crowds).

The best time for canal walks is in late afternoon and early evening—or early in the morning, when the mists still hang over the water. If you're planning to go shopping in the Jordaan, remember that shops in the Netherlands are closed Monday morning. With its many restaurants and cafés, the Jordaan is also fun to visit at night.

What to See

★ ❸❼ **ANNE FRANKHUIS** (Anne Frank House). This unimposing canal house where two Jewish families hid from the Nazis for more than two years during World War II is one of the most frequently visited places in the world. The families were eventually discovered and sent to concentration camps, but young Anne's diary survived as a detailed record of their life in hiding. If you have time to see nothing else in Amsterdam, don't miss a visit to this house. The swinging bookcase that hid the door to the secret attic apartment is still there, you can walk through the rooms where Anne and her family lived, and there is also an exhibition on racism and oppression. *Prinsengracht 263, tel. 020/556–7100. Fl 10 (€4.55). Apr.–Aug., daily 9–9, except May 4 9–7; Sept.–March, daily 9–7, except Dec. 25 and Jan. 1 noon–7. Closed Yom Kippur. www.annefrank.nl*

NEED A BREAK? A traditionally Dutch way of keeping eating costs down is pancakes—laden with savory cheese and bacon, or fruit and liqueur if you have a sweet tooth. The **Pancake Bakery** (Prinsengracht 191, tel. 020/625–1333) is one of the best places in Amsterdam to try them; the menu offers a choice of more than 30 combinations.

❹❷ **BEURS VAN BERLAGE** (Berlage's Stock Exchange). Completed in 1903, the Stock Exchange is considered Amsterdam's first modern building. In 1874, when the Amsterdam Stock Exchange building on the Dam showed signs of collapse, the city authorities held a competition for the design of a new one. The architect who won was discovered to have copied the facade of a French town hall, so he was disqualified and the commission was awarded to a local architect, H. P. Berlage. The building that Berlage came up with proved to be an architectural turning point. Gone are all the fripperies and ornamentations of the 19th-century "neo" styles. The new Beurs, with its simple lines, earned Berlage the reputation of being the "Father of Modern Dutch Architecture." Today it serves as a concert and exhibition hall. The small museum has exhibits about the former stock exchange and its architect, as well as access to the tower. *Damrak 213–277, tel. 020/530–4113. Fl 7 (€3.20). Tues.–Sun. 11–5.*

39 **BROUWERSGRACHT** (Brewers Canal). The pretty, tree-lined canal is lined by residences and former warehouses of the brewers who traded here in earlier centuries. It is blessed with long views down the main canals and plenty of sunlight, all of which makes the Brouwersgracht one of the most photographed spots in town, and a highly desirable address. The canal runs westward from the end of the Singel (a short walk along Prins Hendrikkade from Centraal Station).

NEED A
BREAK? Down a small sidestreet between the Brouwersgracht and the Haarlemmerdijk shopping street you will find **Small World Catering** (Binnen Oranjestraat 14, tel. 020/420–2774), where you can choose from a big selection of fillings served on crunchy, Italian-style *focaccia* bread and accompanied by a fresh-fruit shake or coffee. The place, popular with locals for the varied and international menu of daily dishes, which you can eat in or take away, is open Wednesday–Saturday 10:30–8 and Sunday noon–8.

40 **CENTRAAL STATION** (Central Station). Designed by P. J. H. Cuypers, the architect of Amsterdam's other imposing gateway, the Rijksmuseum, this building is a landmark of Dutch neo-Renaissance style (and does bear a distinct resemblance to the museum on the other side of town). It opened in 1885 and has been the hub of transportation for the Netherlands ever since. From time to time the sumptuous **Koninklijke Wachtkamer**

(Royal Waiting Room) on Platform 2 is opened to the public—and is certainly worth a visit. If it's closed, then you can get a feel for its grandeur from the decor of the **Eerste Klas** restaurant on Spoor 2b (Platform 2b) (☞ *Eating Out*). *Stationsplein*.

41 DAMRAK (Dam Port). This busy street leading up to Centraal Station is now lined with a curious assortment of shops, attractions, hotels, and eating places. It was once a harbor bustling with activity, its piers loaded with fish and other cargo on their way to the weigh house at the Dam. During the 19th century it was filled in, and the only water that remains is a patch in front of the station that provides mooring for canal tour boats.

★ **33 HET KONINKLIJK PALEIS TE AMSTERDAM** (Royal Palace, Amsterdam). Built in the mid-17th century as the city's town hall, the Koninklijk Paleis stands solidly on 13,659 pilings sunk deep into the marshy soil of the former riverbed. Designed by Jacob van Campen, one of the most prominent architects of the time, the Stadhuis (City Hall) is a high point of the Dutch Classicist style. Inside and out, the building is adorned with rich carvings. The prosperous burghers of the Golden Age wanted a city hall that could boast of their status to all visitors—and indeed, the Amsterdam Stadhuis became known as "the Eighth Wonder of the World." When you walk into what was originally the public entrance hall, the earth is quite literally at your feet. Two maps inlaid in the marble floor show Amsterdam not just at the center of the world, but of the universe as well.

During the French occupation of the Netherlands, Louis Napoléon, who had been installed as king in 1808, decided that this was the building most suitable for a royal palace. It has been the official residence of the House of Orange ever since. Louis filled his new palace with fashionable French Empire furniture, much of which remains.

Queen Beatrix, like her mother and grandmother before her, prefers to live in the quieter environment of a palace in a park

Amsterdam's Almshouses—the Hofjes

Hidden behind innocent-looking gateways throughout the city center, most notably along the main ring of canals and in the Jordaan neighborhood, are some of its most charming houses. There are about 30 hofjes (almshouses), mainly dating back to the 18th century, when the city's flourishing merchants established hospices for the old and needy—pensions and social security were unheard of then. Their philanthropy was supposed to be rewarded by a place in heaven.

Most famous is the **Begijnhof** (☞ above). Here is a small selection from the many other less-frequented almshouses that are open to the public during the day, arranged in geographical order for you to hunt down more easily. All you have to do is find the often well-hidden doorways to take a step back into yesteryear, but please remember to respect the privacy of the residents.

There is a small concentration of hofjes around the Egelantiersgracht in the Jordaan. The **Sint Andrieshofje** (Egelantiersgracht 107–114), founded in 1615, is the second oldest almshouse in Amsterdam. Notice the fine gables, including a step gable in the style of Hendrik de Keyser. The **Claes Claeszhofje** (junction of Egelantiersstraat, Eerste Egelantiersdwarsstraat, and Tuinstraat) was established in 1626 by a Mennonite textile trader. The **Zevenkeurvorstenhofje** (Tuinstraat 197–223) was founded around 1645, though the houses standing today are 18th century. The **Karthuizerhof** (Karthuizerstraat 21–131) was founded in 1650 and now accommodates young people around a courtyard with two 17th-century pumps.

The **Van Brienenhofje** (Prinsengracht 89–133), along the main canals, dates from 1804 and has a forbidding, windowless facade. Except for on Sundays, you can enter through the green door to the right and you will find yourself in an oblong courtyard of little houses surrounding an overrun, cottagelike garden.

outside The Hague and uses her Amsterdam residence only on the highest of state occasions. So, once again, the former Stadhuis is open to the public. *Dam, tel. 020/624–8698. Fl 7 (€3.20). Oct.–May, Tues.–Thurs., weekends 12:30–5; June–Sept., daily 12:30–5 Closed occasionally for state events.*

★ **38 JORDAAN.** The renovation generation has helped make the Jordaan (pronounced yohr-dahn)—Amsterdam's Greenwich Village—the winner in the revival-of-the-fittest sweepstakes. In the western part of town, it is one of the most charming neighborhoods in a city that defines charm, basking in centuries-old patina and yet address to chic eateries and boutiques. It was originally called *jardin*, French for "garden." During the French occupation of Amsterdam, the vegetable gardens to the west of the city center were developed as a residential area. The new city quarter was referred to as the jardin, and the streets and canals (which follow the lines of the original irrigation ditches) were named for flowers and trees. In the mouths of the local Dutch, *jardin* became Jordaan, the name by which the quarter is known today.

The Jordaan was a working-class area and the scene of odorous industries, such as tanning and brewing. Its inhabitants developed a reputation for rebelliousness, but their strong community spirit also gave them a special identity, rather like London's Cockneys. Since the 1980s, the Jordaan has gone upmarket, and now it is one of the trendiest parts of town. The narrow alleys and leafy canals are lined with quirky specialty shops, good restaurants, and designer boutiques. Students, artists, and the fashionable fill the cafés. But many of the old Jordaaners are still here—as the sound of jolly singing emanating from some local pubs will testify. The Jordaan is bounded by the Prinsengracht, Looiersgracht, Lijnbaansgracht, and Brouwersgracht canals.

35 NEDERLANDS THEATERMUSEUM (Netherlands Theater Museum). This museum is part of the Theater Instituut Nederland (Netherlands Theater Institute) and occupies two stunning examples of 17th-century houses built for well-heeled merchants. The marble-lined corridors and sweeping monumental staircases provide the backdrop to exhibitions about the history of theater in all its forms: circus, opera, musicals, puppetry, and drama. There are costumes, models of stage sets and other accessories. There is also an extensive library with archives focused on the theatrical scene in the Netherlands. *Herengracht 168, tel. 020/551–3300. Fl 8.50 (€3.85). Tues.–Fri. 11–5, Sat.–Sun. and holidays 1–5.*

③④ NIEUWE KERK (New Church). Begun in the 14th century, the Nieuwe Kerk is a soaring Gothic structure that was never given its spire because the authorities ran out of money. Inside are the graves of the poet Vondel (known as the "Dutch Shakespeare") and Admiral Ruyter, who sailed his invading fleet up the river Medway in England in the 17th century, becoming a naval hero in the process. This church is where the inauguration ceremony has been held for every monarch since 1815. In between times, it serves as a venue for special exhibitions, including the annual presentation of the World Press Photo awards and an exhibition of prize-winning entries that will then travel the world over. *Dam, tel. 020/626–8168. Admission varies according to exhibition. Daily 11–5.*

③⑥ WESTERKERK (West Church). Built between 1602 and 1631, the Westerkerk has a tower topped by a copy of the crown of the Habsburg emperor, Maximilian I. Maximilian gave Amsterdam the right to use his royal insignia in gratitude for help from the city in his struggle for control of the Low Countries. The tower, with its gaudy yellow crown, is an Amsterdam landmark. Its carillon is the comforting "clock" of the canal area of Amsterdam, and its chimes were often mentioned in the diary of Anne Frank, who was hiding just around the corner. Rembrandt and his son Titus are buried here; the philosopher René Descartes lived on the square facing the church. *Prinsengracht (corner of Westermarkt), tel. 020/624–7766. Tower: June–Sept., Tues.–Wed. and Fri.–Sat. 2–5.*

You can seek out the home ports of the seafaring
adventurers who drove the country's economic growth
in the 17th century and turned Amsterdam into such an
important center of commerce. You can cycle through
peaceful farmlands, visit a medieval castle, or wander
around quaint fishing villages. You can check out the
modern cultivation techniques of the Dutch bulb and
flower industry and the sophistication of the
distribution industries that are the motor of today's
flourishing economy.

In This Chapter

VISITING THE BULB FIELDS 113 • What to See 114 • Coming
and Going 117 • HAARLEM 118 • What to See 118 • Coming and
Going 119 • VISITING THE GOLDEN CIRCLE 120 • What to See
120 • Coming and Going 122 • VISITING TEXEL 122 • What to
See 124 • Coming and Going 126 • CONTACTS AND
RESOURCES 127

By Andrew May

side trips

THE PROVINCE OF NOORD-HOLLAND (NORTH-HOLLAND) offers all these things within an hour of the city. There are quick and easy transport links to whisk you away from the cityscape to the bucolic landscape for a day trip that will open up new vistas on Dutch life and history. It's certainly worth taking a look.

Amsterdam is actually in the southeastern corner of the province of Noord-Holland. Reaching westward to Haarlem and the North Sea coast, and north across the Noordzee Kanaal (North Sea Canal) behind Amsterdam's Centraal Station as far as the Kop van Holland (Top of Holland) and the island of Texel, this province offers a taste of unspoiled rural life. South, southwest, and southeast of Amsterdam—and extending partly into Noord-Holland, are the bulb fields, a popular side trip for visitors to the city.

Numbers in the margin correspond to points of interest on the Side Trips from Amsterdam map.

VISITING THE BULB FIELDS
34 km (21 mi) southwest of Amsterdam.

Even if you are in Amsterdam for just a couple of days, it is easy to sample one of the best-known aspects of quintessential Holland—the bulb fields. The flower-growing area to the west of Amsterdam is a modern-day powerhouse of Dutch production techniques that provide Dutch flowers all over the world year-round. In spring, the bulb fields blaze with color: great squares and oblongs of red, yellow, and white look like giant Mondrian paintings laid out on the ground.

What to See

1. **Keukenhof** is a 70-acre park and greenhouse complex where nearly 7 million flowering bulbs provide a carpet of blooms every spring and summer. In the last weeks of April you can catch tulips, daffodils, hyacinths, and narcissi all flowering simultaneously. There are also some 50,000 square ft of more

exotic blooms under glass. The first tulip bulbs were brought to the Netherlands from Turkey in the mid-16th century. During the 17th century, the bulbs became a prized possession and changed hands for extraordinary amounts of money. Today, Dutch botanists use Keukenhof as a showcase for their latest hybrids, so black tulips and gaudy frilled varieties make an appearance. In the summer of 1999, the same gardens were the green stage for the first ever Zomerhof (Summer Garden), with summer bulbs and tuberous plants such as lilies, anemones, begonias, and canna, as well as perennials. N207, Lisse; tel. 0252/465–555. Fl 17.50 (€7.95). Late Mar.–May, daily 8–7:30; mid-Aug.–mid-Sept., daily 9–6.

After visiting Keukenhof, check out the dunes north of **Noordwijk.** You'll find a vast, sandy nature reserve, almost as big as the bulb district itself. Small canals and pools of water are dotted about between the dunes, providing a haven for bird life. The Bulb District Route (☞ Bollenstreek Route, *below*) passes through, in addition to Noordwijk, the beach community of **Katwijk** and **Sassenheim,** where there is an imposing 13th-century ruined castle.

The **Bollenstreek Route** (Bulb District Route) is a special itinerary through the heart of the flower-growing region that was laid out by the Dutch auto club, ANWB. The 62-km (39-mi) circular route, marked with small blue and white signs that read BOLLENSTREEK, begins in Oegstgeest, near Leiden, and continues through the town of Rijnsburg (site of one of Holland's three major flower auction houses), where there is a colorful Flower Parade on the first Saturday in August. On the way, you pass through Lisse, which has a Flower Parade on the last Saturday in April. Lisse is also the site of the flower gardens at Keukenhof (☞ *above*).

➋ The **Bloemenveiling Aalsmeer** (Aalsmeer Flower Auction) is held in Aalsmeer (19 km or 12 mi south of Amsterdam, near Schiphol Airport) five days a week, from the pre-dawn hours until mid-

Back to Nature, Dutch Style

The development of the Netherlands offers insight into countryside as a man-made landscape in flux. For centuries, the low-lying land has been pumped dry, reclaimed from the sea to make it cultivable. However, nowadays many people complain about the recent ribbonlike business developments along highways, akin to the strip malls that have sprung up in the United States. The Dutch government enforces stricter planning laws for the construction of new homes outside already developed areas, but the need for housing results in dense developments between and on the outskirts of cities, encroaching on agricultural land and leading to ever more intensive farming methods.

Tactics to combat this rampant urban spread include "wildlife" corridors of untouched "nature" under railways and highways, so that wild animals can still wander or migrate safely, and "compensatory greenery" exchanged for ground consumed by development. Infrastructure is hidden to stop it "polluting" the view: Railways are dug under meadowlands, and highways are screened behind landscaped hills and sound mufflers.

Although almost no land is untouched by man, the protection and preservation of natural areas has created and preserved places of outstanding beauty and protected indigenous wildlife. Wild boar and roe deer roam protected woodland areas, and mushrooms and toadstools abound in this damp climate. Reed warblers nest in the reed beds on the banks of freshwater lakes, grey herons stand tall and proud, and harriers hover as they hunt the resident voles and harvest-mice. One of the reasons for the ardent nature preservation here is the importance of the country for migratory birds. Eider ducks, barnacle geese, and wigeons pass through on their way to breeding grounds in the north, while golden plovers and curlews spend their winters here, grazing the grasslands. No fewer than 850 species of bird have been spotted in the Dutch countryside.

morning. The largest flower auction in the world, it has three auction halls operating continuously in a building the size of several football fields. You walk on a catwalk above the rolling four-tier carts that wait to move on tracks past the auctioneers. The buying system is what is called a Dutch auction—the price goes down, not up, on a large "clock" on the wall. The buyers sit lecture-style with buzzers on their desks; the first to register a bid gets the bunch. *Legmeerdijk 313, Aalsmeer, tel. 0297/392–185. Fl 7 (€3.20). Weekdays 7:30–11.*

Coming and Going

Public transport is probably your best option for getting to these outlying areas because one-day car rental is often expensive. Train and bus combinations will get you there in comfort and for a cheap fare. Ask about combination tickets offered by the NS (Dutch Railways), which include all transport and reduced entrance fees.

BY BUS

It's best to take a bus or car to **Aalsmeer,** since the train will take you only as far as Schiphol Airport, where you'll need to transfer to a bus. You can take the NZH Bus 172 from the stop opposite American Hotel near Amsterdam's Leidseplein, or catch either Bus 172 or 171 from Centraal Station.

BY CAR

To join the **Bulb District Route,** take the A4 southbound from Amsterdam toward Leiden. At Junction 4 take the N207 exit for Lisse, then turn left when you reach the N208. **Keukenhof** is signposted from here. To reach **Aalsmeer** by car, take the A4 highway from Amsterdam, and exit at Junction 3 onto the N201, immediately after Schiphol Airport.

BY TRAIN

To get to **Keukenhof** by train, take the Keukenhof Express train from Amsterdam, then bus 54. For information, contact national train information (tel. 0900/9292, Fl 0.75 [€0.35] per minute).

118

HAARLEM

20 km (12 mi) west of Amsterdam.

With buildings notable for their secret inner courtyards and step gables, many of Haarlem's streets and vistas resemble a 17th-century canvas, perhaps one by Frans Hals, the city's greatest painter. The two museums here are superb.

What to See

The area around the **Grote Markt** (market square) provides an architectural stroll through the 17th and 18th centuries. Some of the facades are adorned with such homilies as "The body's sickness is a cure for the soul."

The **Grote Kerk** (Great Church) is also known as the St. Bavo, to whom it is dedicated. Built between 1400 and 1550, it houses one of the world's finest organs, which has 5,000 pipes and was played by both Mozart and Handel. A world-class organ festival is held here in July every year. *Grote Markt, tel. 023/533–0877. Apr.–Aug., Mon.–Sat. 10–4; Sept.–Mar., Mon.–Sat. 10–3:30.*

NEED A BREAK? **Café Restaurant Brinkman** (Grote Markt 9–13, tel. 023/532–3111) is an elegant, classic grand-café that overlooks the magnificent Grote Kerk. Pop in for a sandwich at lunchtime, or you can while away the afternoon contemplating the medieval view over coffee and apple pie. In the evening the kitchens prepare an extensive menu of traditional Dutch and continental fare.

The **Vleeshal** (meat market), close to the medieval Stadhuis (City Hall), dates from the early 1600s and has an especially fine step-gable facade. It now serves as an annex for temporary exhibitions organized by the Frans Hals Museum, often featuring contemporary art (☞ below). *Grote Markt 16, tel. 023/511–5775. Fl 7.50 (€3.40). Mon.–Sat. 11–5, Sun. and holidays noon–5.*

★ The **Teylers Museum** is the oldest in the country. It was founded by a wealthy merchant in 1778 as a museum of science and the arts, and has antique showcases filled with mineral specimens as well as an intriguing collection of historic scientific instruments. On the artistic side there is a fine collection of The Hague school of painting as well as drawings and sketches by Michelangelo, Raphael, and other non-Dutch masters. As the canvases in this building are shown in indirect natural light, try to visit on a sunny day. The modern wing includes a café. *Spaarne 16, tel. 023/531–9010. Fl 10 (€4.55). Tues.–Sat. 10–5, Sun. and holidays noon–5. www.teylersmuseum.nl*

★ The **Frans Hals Museum** occupies the buildings of a 17th-century hospice and contains a marvelous collection of works by Hals (1585–1666); his paintings of the guilds of Haarlem are particularly noteworthy. The museum also has works by the artist's 17th-century contemporaries and an extensive contemporary collection, including paintings by members of the CoBrA movement (its name deriving from Copenhagen/Brussels/Amsterdam, the capital cities of the founders' countries of origin), such as Corneille, Constant, and Appel. *Groot Heiligland 62, tel. 023/511–5775. Fl 10 (€4.55). Mon.–Sat. 11–5, Sun. and holidays noon–5. www.franshalsmuseum.nl*

Coming and Going

Public transport is probably your best option for getting to nearby Haarlem. The train service is quick and direct.

BY CAR
You can drive directly to **Haarlem** from Amsterdam via the N5, which becomes the N200/A200, but traffic is often backed up, especially during rush hour.

BY TRAIN
There are direct trains to **Haarlem** four times every hour. For train information, contact national train information (tel. 0900/9292, Fl 0.75 [€0.35] per minute).

VISITING THE GOLDEN CIRCLE

43 km (27 mi) northwest of Amsterdam to Hoorn, 62 km (39 mi) to Enkhuizen.

The characterful towns encircling the IJsselmeer were once home to the Dutch fishing fleets and ports from which the adventurous captains of the Dutch Golden Age set out for the East and West Indies and beyond. The *Afsluitdijk* (Enclosing Dike) cut off the former Zuider Zee sea inlet from the ocean, creating the IJsselmeer lake. This extraordinary piece of civil engineering was completed in 1932, protecting the low-lying land from the ravages of the open seas and creating a massive freshwater lake. The former ports are now busy harbors for the leisure craft that ply the protected waters, but the province's heritage has been preserved in the many museums that recall the activities of yesteryear.

The former capital of West-Friesland, Hoorn was an important center for the fleets of the *Verenigde Oostindische Compagnie* (VOC, or United East India Company) during the 17th century. Willem Cornelis Schouten, one of the town's sons, sailed round the southern cape of America (in 1616) and christened it Cape Hoorn. Jan Pieterszoon Coen, whose statue lords over the Rode Steen square, founded the city of Batavia in Java, the present-day Jakarta, and governed it from 1617 until his death in 1629. Hoorn's decline was precipitated by the growing naval power of the British during the 18th century and the opening of the *Noordzeekanaal* (North Sea Canal) linking Amsterdam directly to the North Sea. Nowadays it is a leisurely yacht harbor on the enclosed IJsselmeer lake.

What to See

❸ Only a short diversion off the direct route from Amsterdam to Hoorn, the **Zaanse Schans** is a gem of windmill-studded countryside. A row of windmills stands alongside the village on the banks of the Zaan river in the province of Noord-Holland, 16 km (10 mi) northwest of the city. In the 17th and 18th centuries, this area was a hive of industrial activity with hundreds of mills and timber yards along the river banks, originally powered by wind, later by steam. The Zaanse Schans is just north of the town of Zaandam, where Peter the Great of Russia learned the craft of shipbuilding. The historic village is filled with classic green wooden houses. Many have been restored as private homes, but a whole cluster is open to the public, including the workshop of a clog maker, the shop of a traditional cheese maker, a bakery museum, and the working windmills themselves. *Kraaienest, Zaandam, tel. 075/616 8218. Free. Daily 8:30–6.*

4 The **Westfries Museum** (West Frisian Museum) is housed in the provincial government building from 1632, where the delegates from the seven cities of West-Friesland used to meet. The cities are represented by the coats of arms decorating the stunning facade, a testimony to the province's former grandeur. The council chambers are hung with portraits of the region's grandees, and the exhibitions explain the town's maritime history and the exotic finds of its adventurous sailors. *Rode Steen 1, Hoorn, tel. 0229/280–028. Fl 5 (€2.25). Weekdays 11–5, weekends 2–5. www.westfriesmuseum.nl*

NEED A **De Waag** (The Weigh House; Rode Steen 8, tel. 0229/215–195) is
BREAK? a monumental weigh house dating from 1609, designed by Hendrick de Keyser, with wooden beams and the antique weighing equipment still intact. The café-restaurant offers soups, salads, and well-filled sandwiches during the day, and at dinnertime you can choose from fish specialties or French cuisine. The terrace affords a stunning view of the Westfries Museum's towering ornamental facade across the square.

5 Near the former harbor town of Enkhuizen is the **Zuiderzee Museum,** one of the Netherlands' most complete outdoor museums, with streets, neighborhoods, and harbors lined with historic buildings. There are 130 houses, shops, and workshops where old crafts are still practiced. To reach the museum you have to take a boat from the main entrance. At the children's island, youngsters get a taste of life in the former fishing village of Marken during the 1930s. *Wierdijk 12–22, Enkhuizen, tel. 0228/ 351–111. Fl 17.50 (€7.95); indoor museum only, Fl 7.50 (€3.40). Indoor museum, daily 10–5; outdoor museum, Apr.–Oct., daily 10–5.*

Coming and Going

If you don't mind short walks from stations to the sights, then the rail service to rural destinations in this area is fast and efficient, and allows you to take in the countryside. Traveling by car will demand your close attention in order not to miss exits, especially on small country roads, so it is not really advised.

BY CAR

To get to the **Zaanse Schans,** you need to navigate the most confusing part of the country's road system, Amsterdam's A10 ring road, from which you take the exit for A8 toward Zaandam. Take the Zaandam exit, then follow local signs. **Hoorn** is north of Amsterdam just off E22/A7. To reach **Enkhuizen** take the Hoorn exit from E22/A7 and continue eastward on N302.

BY TRAIN

Koog-Zaandijk is the station nearest to **Zaanse Schans,** on the local line from Amsterdam to Alkmaar. The village can be reached on foot in a few minutes. Local trains operate once an hour direct from Amsterdam to **Hoorn** and **Enkhuizen.** For train information, contact national train information (tel. 0900/9292, 75¢ per minute).

VISITING TEXEL

85 km (53 mi) north of Amsterdam.

The largest of the Wadden Islands is also the easiest to reach. With an early start you can tour the island by bike in a day. Otherwise take a night or two to enjoy the nature, sea breeze, sports, and clear skies. Texel is nicknamed "Holland in

A Sporting Island

Cycling is the recommended way to travel around the compact island of Texel. Bicycles can be rented from the ferry terminal, and at outlets all over the island for about Fl 7.50 (€3.40) per day. You will be able to cross from one side of the island to the other in a day, and the fit may even zip around the whole island in that time. You will ride along quiet, hedged roadways and past verdant meadows that are sometimes filled with seasonal flowers. Along the perimeter of the island are sand dunes and some sheltering tidal inlets where you can spot migratory birds. Take some bottled water and a packed lunch with you for a contemplative repast in these wonderful untouched surroundings.

The sand flats around the island make it ideal for sailing, and in mid-June each year there is the Ronde van Texel (Circuit of Texel), a 100-km (62-mi) catamaran race around the island preceded by a week of other maritime events. Catamaran sailing training courses and rentals are available at **Zeilschool De Eilander** (Paal 33, De Cocksdorp, tel. 0222/316–500). **J. Schuringa** (Westerslag, Paal 15, De Koog, tel. 0222/314–847) also offers rentals and courses.

If you prefer paddling under your own steam, and that of the tides, there are supervised sea-kayaking excursions and training courses offered by **Zeekanocentrum Texel** (Lijnbaan 37, Den Burg, tel. 0222/315–066). **SeaMount Tracks** (Rommelpot 19, Den Hoorn, tel. 0222/319–393) offers weeklong sea-kayaking certificate courses. Going out on your own is dangerous in the unpredictable currents of the shallow mudflats around the island.

Daredevils might be interested in the parachuting training and jumps organized by **Paracentrum Texel** (tel. 0222/311–464) at Vliegveld Texel (Texel Airfield). For the more leisurely visitor—and those who don't wish to get wet or dizzy—there is a 9-hole links course and a 9-hole practice course at golf club **De Texelse** (Roggeslootweg 3, De Cocksdorp, tel. 0222/316–539).

Miniature" because of the variety of landscape and natural features: woodlands, open meadows, saltwater marshes, dunes, and broad beaches. The many nature reserves make it a paradise for bird-watchers. The island is also known for its organic dairy products and vegetables. Texel's sheep outnumber the human population, and their lambs are famous for their succulent pré-salé saltiness, acquired from grazing in meadows sprayed by the salt-laden sea winds.

What to See

🐚 The **Ecomare** nature center for the Wadden Sea and the North Sea is a good starting point for discovering the natural wonders of these abundant habitats. There is a seal rehabilitation center with an underwater viewing gallery, a bird sanctuary, as well as guided tours and fieldwork programs for the public. *Ruyslaan 92, De Koog, tel. 0222/317–741. Fl 12.50 (€5.65). Apr.–Oct., daily 9–5; Nov.– Mar., Mon.–Sat. 9–5. www.waterland.net/ecomare*

One of Texel's most remarkable natural features is **De Hoge Berg** (the High Mountain), the 50-ft-high ridge formed by glacial movement during the last Ice Age and declared a natural monument in 1968. Climbing its grass-covered pathways is hardly a problem, and it offers a stunning overview of the whole island. All over the island you can spot the unusual *schapeboet*, sheep shelters that look like truncated barns, some thatched with local reed, with their sloping rumps turned to the westerly winds. The characteristic *tuinwallen* (garden walls) that were used to divide plots of farmland were built up from sods of earth. These have become a habitat for all kinds of plants, animals, and insects.

❻ **Den Burg** is at the center of the island, geographically and for restaurants and shopping. The step-gabled house occupied by the **Oudheidkamer** (Museum of Antiquities) dates from 1599 and gives a sense of local life in times gone by, with exquisitely tiled fireplaces, antique furniture and traditional costumes displayed in a homey setting. *Kogerstraat 1, tel. 0222/313–135. Fl 3.50 (€1.60). Apr.–Oct. weekdays 10–12:30 and 1:30–3:30.*

NEED A
BREAK? **Hotel De Lindeboom** (*Groeneplaats 14, tel. 0222/312–041*) is a popular café-restaurant with a sunny terrace that overlooks an open square in the peaceful center of town. For an overnight stay, there are spacious, light rooms with simple modern furnishings.

7 **Oudeschild** is the island's historic harbor town, still used as a port by Texel's modern fishing fleet. During the 17th century, VOC ships would anchor here, awaiting favorable winds to take them off on their adventurous journeys, and smaller boats would bring them provisions. Sports fishing trips and shrimping fleets now set out from here.

The **Maritiem en Jutters Museum** (Maritime and Beachcomber's Museum) contains an amusing collection of beachcombers' finds, exhibits about the local fishing industry, and finds from a VOC ship that sank in the Wadden Sea in 1640. The **Traanroier molen** (Tear Rower windmill), just next door, was used for hulling grain. *Barentszstraat 21, Oudeschild, tel. 0222/314–956. Fl 8 (€3.65). Sept.–June, Tues.–Sun. 10–5; July–Aug., daily 10–5.*

NEED A
BREAK? **Hotel-Restaurant De Zeven Provinciën** (*De Ruyterstraat 60, tel. 0222/312–652*) is an old-fashioned tavern that nestles safely behind the sea dike on the eastern side of the island. The restaurant serves traditional Dutch food throughout the day, and the hotel has simple rooms.

One of Texel's oldest constructions is **Fort De Schans.** Built in the 15th century, this fort is surrounded by water-filled moats. It was extended in 1811 on the orders of Napoléon. *Schansweg, 1 km (½ mi) south of Oudeschild. Guided tours Fl 10 (€4.55). Tours: Apr.–Oct., Wed. 10.*

8 **De Koog,** a modern seaside town, is a practical base for exploring the North Sea coastline and its nature reserves. In high season it is subject to hordes of sun-seeking tourists. Much of northwestern Texel is new, the result of dikes built early in the 17th century. Sand was deposited on the seaward side of these dikes, forming a second row of dunes that protected the land behind. However, if the sea breaks through the dunes or man-made dikes during a storm, the valleys behind them can become tidal salt marshes. This is how **De Slufter** and **De Muy** nature reserves were formed, ideal feeding and breeding grounds for birds such as the spoonbill, sandpipers, and even the rare avocet.

Coming and Going

Texel is just over an hour from Amsterdam by road or rail, plus 20 minutes from the mainland by ferry.

BY CAR
To reach **Texel,** travel north from Amsterdam on N203, N9, and N250 to the port of Den Helder, where the ferry departs.

BY FERRY
The ferry (tel. 0222/369–600) to the island of Texel runs hourly from 6 AM to 9 PM daily in summer. In winter the service is reduced. The **TelekomTaxi** (tel. 322–211, local calls only) minibus serves the ferry terminal.

BY TRAIN
Intercity trains run direct to Den Helder every hour, with connecting buses to the ferry terminal. The **Waddenbiljet** all-inclusive return ticket, the easiest and most economical method for getting to Texel, includes bus services on the island itself. For train information, contact national train information (tel. 0900/9292, Fl 0.75 [€0.35] per minute).

CONTACTS AND RESOURCES

VISITOR INFORMATION

VVV/ANWB Aalsmeer (Drie Kolommenplein 1, 1431 LA, Aalsmeer, tel. 0297/325–374, fax 0297/354–255). **VVV Haarlem** (Stationsplein 1, 2011 LR, tel. 0900/616–1600, Fl 1 [€0.45] per min, fax 023/534–0537). **VVV Lisse** (VVV, Grachtweg 53, 2160 AG, tel. 0252/414–262, fax 0252/418–639). **VVV Noord-Holland** (Oranjekade 41, 2011 VD, Haarlem, no tourist information by phone, www.noord-holland-tourist.nl). **VVV Texel** (Emmalaan 66, 1791 AV, Den Burg, tel. 0222/314–741, fax 0222/310–054). **VVV West-Friesland** (Veemarkt 4, 1621 JC, Hoorn, tel. 0900/403–1055, 75¢ per min; fax 0229/215–023). **VVV Zaanstreek/Waterland** (Gedempte Gracht 76, 1506 CJ, Zaandam, tel. 075/616–2221, fax 075/670–5381).

There is truly something for everyone in Amsterdam, from the most genteel to the most sordid. In general: anything goes. Fun loving Amsterdammers are extremely spontaneous and it is not unusual to have small groups breaking into song in some of the neighborhood places.

In This Chapter

Brown Cafés 132 • Cabarets 133 • Casino 133 • Cocktail Bars and Grand Cafés 134 • Coffee Shops 135 • Dance and Rock Clubs 135 • Gay Bars 136 • Lesbian Bars 138 • Jazz Clubs 138 • Lounges 139 • World Music 139

By Barbara Krulik

nightlife

AMSTERDAM AT NIGHT IS VIBRANT AND COLORFUL. Homey brown bars, artsy dance clubs, chic wine bars, mellow jazz clubs, and laid back lounges are a few of the venues where all are welcome. It is particularly pleasant to find young people mixing comfortably with older people in cafés of every type. Every night is reason to celebrate, so men selling single red roses and taking Polaroids pop in and out of every kind of venue.

Lounges are a totally new phenomenon in Amsterdam and have added a new vitality to the nightlife. They tend to be small and concentrated along the Nieuwezijds Voorburgwal, but others are springing up in the city. As hip as big dance clubs, the lounges generally have a relaxed atmosphere and DJs spinning club music.

Amsterdam, being one of the most liberal cities in the world, has a reputation for its tolerant attitude towards prostitution and soft drugs. It is somewhat shocking for first-time visitors to the city to see the world famous Red Light District and it hundreds of "coffee shops." The pragmatic Dutch, knowing that the sex and drug trade will always exist as it does around the world, actually choose to accept and control the trade, earning tax revenues and protecting the health concerns of people in the business. Prostitutes have regular medical examinations and practice safe sex, and—to address the concerns of timid customers—there is a storefront information center (☞ Sensual Pleasures in Introducing Amsterdam). The Red Light District is organized according to preference: either skin color or fetish.

It is not actually legal to deal in marijuana and hashish, and only small amounts (1 ounce) for personal use are tolerated. Although there is a tolerant attitude towards smoking marijuana in the hundreds of "coffee shops" in Amsterdam, many people still frown upon smoking in restaurants, bars, and cafés. The coffee shops are populated by Dutch teenagers (who usually gravitate to more socially acceptable alcohol as they reach their twenties) and enthusiastic tourists. Since 1999, the police have been cracking down on all other drugs, which are strictly illegal.

How and Where

Amsterdam nightlife centers mainly on two city squares: Leidseplein, where the cafés and discos tend to attract young visitors to the city, and Rembrandtplein, which fills up with a more local crowd. Trendier nightspots and many of Amsterdam's gay venues are on the streets in between the two squares; Reguliersdwarsstraat is a particularly happy hunting ground, while Warmoestraat and other streets in the Red Light District are the scene of leather-oriented gay bars and throbbing rock clubs. The gay scene in Amsterdam is concentrated mostly on Reguliersdwarsstraat, Amstelstraat, Kerkstraat (near the Leidseplein), and along the Amstel River—in addition to Warmoestraat.

The Dutch are very social people and enjoy going out either after work or after dinner. Sunday and Monday nights tend to be quiet in town, and of course, on Friday and Saturday nights the streets are teeming with people. Most bars and cafés close around 2 AM, but *nachtbars* (night bars) open after 10 pm and are licensed to stay open until about 4 or 5 am.

Sources

The **AUB (Amsterdam's Uit Buro)** on Leidseplein, on the corner of the Marnixstraat (tel. 020/621–1211), is a great source for everything happening in the city. Publications and brochures

Sybaritic Pleasures

If you're interested in relaxing and sensual—but not sexual—activities, spend a delightful fall or winter evening at **Sauna Deco** (Herengracht 115, tel. 020/623–8215), an institution for Amsterdam literati, and cognoscenti. On entering the canal house designed by Henrick P. Berlage (in his early neoclassical period), one descends several steps and is dazzled: the interior is truly spectacular.

Two decades ago (the sauna celebrated its 20th anniversary in 2000), when the board of directors of Paris's Au Bon Marché department store decided to strip the elegant interior of its art deco ornamentation from the 1920s and modernize, the enterprising Renske Visser and her partner negotiated with the directors and were able to remove the material, transport it to Amsterdam, and reassemble it painstakingly in its new home in the Sauna Deco. They salvaged the magnificent deco tile work from the Dutch Twentsche Bank and chairs from the Hotel Suisse. A staircase with patterned railings, gilt decorations, lamps, stained and sandblasted glass, and wood wainscot were incorporated into this elegant sauna.

This is not a place to come for a quick sauna; plan on spending several hours. Guests are rented towels and robes and given lockers. There are no separate sections for men and women; everyone goes together into the saunas and lounges. Because every age and body type comes to the sauna, there is no need to be inhibited about your body. The point is to relax, read, chat. Amenities include two sauna cabins, Turkish bath, tanning booth, footbaths, and lounges. Light meals and snacks as well as healthy soft drinks are available throughout the day and evening. A team of masseurs and masseuses are trained in Swedish massage, sports massage, and deep-tissue and shiatsu massage techniques. The adjoining Salon Deco offers facial treatments, body wraps, pedicures, and manicures. Reservations are not necessary for the sauna, but are for massages and the salon.

from high-culture to pop-culture venues line the walls by category. The monthly Dutch-language *UitKrant*, published by AUB, has current and clear listings for every entertainment possibility. Every Thursday, *De Volkskrant* newspaper has a special listings section that covers films and arts and cultural events in the entire country, with special emphasis on Amsterdam.

Major newsstands carry specialized publications that include ads and listings for entertainment possibilities oriented to the interests of gays and lesbians. The action group **COC** (Rozenstraat 14, tel. 020/626–3087) is a good information source and also operates as a coffee shop, youth café, and dance club. The **Gay & Lesbian Switchboard** (tel. 020/623–6565) can provide information from 10 AM to 10 PM.

BROWN CAFÉS

Coffee and conversation are the two main ingredients of *gezelligheid* (a good time) for an Amsterdammer, and perhaps a beer or two as the evening wears on. The best place for these pleasures is a traditional brown café. Wood paneling, wooden floors, comfortably worn furniture, and walls and ceilings stained with eons' worth of tobacco smoke give the cafés their name—though today a little carefully applied paint achieves the same effect. Traditionally, there is no background music, just the hum of chitchat. You can meet up with friends or sit alone and undisturbed for hours, enjoying a cup of coffee and a thorough read of the newspapers and magazines from the pile in the corner.

Bierbrouwerij 't IJ (Funekade 7, tel. 020/622–8325) is a micro-brewery located in a windmill and is only open 3–8 PM, Wednesdays–Sundays. Once the tasting house of an old family distillery, **De Admiraal** (Herengracht 319, tel. 020/625–4334) still serves potent liqueurs—many with obscene names.

De Reiger (Nieuwe Leliestraat 34, tel. 020/624–7426) has a distinctive Jugendstil bar and serves food. If you want to hear the locals sing folk music on Sunday afternoon, stop by **De Twee Zwaantjes** (Prinsengracht 114, tel. 020/625–2729).

A busy, jolly brown café, **In de Wildeman** (Kolksteeg 3, tel. 020/ 638–2348), attracts a wide range of types and ages. **Nol** (Westerstraat 109, tel. 020/624–5380) resonates with lusty-lunged, native Jordaaners having the time of their lives.

Rooie Nelis (Laurierstraat 101, tel. 020/624–4167) is one of the cafés that has kept its traditional Jordaan atmosphere despite the area's tendency toward trendiness. The high-ceiling **'t Smalle** (Egelantiersgracht 12, tel. 020/623–9617) has a waterside terrace and is a favorite after-work gathering place.

CABARETS

Boom Chicago (Leidseplein 12, tel. 020/530–7306), at the Leidseplein Theater, belongs to a bunch of zany ex-pat Americans who opened their own restaurant-theater to present improvised comedy inspired by life in Amsterdam; dinner and seating begin at 7, show time is at 8:15. **Kleine Komedie** (Amstel 56–58, tel. 020/624–0534) has for many years been the most vibrant venue for cabaret and comedy (mainly in Dutch).

One of the best additions to Amsterdam's nightlife scene in recent years is the **Lido Dinner Show** (Leidsestraat 105, tel. 020/ 626–2106), which offers cabaret and light entertainment while you dine.

CASINO

The **Holland Casino Amsterdam** (Max Euweplein 62, tel. 020/ 620–1006) is part of the Lido complex near Leidseplein (☞ Cabarets, *above*). It is one of the largest casinos in Europe (more than 90,000 square ft) and offers everything from your choice of French or American roulette to computerized bingo, as well as the obligatory slot machines to eat up your supply of loose guilders. On your way out-of-town via Schiphol airport, Holland Casino has lounges in many of the wings of the airport leading to your gate.

COCKTAIL BARS AND GRAND CAFÉS

Café de Jaren (Nieuwe Doelenstraat 20, tel. 020/625–5771) is a large, airy multi-level bar with a lovely terrace overlooking the Amstel. **Ciel Bleu Bar** (Hotel Okura, Ferdinand Bolstraat 333, tel. 020/678–7111) has a glass-wall lounge 23 stories high, where you can enjoy the sunsets over Amsterdam and watch the night lights twinkle to life.

In the Stopera complex next to the Waterlooplein Market is the lovely **Dantzig** (Zwanenburgwal 15, tel. 020/620–9039). With a view of the Amstel River, it is the perfect location before or after the ballet or opera. **De Kroon** (Rembrandtplein 17, tel. 020/625–2011) is a grand café with intimate seating arrangements and a U-shape bar surrounding old-style wood museum cases filled with specimens. The bar attracts a fashionable yuppie clientele in the evenings.

Freddy's (Hotel de l'Europe, Nieuwe Doelenstraat 2–8, tel. 020/623–4836), cozy and stylish, is a favorite meeting place for businesspeople. Comfy leather chairs and soft lighting give the **Golden Palm Bar** (Grand Hotel Krasnapolsky, Dam 9, tel. 020/554–9111) something of the atmosphere of a British gentlemen's club.

Luxembourg (Spui 22-24, tel. 020/620–6264) has an art deco interior and glass terrace for people-watching on the Spui square. In the afternoon, **Wildschut** (Roelof Hartplein 1-3, tel. 020/676–8220), in a 1920s Amsterdam school, is a delightful place for coffee, and this is the place to go to meet suited yuppies in the evenings. The terrace is large and has great views for architecture enthusiasts.

COFFEE SHOPS

As a group, the "coffee shops" where marijuana and hashish are smoked are not the most delightful of local establishments, but the following are among the more "reputable" establishments. One should always use caution, because the quality of the merchandise is good and those that partake may become too high (☞ chapter introduction, *above*). **Greenhouse** (Tolstraat 4, tel. 020/673–7430) serves alcohol, burgers, and fries. **Kandinsky** (Rosemarijnsteeg 9, tel. 020/624–7023) offers mellow jazz and scrumptious chocolate chip cookies. The clientele at the **Other Side** (Reguliersdwarsstraat 6, tel. 020/625–5141) is primarily gay. **Paradox** (del Eerste Bloemdwarstraat 2, tel. 020/623–5639), a storefront in the charming Jordaan, is more like a health food café than a coffee shop. **Tweede Kamer** (Heisteeg 6, tel. 020/627–5709) is a pun meaning "second room" and refers to the Dutch parliamentary structure.

DANCE AND ROCK CLUBS

Arena ('s-Gravensandestraat 51, tel. 020/694–7444), a hostel complex, is gaining favor as a venue for its weekend club and events. Unabashedly commercial, **Cash** (Leidseplein 12, tel. 020/422–0808) attracts Dutch youth from the provinces and reveling tourists. The huge, popular **Escape** (Rembrandtplein 11–15, tel. 020/622–1111) can handle 2,500 people dancing to a DJ or live bands; attractions include laser light shows, videos, and shops selling club wear.

iT (Amstelstraat 24, tel. 020/625–0111), with four bars, special acts and bands, and celebrities, tends toward a gay crowd on Friday and Saturday nights, straight on Thursday and Sunday nights. **Mazzo** (Rozengracht 114, tel. 020/626–7500) is the rising star of club life in Amsterdam. If you feel like dancing in a gracious old canal house, head for **Odeon** (Singel 460, tel. 020/624–9711), where jazz and rock play in various rooms, many of which retain their spectacular painted and stucco ceilings.

The famous **Paradiso** (Weteringschans 6-8, tel. 020/626–4521) hosts bands and dance nights with guest DJs in a former church that reverberates nightly to unusual sounds—anything from the latest rock band to a serious contemporary composer. Flexible staging arrangements make this a favorite venue for performance artists and multimedia events.

A group of artists runs **Seymour Likely Too** (Nieuwezijds Voorburgwal 161, tel. 020/420–5663), giving vent to their creativity in the decor—such as the Beuys Bar, decorated in the style of Joseph Beuys, a father of the avant-garde. Sound is in the capable hands of some of Amsterdam's most popular DJs. **West Pacific** (Haarlemmerweg 8-10, tel. 020/681–3068), on the historic 19th-century Westergasfabriek (gas factory) grounds, is a relaxed café and club in the evenings.

GAY BARS

Tankards and brass pots hang from the ceiling in the **Amstel Taveerne** (Amstel 54, tel. 020/623–4254), and the friendly crowd of Amsterdammers around the bar bursts into song whenever the sound system plays an old favorite. **April** (Reguliersdwarsstraat 37, tel. 020/625–9572) has a lounge in the front and a fabulous rotating bar in the back, which is open when the bar is particularly crowded on the weekends. April's late night multi-level bar and disco, **April's Exit** (Reguliersdwarsstraat 42, tel. 020/625–8788) attracts a smart young crowd of gay men and is women-friendly.

Club Havana (Reguliersdwarsstraat 17, tel. 020/620–6788) has a comfortable atmosphere with large wicker chairs and banquet seating. For a heavy cruise scene, the men-only **Cockring** (Warmoesstraat 96, tel. 020/623–9604) runs well into the morning hours. **Downtown** (Reguliersdwarsstraat 31, tel. 020/ 622–9958) is a pleasant daytime coffee bar with a sunny terrace.

Le Montmartre (Halvemaansteeg 17, tel. 020/620–7622) attracts a hip crowd of younger gay men, who stop for a drink

The Gay Community

Though many of Amsterdam's native inhabitants declare that the Dutch are becoming homomoe (tired of homosexuals), such an opinion is quickly put to rest by the lively and welcoming scene offered to gay and lesbian travelers by Amsterdam.

Homosexuality was officially decriminalized in Amsterdam in 1811; recent estimates put the homosexual population between 20% and 30% One can feel the city's tolerance in everything from the locals' nonchalant attitude toward public affection to the recent vote to convert the country's registered same-sex partnerships into full-fledged marriages, with divorce guidelines and wider adoption rights. In the early '80s, Amsterdam was quick to cope constructively with the AIDS crisis, and in 1987, it unveiled the Homomonument, a world's first. The three pink granite triangles memorialize gays and lesbians persecuted by the Nazis and are often at the center of a party, protest, or commemoration. The COC (Cultuur en Ontspanningscentrum, or Cultural and Social Center, pronounced say-o-say) of the Nederlandse Vereniging tot Integratie van Homoseksualiteit (Dutch Association for the Integration of Homosexuality), which is subsidized by the government, is one of the country's largest gay and lesbian rights organizations and provides a social haven in the center of town. At the School of International Training, "Homo" Studies have now been added to the official curriculum, and 1998 found Amsterdam host to the Gay Games.

Roze Zaterdag (Pink Saturday) takes place in a different Netherlands city each June and attracts the most tourists of any gay pride event. Since the mid-'90s, Amsterdam has had its own parade, early in August, with a boat parade up the Prinsengracht. Every weekend visitors flock to the many gay venues that dot Amsterdam. As is often the case, the lesbian scene is less developed. In Amsterdam, unlike what happens in many other cities, gay establishments do not have covered windows but harbor an open attitude toward anyone. Free gay maps of Amsterdam and other informational leaflets, often bilingual or in English, are available at many venues (☞ Practical Information).

138

before heading out clubbing. Leather, piercing, and tattoos predominate at the **Web** (St. Jacobstraat 6, tel. 020/623–6758), a local bar.

Lesbian Bars

Amsterdam offers lesbians very few places to meet and party. Women should check at the bars, the gay and lesbian bookstore, or the COC for women's parties and events (☞ Sources, *above*). Amsterdam's best women-only bar, **Saarein** (Elandsstraat 119, tel. 020/623–4901) has a cozy brown-café atmosphere in the Jordaan. **Vive-la-Vie** has a lively bar scene and is men- and straight-friendly (Amstelstraat 7, tel. 020/624–0114).

JAZZ CLUBS

In the smoky, jam-packed atmosphere of **Alto** (Korte Leidsedwarsstraat 115, tel. 020/626–3249), you can hear the pick of local bands. **Bamboo Bar** (Lange Leidsedwarsstraat 64, tel. 020/624–3993) has a long bar and cool Latin sounds. At **Bimhuis** (Oude Schans 73–77, tel. 020/623–3373), the best-known jazz place in town, you'll find top musicians, including avant-gardists, performing on Friday and Saturday nights, and weeknight jam sessions.

Bourbon Street Jazz & Blues Club (Leidsekruisstraat 6–8, tel. 020/623–3440) presents mainstream blues and jazz to a largely tourist clientele. **Casablanca** (Zeedijk 26, tel. 020/625–5685) on the edge of the Red Light District is an institution in the neighborhood, with jazz during the week and karaoke on the weekends.

Café Meander (Voetboogstraat 3b, tel. 020/625–8430) offers a mixed selection of live music, from soul to swing. **Joseph Lam Jazz Club** (Van Diemenstraat 242, tel. 020/622–8086) specializes in Dixieland and is open only on Saturday.

LOUNGES

At press time, the **NZ Lounge** (Nieuwezijds Voorburgwal 169, no phone) is the hippest of the new lounges. It changes its name from time to time (originally, it was called the "NL Lounge"), but the location stays the same. Since it opened, **Bep** (Nieuwezijds Voorburgwal 260, tel. 020/626–5649) has attracted a smart artist crowd for mellow afternoons and lively evenings. A group of artists runs **Seymour Likely** (Nieuwezijds Voorburgwal 250, tel. 020/627–1427); it was one of the first hip lounges to become the rage.

Lux (Marnixstraat 397, tel. 020/422–1412) has a fantastic '6os decor and an attractive young crowd. At the **Supper Club** (Jongeroelensteeg 21, tel. 020/638–0513), a breathtakingly hip lounge/restaurant, you can recline on mats and white pillows and listen to DJs spin music while being served an expensive fixed-price multi-course meal.

WORLD MUSIC

Akhnaton (Nieuwezijdskolk 25, tel. 020/624–3396) is a multicultural stage and dance club renowned for its world music. African nights are especially good, but there's lots of salsa and jazz, too, and even hip-hop.

De Melkweg (The Milky Way; Lijnbaansgracht 234A, tel. 020/624–1777 or 020/624–8492) is internationally known as a multicultural center for music, theater, film, and dance, with live music performances at least four nights a week and an innovative programming policy that tends increasingly toward multimedia events. **Tropeninstituut** has dance and music from Africa, Asia, Latin American, the Caribbean, and other tropical regions. (Mauritskade 63 en Linnaeusstraat 2, tel. 020/568–8500).

Crossover shows and combinations of high and low culture are hallmarks of the contemporary Amsterdam arts scene. Imagine Beethoven's Fifth Symphony performed with break dancers, conducted by one of Holland's most important conductors. Some venues offer a mixture of programming, including films, lectures, debates, concerts, and vocal productions. If the programs are multicultural, English may well be the language of presentation.

In This Chapter

GALLERIES 142 • FILM 145 • MULTIPURPOSE VENUES 145 • MUSIC, DANCE, AND THEATER 146 • Music 146 • Opera and Dance 148 • Puppets and Children's Theater 148 • Theater 149

By Barbara Krulik

the arts

FOR A THOROUGH OVERVIEW OF THE RICHNESS of the Amsterdam cultural scene, check out the UitMarkt (Going Out Market), the last weekend in August. This festival has city streets and squares teeming with culture vultures of all ages previewing the coming year's attractions. Amsterdam's theater and music season begins in September and runs through June, when the Holland Festival of Performing Arts is held.

Theater and music concerts are reasonably priced, even for the most internationally acclaimed artists. Therefore, the audiences span a broad age range, making for a simulating program in even the most traditional of venues.

Sources

Unfortunately, there's no English-language guide to events around the city. On Thursday, the daily newspaper De Volkskrant has excellent listings of events. If you can get translations, the arts and literature reviews are thoughtful. Other daily newspapers have listings, too, but tend to be more national in scope.

Reserve tickets to performances at the major theaters before your arrival through the **Netherlands Reservation Center** (Postbus 404, 2260 AK Leidschendam, tel. 070/419–5500, fax 070/419–5519). Upon arrival, you can buy tickets at theater box offices or in person at the tourist information offices through the **VVV Theater Booking Office** (Stationsplein 10) Monday through Saturday, 10–4.

The **AUB Ticketshop** (Leidseplein, corner Marnixstraat, tel. 020/ 621–1211) is open Monday–Saturday 9–9 and is generally less crowded than other ticket outlets, though the prices include a small service fee. AUB (the acronym for Amsterdam's Uit Buro, or Amsterdam Going Out Office) also has brochures from all of the major venues (organized by discipline), and the staff is very friendly. The Dutch-language *UitKrant*, published by AUB, is a free monthly magazine listing all sorts of cultural events; you can pick it up throughout the city.

GALLERIES

Many of the galleries that deal in modern and contemporary art are centered on the Keizersgracht and in the charming neighborhood of the Jordaan. *Exhibitions Amsterdam/ Tentoonstellings Agenda* is a bimonthly four-fold brochure and the most comprehensive and current listing of exhibitions in contemporary art galleries and museums. The brochure is available in most galleries for free. Another good source of information on the art scene is the Dutch-language publication *Alert*, which has the most comprehensive listings available. Galleries are generally open on Tuesdays or Wednesdays through Saturday. Check carefully to avoid disappointment. Many galleries are also open the first Sunday afternoon of the month, 2–5 PM.

The **KunstRAI**, in the first week of June, is an annual art trade fair. ("RAI"—from Rijwiel Automobiel Industrie, or Bicycle Automobile Industry, a trade fair begun in 1893 and later expanded to include cars—has come to stand for any trade fair that is held at the Amsterdam convention center, which is itself known as the Amsterdam RAI.) Dealers from all over the Netherlands gather for the largest art fair of the year. Most of the art presented is by Dutch artists, and all of it is from the 20th century. All of the "high" art galleries pull out their very finest objects, so the fair is filled with treasures. A 40-gallery

Kunstenaarsinitiatieven

In Holland the phenomenon of Kunstenaarsinitiatieven (artists' initiatives) has developed since the mid-1980s and virtually exploded since the mid-1990s. Initiatives are exhibition opportunities or projects that are created by artists but don't fit neatly into the traditional venues for art. Impromptu public manifestations and small presses for artists' books, magazines, and newspapers exist alongside installations, video, and body-art performances.

The artist initiatives have roots in the Fluxus movement that created the art happenings of the 1960s and 1970s and operate either singly, collaboratively, or collectively. The initiatives exist for four primary purposes: to provide a counterpoint to the limited number of galleries for contemporary art; so that there is a self-directed platform for presentations that are free of curatorial or dealer's choice; to serve as forums for artists' work that exists alongside their main body of work (as when painters with gallery representation also make small edition magazines); and, in some cases, to share studio space in groups of artists. This final purpose is connected to the anarchist/squatters movement of the early 1970s.

Jos Houweling, director of the Sandberg Institute of Amsterdam's Gerrit Rietveld Academy, recognized these phenomena and, beginning in 1996, organized an event to gather these initiatives together. An alternative art fair called Kunstvlaai (art pie) is held annually in May in a group of 19th-century factory buildings in the western part of Amsterdam, the historic Westergasfabriek. As many as 80 initiatives involving 200 artists were presented in the huge and impressive spaces. Most of the initiatives were based on one object, one theme, or one collective concept, and at other times of the year many can be visited at their home sites such as W139 at Warmoestraat 139 or Consortium on the Oostelijke Handelskade 29.

association calls itself "Art Amsterdam" and stands for the highest quality contemporary art, in opposition to some of the crafts and kitsch galleries in this large art fair. (The Maastricht Art Fair is largely for pre-20th century art and antiques and is held in March or April.)

In the Jordaan, the newest and hippest gallery scene is home to **Annet Gelink Gallery** (Laurierstraat 187-189, tel. 020/330–2066). Among not-for-profit exhibition centers known for their challenging content or new media is **Arti en Amicitiae** (Rokin 112, tel. 020/626–5206). **Collection D'Art** (Keizersgracht 516, tel. 020/622–1511) specializes in 20th-century art and has a noteworthy modernist interior and balconies overlooking a central atrium.

De Appel (Nieuwe Speigelstraat 10, tel. 020/625–5651) is another not-for-profit exhibition venue. For serious art with a touch of humor, visit **Fons Welters** (Bloemstraat 140, tel. 020/423–3046). **Galerie Espace and Metis** (Keizersgracht 548, tel. 020/624–0802 Gallerie Espace or 020/638–9863 Metis) share a building and a 20th-century specialty. Several well-known Dutch artists are represented by **Galerie Rob Jurka** (Singel 28, tel. 020/627–6343).

The roster of artists at **Hof en Huyser** (Bloemgracht 135, tel. 020/420–1995) is international and displays powerful human content. **Kunsthandel M.L. De Boer** (Keizersgracht 542, tel. 020/623–4060) offers realistic paintings and has a regal clientele. Innovative and emerging artists have installations and exhibitions in **Loerakker's** (Keizersgracht 380, tel. 020/622–1732) labyrinthian canal house gallery. **Nederlands Instituut voor Mediakunst Montevideo** specializes in video and new media art and also has a very special video-library (Keizersgracht 264, tel. 020/624–4423). **Paul Andriesse** (Prinsengracht 116, tel. 020/623–6237) handles internationally known contemporary artists. Gestural abstraction and color field painting can be found at **Slewe** (Kerkstraat 105-A, tel. 020/625–7214). The **Stedelijk Museum Bureau Amsterdam** (Rozenstraat 59, tel. 020/422–

0471) is a venue for young Amsterdam artists, occasionally in collaboration with artists from abroad.

FILM

Mainstream *bioscopen* (cinemas) are concentrated near the Rembrandtplein and the Leidseplein. **Bellevue Cinerama and Calypso** (Marnixstraat 400, tel. 020/620–8417) screens first-run movies and small budget European films. Not so recent releases are shown at the intimate and worn, **De Uitkijk** (Prinsengracht 452, tel. 020/623–7460).

The podium for Dutch filmmakers is at the **Ketelhuis** (Haarlemerweg 8-10, tel. 020/684–0090) outside the center of town at the former factory buildings of the Westergasfabriek. The **Kriterion** (Roeterstraat 170, tel. 020/623–1708) screens highly artistic European films that attract an intellectual crowd. The bar is a great meeting place, too. Amsterdam's largest cinema is the seven-screen **Pathé City Theatre** (Kleine Gartmanplantsoen 15–19, tel. 020/623–4570). Worth visiting, if only for the pleasure of sitting in its magnificent art deco auditorium, is the **Tuschinski** (Reguliersbreestraat 26, tel. 020/626–2633).

MULTIPURPOSE VENUES

Several of Amsterdam's venues host a variety of arts performances. **De Balie** (Kleine-Gartmanplantsoen 10, tel. 020/553–5100) is often the site of debates, lectures, and film presentations. For German programming, try the **Goethe Institute** (Herengracht 470, tel. 020/623–0421). **Maison Descartes** (Vijzelgracht 2A and Prinsengracht 644A, tel. 020/531–9500) presents events in French.

The **Westergasfabriek** (Haarlemmerweg 8-10, tel. 202/681–3068) complex—which includes the **Gashouder**, the **Ketelhuis**, and **Machinegebouw**—hosts film presentations, art exhibitions, music festivals, and theater productions.

MUSIC, DANCE, AND THEATER
Music

There are two concert halls under one roof at the **Concertgebouw** (Concertgebouwplein 2–6, tel. 020/671–8345). Completed in 1888 and renowned for its marvelous acoustics, the main hall, Amsterdam's critically acclaimed Koninklijk Concertgebouworkest (Royal Concert Orchestra) often hosts international performers. The smaller hall is a venue for chamber music and shows by up-and-coming musicians. There are free lunchtime concerts in the Concertgebouw on Wednesday at 12:30.

A good venue for classical music is the architecturally magnificent **Beurs van Berlage** (Damrak 243, tel. 020/627–0466). Designed by Hendrick P. Berlage (the Netherlands equivalent of Frank Lloyd Wright), the former stock exchange building is one of the city's most important 20th-century structures. In addition to having concert halls that host everything from large philharmonic performances to intimate piano recitals, it has a remarkable exhibition space.

The internationally acclaimed **Conservatorium van Amsterdam** (Van Baerlestraat 27, tel. 020/571–2500) has concerts by their accomplished students for free at 5:30 PM. At **Felix Meritis** (Keizersgracht 324, tel. 020/623–1311) you can enjoy concerts of young composers as well as dance productions and lectures.

The **Muziekcentrum De IJsbreker** (Weesperzijde 23, tel. 020/668–1805) is at the cutting edge of contemporary music and often hosts festivals of international repute. The **Tropeninstituut** (Mauritskade 63 en Linnaeusstraat 2, tel. 020/568–5800) concert hall is the site of world music shows that complement the institute's exhibitions focusing on the world's tropical regions. It also hosts children's theater productions, marionette shows, and lectures.

Warner and Company: The Art of Street Theater

Warner en Consorten (Warner and Company; Middenweg 67/D, tel. 020/663–2656), formed in 1993, is unique in the world. Its founder, Warner van Wely, created an interdisciplinary concept of street theater, where sculpture, dance, physical acting (such as mime), and music collide and challenge the concepts of theater, urban life, and reality. Although their background is complex and theoretical, their power comes from paring down their performance to essential elements. The results are simply hilarious.

Public space is the starting point for Warner and Company. Streets are analyzed, crowd behavior is studied, passersby are observed. Van Wely describes the city as a man-made collective fantasy that inhabitants see as reality, a reality that can be reinterpreted as a new collective fantasy. This is precisely what Warner and Company achieves. It engages the often-unsuspecting audience and encourages people to interact actively with each other and with the company.

The company creates a sort of primordial environment with their music, movement, and costumes. Their props are simple daily objects that have been adapted to new uses as costumes or instruments. For example, white handbags are used as hats and filled with talc: when they are drummed on, puffs of powder emanate from the heads of the performers. Old-fashioned rotary lawn mowers become percussion instruments that rhythmically batter the cobblestone streets, both attracting and scattering crowds. Warner and Company provides a total sensory experience: members of the audience may smell talc, taste powdered sugar, be wrapped in packing tape, have their hair mussed, be sprayed with water, or offered a soda. With either provocation or tenderness, the company's goal is to alter the reality and perceptions of its public.

During the winter months the company finds indoor spaces to perform, such as abandoned warehouses and factories, and in the summer they find locations in city streets and worldwide festivals.

Concerts of all types are held in historic locations around the city. Churches provide stunning environments for classical, chamber music, and jazz. Concerts are played on the early 18th-century organ in the 14th-century **De Oude Kerk** (Oudekerkplein 23, tel. 020/625–8284). **De Rode Hoed** (Keizersgracht 102, tel. 020/638–5606) is a venue for contemporary composers and chamber music. **Mozes en Aäronkerk** (Waterlooplein 207, tel. 020/622-1305), behind the Stopera, offers chamber and baroque music. **Uilenberger Synagoge** (Nieuwe Uilenburgerstraat 91, tel. 020/623–7791) is a venue for music from Bach to jazz. **Waalse Kerk** (Oudezijds Achterburgwal 159, tel. 020/623–2074) hosts chamber-music concerts sponsored by the Network for Old Music. Saturday afternoon concerts of acoustic chamber music are held at the **Noorderkerk** (Noordermarkt 44, tel. 020/623–5149).

Opera and Dance

The grand and elegant **Muziektheater** (Waterlooplein 22, tel. 020/551–8911) seats 1,600 people and hosts international opera, ballet, and orchestra performances throughout the year. The Muziektheater is home to De Nederlandse Opera (the Netherlands National Opera) and the Nationale Ballet (the Netherlands National Ballet). Both offer largely classical repertoires, but the dance company has, in recent years, gained a large measure of fame throughout Europe for its performances of 20th-century ballets, and the opera company is gaining international praise for its imaginative and adventurous stagings. Scarpino Rotterdam, the innovative modern dance company from nearby Rotterdam, also resides at the Muziektheater when performing Amsterdam.

Puppets and Children's Theater

The young and the young at heart can enjoy puppet and marionette shows at **Amsterdams Marionetten Theater** (Nieuwe Jonkerstraat 8, tel. 020/620–8027).

The children's theater **Jeugdtheater de Krakeling** (Nieuwe Passeerdersstraat 1, tel. 020/624–5123) has a variety of programming for children, from circuses to dance theater. Performances are targeted to children by age group.

Children between 7 and 12 years old can go to a sound installation designed by artists at **De Klankspeeltuin** (Swammerdamstraat 40, tel. 020/693–9093).

Theater

Built in the 19th century as permanent home to a circus, the **Koninklijk Theater Carré** (Amstel 115–125, tel. 020/622–5225) is the site of lavish, mainstream theater productions and concerts by rock, pop, and jazz greats.

Amsterdam's municipal theater, the **Stadsschouwburg** (Leidseplein 26, tel. 020/624–2311), mainly stages theater in Dutch but sometimes hosts smaller visiting opera companies and is beginning to turn its eye to the profitable possibilities of multicultural programming.

Amsterdam's Off-Broadway–type theaters are in an alley called Nes, which leads off the Dam. They collectively promote themselves as the [NES]. **De Brakke Grond** (Nes 45, tel. 020/ 626–6866) is part of the Vlaams Cultuuralhuis (Flemish Cultural House) that promotes productions from Belgium. **Frascati** (Nes 63, tel. 020/623–5723 or 020/623–5724) has been at the forefront of innovative performance, from theater to hip-hop dance. Open podium nights are held to promote new talents in poetry, literature, and music at the **Theatre Cosmic** (Nes 75, tel. 020/623–7234). Established in 1975, the **Theatre De Engelenbak** (Nes 71, tel. 020/626–3644) offers a stimulating range of perfomances, from one-person shows to dance groups.

Lodging in Amsterdam ranges from homey bed and breakfasts to super-exclusive suite guest houses and elegant and palatial city monuments. Amsterdam has an intimate character and its inhabitants pride themselves on their singularity, so their hotels are each unique. Some are delightfully quirky, and others breathtakingly beautiful. In almost all instances— across all price categories—the owners and staff are very warm, hospitable, and helpful.

In This Chapter

Amsterdam South and de Pijp 153 • East of the Amstel 156 • Grachtengordel: The Canal Ring 157 • Jordaan 161 • Leidseplein 162 • Museum Quarter and Vondelpark 162 • Nieuwezijde and the Dam 169 • Oudezijde and de Wallen 170 • Rembrandtplein 172

By Barbara S. Krulik

where to stay

THERE ARE SOME 300 HOTELS FROM WHICH to choose in Amsterdam. Most are small mom-and-pop operations, best described as pensions, found along and among the canals or in residential neighborhoods beyond the center, such as the Museum District. These smaller canal-side hotels, often in historic buildings with antique furniture, capture the charm and flavor of Amsterdam. The larger hotels, including the expensive international chains, are clustered around Centraal Station, at Dam Square, and near Leidseplein. The following list does not include the huge multinational chains where there is worldwide consistency of rooms and service.

Amsterdam is a busy city; reservations are advised at any time of the year and are essential in tulip season (late March–June) and through the summer. Annual conventions fill the city for weeks in the beginning of September. Try to plan well in advance so you have the widest range of possibilities. Some of the hotels are very small and benefit from excellent word-of-mouth, so they book quickly. The Amsterdam tourist office known as the VVV (Vereniging voor Vreemdelingenverkeer, ☞ Practical Information) can book hotel rooms for you in all categories if you arrive without reservations. They charge a fee of Fl 6 (€2.70) per reservation and also receive a commission from the hotel, which has a tendency to drive prices up. The VVV books for everything—including tickets for tours, theater, and concerts—and the offices are ridiculously crowded in summer with all manner of visitors needing same-day booking and with an unsavory local crowd of opportunists offering sleazy accommodations to desperate students and backpackers.

The lodgings we list are the cream of the crop in each price category. All hotels listed have private bath unless otherwise noted. We always list the facilities that are available—but we don't specify whether they cost extra: when pricing accommodations, always ask what's included and what costs extra. Amsterdam is a pedestrian's paradise but a driver's nightmare. Few hotels have parking lots, and cars are best abandoned in one of the city's multistory lots for the duration of your stay. Some hotels have parking services available, but it is never included in the hotel price.

Prices

Given the world standard for hotel pricing, the Dutch generally do NOT overprice and they relish the *goedkoop* (bargain). Most often you will get more than you expect in friendliness, efficiency, service, and charm. Haggling over the price of a room is not advisable, but a politely requested upgrade depending upon availability (in the large hotels) can never hurt as long as you don't really expect it. Because there are relatively few hotels for a city that attracts so many visitors, the charming family or small-hotel owner will have little problem turning you away if you try to drive the price down.

Prices are seasonal in most hotels. The low season runs from several days after the new year until spring (either the first of March or first of April), and from November until Christmas. Weekend rates are somewhat lower than weekday rates and sometimes, if you are staying for quite a few nights, you may get weekly rates.

Most of the pricing includes a VAT (Value Added Tax) of 6% and in some cases the city tax of 5% may be included. Always be sure to ask which of the taxes are included in the pricing. Most hotels operate on the **European Plan** (EP, with no meals) and some on

Paris, France.

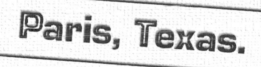

Paris, Texas.

When it Comes to Getting
Local Currency at an ATM,
Same Thing.

Whether you're in Yosemite or Yemen, using your Visa® card or ATM card with the PLUS symbol is the easiest and most convenient way to get local currency. For example, let's say you're in France. When you make a withdrawal, using your secured PIN, it's dispensed in francs, but is debited from your account in U.S. dollars. This makes it easy to take advantage of favorable exchange rates. And if you need help finding one of Visa's 627,000 ATMs in 127 countries worldwide, visit **visa.com/pd/atm**. We'll make finding an ATM as easy as finding the Eiffel Tower, the Pyramids or even the Grand Canyon.

It's Everywhere You Want To Be.®

SEE THE WORLD
IN FULL COLOR

Fodor's Exploring Guides bring all the great sights vividly to life with hundreds of photographs, fascinating historical background, and colorful anecdotes. Detailed maps and practical information keep you headed in the right direction.

Pair a Fodor's Exploring Guide with your trusted Fodor's Pocket Guide for a complete planning package.

Fodor's EXPLORING GUIDES

At bookstores everywhere.

the **Continental Plan** (CP, with a Continental breakfast). In fact, although neither a real Modified American Plan (MAP, with breakfast and dinner) nor a real Full American Plan (FAP, with all meals) exists in Amsterdam, breakfast, from vast breakfast buffets to breakfast of eggs, ham, cheese, bread and jam, and coffee or tea, is included in the rate at most hotels.

CATEGORY	COST*
$$$$	over Fl 550 (€250)
$$$	Fl 400–Fl 550 (€180–€250)
$$	Fl 275–Fl 400 (€125–€250)
$	under Fl 275 (€125)

*All prices are for a double room, including tax and service

AMSTERDAM SOUTH AND DE PIJP

$$$–$$$$ **OKURA AMSTERDAM.** This modern hotel complex has all the luxury of an Amsterdam business hotel—with a Japanese accent. The lobby is natural wood, glass, and marble. Lights on the hotel roof change color according to the weather and give a new focus to the Amsterdam skyline. The rooms are comfortable, with large windows overlooking the city from the south. Every room has Internet access with a keyboard connected to ISDN/cable TV and room faxes. The two Japanese restaurants are the best in Amsterdam; the health club is the most glamorous in the city. *Ferdinand Bolstraat 333, 1072 LH, tel. 020/678–7111, fax 020/671–2344. 321 rooms, 49 suites. 4 restaurants, 2 bars, air-conditioning, in-room data ports, in-room safes, minibars, room service, pool, massage, health club, dry cleaning, laundry service, business services, meeting rooms, parking (fee). AE, DC, MC, V. EP. www.okura.nl*

$ **HOTEL DE STADHOUDER.** This simple, well-kept hotel is well located in the residential neighborhood De Pijp. Though the facilities are limited, with no telephones or TVs in the rooms, there is an elevator, unusual for hotels in this price category—and necessary given the steep and narrow *trappenhuis* (walk-up) stairway. The lovely couple who own the hotel and their friendly

Ambassade, 14

American, 22

Amstel Botel, 1

Amstel Inter-Continental Hotel, 26

Atlas Hotel, 37

Avenue Hotel, 2

Blake's, 13

Canal House, 4

Dikker and Thijs Fenice Hotel, 20

Golden Tulip Schiller, 19

Grand Hotel Krasnapolsky, 9

Grand Sofitel Demeure Amsterdam, 11

Hotel Aalders, 36

Hotel Acro, 34

Hotel Amsterdam, 8

Hotel Arena, 25

Hotel Armada, 24

Hotel Concert Inn, 41

Hotel de Compagnie, 18

Hotel De Filosoof, 28

Hotel de l'Europe, 16

Hotel De Stadhouder, 39

Hotel Estheréa, 7

Hotel Hestia, 30

Hotel New York, 3

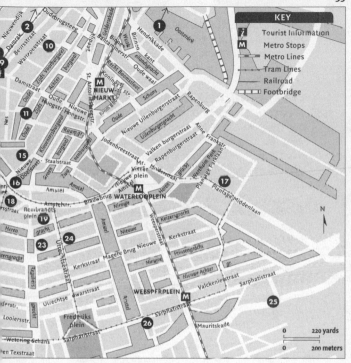

Hotel Owl, **29**	Hotel Winson, **10**	Quentin England Hotel, **31**
Hotel Rembrandt, **17**	Jan Luyken, **35**	Seven Bridges Hotel, **23**
Hotel Résidence Le Coin, **15**	Memphis Hotel, **42**	
	Museumzicht, **33**	Seven one Seven, **21**
Hotel Sander, **44**	Okura Amsterdam, **40**	Smit Hotel, **32**
Hotel Toren, **5**		Toro Hotel, **45**
Hotel Vondel, **27**	Omega Hotel, **43**	Weichmann Hotel, **12**
Hotel Washington, **38**	Pulitzer, **6**	

156

dog have created a very cozy atmosphere, and the delightful breakfast room is filled with blue and white Delft-style pottery and red flowers. There is an additional 5% charge if you pay with a credit card. *Stadhouderskade 76, 1072 AE, tel. 020/671–8428, fax 020/664–7410. 20 rooms, 10 with bath. Breakfast room. AE, MC, V. CP.*

EAST OF THE AMSTEL

$$$$ AMSTEL INTER-CONTINENTAL HOTEL. This grand 125-year-old hotel has an interior designed in 1992 by Pierre Yves Rochon of Paris, who has created a Dutch atmosphere with a European touch. Rooms are the most spacious in the city; the decor resembles that of a gracious home, with Oriental rugs, brocade upholstery, Delft lamps, and a color scheme inspired by the warm tones of Makkum pottery. Fresh tulips are placed in all rooms and the glorious bathrooms have showerheads the size of dinner plates. The generous staff-guest ratio and the top-notch food explain the hotel's popularity among royals and celebrities. *Professor Tulpplein 1, 1018 GX, tel. 020/622–6060, fax 020/622–5808. 55 rooms, 24 suites. 2 restaurants, bar, lounge, in-room data ports, in-room safes, in-room VCRs, minibars, room service, indoor pool, health club, dry cleaning, laundry service, business services, convention center, meeting rooms, parking (fee). AE, DC, MC, V. EP. www.interconti.com/netherlands/amsterdam/hotel_amsic.html*

$–$$ HOTEL ARENA. This grand complex in a late-19th-century Roman Catholic orphanage consists of the hotel, a café restaurant, and a dance-club with frescoed walls that was the church. For those that like spare minimal style the hotel is stunningly austere. The lobby is minimalist white, which draws attention to the impressive cast iron staircase leading to the rooms. The hotel has commissioned the hottest young Dutch architects and designers to supervise the renovation and graphic identity and will surely shake off its reputation as a youth hotel. Rooms are painted in white, grey, and mauve tones and are furnished with modernist furniture by Gispen, Eames, and Martin Visser. *s'Gravesandestraat*

51, 1092 AA, tel. 020/663–3201, fax 020/663–2649. 121 rooms. Bar, café, dance club, meeting rooms, parking (fee). AE, MC, V. EP. www.hotelarena.nl

$ **HOTEL REMBRANDT.** Because it is close to the University of Amsterdam, the zoo Artis, Hortus Botanicas, and Tropenmuseum, the Hotel Rembrandt is often populated with academics and museum people. A remarkable and unique feature of this hotel is the breakfast room, with 18th-century paintings and exquisitely painted woodwork on the ceiling; wood paneling and beams, carved and dated 1558, were transported to their current location in the 19th century. Most of the rooms at the back of the hotel facing the garden are quiet. Duplex Room 21, in the front, can accommodate a family of six, and six rooms can house three or four. All rooms are immaculately clean. *Plantage Middenlaan 17, 1018 DA, tel. 020/627–2714, fax 020/638–0293. 15 rooms, 1 suite. Breakfast room. AE, MC, V. CP.*

GRACHTENGORDEL: THE CANAL RING

$$$$ **BLAKE'S.** Everything about this 18th-century canal house is consistent with the theme of East meets West, inspired by the tradition of travel to the Dutch East Indies. Known for her chic London hotels, Anouska Hempel's newest is simply elegant. The furnishings combine lacquered trunks, mahogany screens, and modernist hardwood tables with cushions in fine fabrics. Only one suite is on the canal; other rooms overlook a central courtyard and are serenely quiet. The palette of each room breathes with Zen calm: grey to blue, terra-cotta to chocolate brown, or ruby red and cream. The unique flow of water in the bathroom sinks is more like a fountain than a tap. The exclusive restaurant has an Asian and Western menu. *Kiezersgracht 384, 1016 GB, tel. 020/530–2010, fax 020/530–2030. 15 rooms, 10 suites. Restaurant, bar, lounge, in-room data ports, in-room fax, in-room VCR, meeting rooms. AE, DC, MC, V. EP. www.slh.com/blakesam*

Amsterdam's Star System

The Benelux hotel-classification star system, used in Belgium, the Netherlands, and Luxembourg, is based exclusively on the facilities offered and not on quality, location, or level of personal service. A checklist provides the minimum requirement for hotels and their guest rooms in every star category. Often a very lovely small hotel will have a low star rating simply because there is no elevator, and it may be misleading to relate the star system directly to price. The largest differentials in quality and level of service are between the two- and three-star hotels and the four- and five-star hotels.

The one- and two-star categories include very simple accommodations, some rundown, some simple, clean, and cheerful. Most one-star hotels are family or individually run; they provide a bed, sink, towel, soap, breakfast, and a reception area that is open for a specified period of time. Generally, all taxes as well as breakfast are included in the price. Rates may be per room rather than per person, as in higher star categories. Two-star hotels that are over three stories must have an elevator; and 35% of guest rooms must have bathrooms.

Three-star hotels must provide greater in-room amenities (including TV, desk, chair, and bath), an elevator, and restaurants or cafés, but breakfast is an additional cost. Four-star hotels are geared towards the business traveler and must have room service, minibars, telephones, wake-up service, and hotel safes.

Five-star hotels offer extremely comfortable accommodations, meeting rooms, shops with periodicals and books, available taxis, and ticket services. Many provide massages and boat tours and place fruit or flowers in the guest rooms. Rooms are equipped for Internet access, fax machines, VCRs, CD players, and in-room safes. The chain business hotels such as Marriott, Radisson, Hilton, and Sheridan are five-star hotels. The five-star deluxe hotels provide an even higher level of luxury, and there are currently three in Amsterdam: Amstel, Hotel de L'Europe, and the Grand.

$$–$$$$ **PULITZER.** Twenty-four 17th- and 18th-century houses were
★ combined to create this hotel, which faces both the Prinsengracht
and the Keizersgracht canals and is just a short walk from Dam
Square. The place retains a historic ambience: most guest rooms
have beam ceilings, there are gardens in the middle of the block,
and you can hear the hourly chiming of the Westerkerk clock. The
hotel was completely refurbished in 2000 to increase comfort
and convenience; modern furnishings are gradually being replaced
with more appropriate antique styles. *Prinsengracht 315–331, 1016
GZ, tel. 020/523–5235, fax 020/627–6753. 226 rooms, 7 suites.
Restaurant, bar, café, air-conditioning, in-room safes, room service, baby-
sitting, dry cleaning, laundry service, business services, convention center,
meeting rooms, parking (fee). AE, DC, MC, V. EP. www.pulitzer.nl*

$$$–$$$$ **SEVEN ONE SEVEN.** More an exclusive guest house than a hotel,
Seven one Seven is a boutique hotel in the common sense of the
word. The owner is a fashion designer and used men's suiting
fabrics to upholster all of the overstuffed armchairs and sofas. The
rooms seem to have come from a museum, with classical
antiquities, art, and objets d'art, flowers, and candles on tables
and fireplace mantles. The suites are splendid, each honoring a
composer, artist, or writer. Breakfast is served in the suites; coffee,
tea, cakes, wine, and beer are available during the day and evening
for the asking. There is a video and CD library. *Prinsengracht 717,
1017 JW, tel. 020/427–0717, fax 020/423–0717. 8 suites. Air-conditioning,
in-room data ports, in-room safes, in-room VCRs, meeting room. AE, DC,
MC, V. CP. www.717hotel.nl*

$$–$$$ **HOTEL ESTHERÉA.** On a convenient and quiet part of the Singel
canal, this hotel has been run by the same family for three
generations. Three elegant 17th-century houses front the hotel,
with two additional houses behind. The lobby is filled with antiques
and brass chandeliers. The rooms are bright white with pastel
highlights in the Adamsesque ceilings and doors, and each is
different, some with clever headboards made of finely upholstered
pillows hung from brass rods. Some rooms have minibars. Family

rooms for three or four are available. The owners and staff are young, enthusiastic, and highly professional. *Singel 303–309, 1012 WJ, tel. 020/624–5146, fax 020/623–9001. 70 rooms. Bar, breakfast room, in-room data ports, in-room safes, room service, dry cleaning, laundry service. AE, DC, MC, V. EP www.estherea.nl*

$$ AMBASSADE. Ten 17th- and 18th-century houses have been joined
★ to create this hotel on the Herengracht near the Spui square. Two lounges are elegantly decorated with Oriental rugs, chandeliers, and antiques. The canal-side rooms are spacious, with large windows and solid, functional furniture. The rooms at the rear are quieter, but smaller and darker. Attic rooms have beamed ceilings, providing a period atmosphere. Service is attentive and friendly. *Herengracht 341, 1016 AZ, tel. 020/555–0222, fax 020/555–0277. 59 rooms, 6 suites, 1 apartment. Bar, in-room safes, room service, spa, baby-sitting, dry cleaning, laundry service, business services, meeting rooms, car rental, parking (fee). AE, DC, MC, V. EP. www.ambassade.hotel.nl*

$$ CANAL HOUSE. This is what you imagine a 17th-century (1640) canal-house hotel to be: a beautiful old home with high plaster ceilings, antique furniture, old paintings, and a backyard garden bursting with plants and flowers. Every room is unique in both size and decor, and there isn't a television in sight. The elegant chandeliered breakfast room with burled wood grand piano overlooks the garden, and there is a small bar in the front parlor. Wandering the halls is a treat. The owners have put a lot of love and style into the Canal House—the result is an intimate hotel for adults. *Keizersgracht 148, 1015 CX, tel. 020/622–5182, fax 020/624–1317. 26 rooms. AE, DC, MC, V. CP. www.canalhouse.nl*

$–$$ HOTEL TOREN. A perfect example of a low-cost and high-Benelux-rating hotel, this consists of two canal-side buildings from 1638 and offers every facility for business travelers. Family-run for several generations, the Hotel Toren is located in the shadow of the Westerkerk *toren* (Western Church tower), but the "*toren*" is also the family name. There is a very beautiful carved wooden and mirrored bar. The in-room minibar offers the same low prices. *Keizersgracht 164, 1015 CZ, tel. 020/622–6033, fax 020/626–9705. 40 rooms. Bar, air-conditioning, in-room safes, minibars, room service, meeting room. AE, DC, MC, V. EP. www.toren.nl*

$ **HOTEL ARMADA.** The Hotel Armada offers a superb canal-side location at the corner of the Utrechtsestraat, where there is excellent shopping and restaurants. The rooms are simple, and some doubles can be adjusted to accommodate additional guests. Eight rooms have neither bath or shower but share facilities down the hall. The breakfast room has an aquarium and small oriental carpets covering the tables, in the 17th-century style. *Keizersgracht 713–715, 1017 DX, tel. 020/623 2980, fax 020/623–5829. 26 rooms, 14 with bath. Bar. AE, MC, V. CP.*

$ **HOTEL NEW YORK.** This small, very popular (make reservations early) hotel is well located at a beautiful corner of the Herengracht and Brouwersgracht. Cheerful and immaculately clean, this is one of the few gay hotels in the city that is very "charming" (many of the others target a rough leather crowd). The staff is nice, helpful, and informative. There are plenty of gay guides and literature around, so that a newly arrived guest can figure out the scene or get advice. *Herengracht 13, 1015 BA, tel. 020/624–3066, fax 020/620–3230. 15 rooms. AE, DC, MC, V. CP.*

JORDAAN

$ **WEICHMANN HOTEL.** This hotel is a maze of hallways leading through the three buildings to the rooms, which are of wildly varying sizes. Run for 50 years by the Boddys, the Weichman Hotel has delightful personal touches throughout the lobby and adjoining breakfast room. Mrs. Boddy has a fantastic collection of tea pots, toys, and antiques visible from the street and cheerfully decorating the breakfast room. The hotel was a favorite with rock and country musicians in the '70s, and Mr. Boddy's collection of gold records are hung in the lobby by the desk. Although the hotel could use some upgrading, it is as enchanting as are its owners.

Prinsengracht 328–330, 1016 HX, tel. 020/626–3321, fax 020/626–8962. 38 rooms. Breakfast room. MC, V. CP.

LEIDSEPLEIN

$$$–$$$$ ★ **AMERICAN.** The American, one of the oldest hotels in Amsterdam, is housed in one of the city's most fancifully designed buildings. Directly on Leidseplein, it's in the middle of everything—nightlife, dining, sightseeing, and shopping are all at hand. Rooms are sizable and furnished in art deco style. The rooms with balconies over the Leidseplein are small but special. The hotel entered the new millennium under new ownership, being upgraded. The decor at the café restaurant is one of the finest in Amsterdam, with original lamps and murals from 1930 depicting *A Midsummer Nights Dream*; there is a jazz brunch on Sundays. *Leidseplein 28, 1017 PN, tel. 020/556–3000, fax 020/556–3001. 178 rooms, 10 suites. Restaurant, 2 bars, room service, sauna, exercise room, dry cleaning, laundry service, meeting rooms, parking (fee). AE, DC, MC, V. EP. www.interconti.com*

$$$–$$$$ **DIKKER AND THIJS FENICE HOTEL.** Of the upper-price hotels, this is one of the few that offers a breakfast buffet. The hotel has had a reputation for an excellent restaurant since soon after its founder, A. W. Dikker, took up partnership in 1915 with H. Thijs, who had apprenticed with the famous french chef August Escoffier. The busy location is convenient to the major shopping areas and one block from the Leidseplein, nightlife center of the city. The rooms are fully modernized, although showing some wear. *Prinsengracht 444, 1017 KE, tel. 020/620–1212, fax 020/625–8986. 42 rooms, 1 suite. Restaurant, bar, in-room safes, minibars, room service, baby-sitting, laundry service, business services. AE, DC, MC, V. CP. www.dikkerenthijsfenice.nl*

MUSEUM QUARTER AND VONDELPARK

$$$ **HOTEL VONDEL.** On a quiet street next to Vondelpark and very close to the Leidseplein, the hotel in three buildings is refined and contemporary. All in beige and light wood tones, the lobby and bar are filled with comfortable suede sofas, sunlight, and flowers. The similarly colored rooms are generous in size. Suites are on the top floor and have large windows that mimic the shape of the roof. Children's rooms can be joined to some doubles for families. Throughout the hotel are paintings by Amsterdam artist Peter Keizer. A lavish breakfast buffet is not included in the rate. *Vondelstraat 28–30, 1054 GE, tel. 020/612–0120, fax 020/685–4321. 67 rooms, 3 suites. Bar, in-room safes, minibars, room service, baby-sitting, dry cleaning, laundry service, business services. AE, DC, MC, V. EP. www.srs-worldhotels.com*

$$$ JAN LUYKEN. This small, stylish hotel is perfectly located for
★ those who want a subdued environment. It is nestled among homes and offices in a 19th-century residential neighborhood yet is just one block away from the Museumplein and fashionable shopping streets. The personal approach is a relaxing alternative to the large business hotels, but the Jan Luyken is itself well equipped to handle the needs of the business traveler. There is a lovely little "relax" room with a tanning lounge, Turkish bath, and Jacuzzi. *Jan Luykenstraat 58, 1071 CS, tel. 020/573–0730, fax 020/676–3841. 63 rooms. Bar, lounge, air-conditioning, in-room safes, minibars, room service, dry cleaning, laundry service, business services, parking (fee). AE, DC, MC, V. EP. www.janluyken.nl*

$$$ MEMPHIS HOTEL. The ivy-covered facade of the Memphis has classical proportions and a mansard roof. A red-carpeted entrance sets the tone for this very elegant and particularly spacious hotel. Grand white columns flank the reception desk. As formal as the deluxe hotels, but more reasonably priced, the hotel is across the street from the auction house Christie's and very near the Concertgebouw. The rooms are decorated in a light palette of blues, greens, and peach with swagged draperies and quilted bedspreads. Extra beds are available and children under 12 years are welcome for no additional charge. The bar is large, with comfortable armchairs and tables and serves light meals. *De Lairessestraat 87,*

1071 NX, tel. 020/673–3141, fax 020/673–7312. 74 rooms. Bar, minibars, no-smoking rooms, exercise room, dry cleaning, laundry service, meeting rooms. AE, DC, MC, V. EP. www.memphishotel.nl

$$ HOTEL CONCERT INN. This is a family run hotel that offers simple, basic accommodations. The hotel is located across from the Concertgebouw and there is a certified kosher restaurant right next door. The rooms are immaculately clean; most are at the back of the hotel and thus are quiet. For longer stays, you can rent apartments equipped with fax machines and kitchenettes. There is a fabulous large garden where guests can lounge or have breakfast. De Lairessestraat 11, 1071 NR, tel. 020/305–7272, fax 020/ 305–7271. 25 rooms. Breakfast room, dry cleaning, laundry services. AE, MC, V. CP. www.concert-inn.demon.nl

$$ OMEGA HOTEL. This hotel is a find, on a quiet villagelike square. It has been extended and redecorated personally by the owner, Renee Toonen, with a brilliant color scheme and combinations of patterns, stripes, and solids. The all-female staff contributes to the informal, but professional atmosphere. Breakfast hours are extended until 11 to accommodate tourists who wish to start the day slowly. The bar is extremely attractive and offers small meals and snacks from a spotless open kitchen. The hotel offers a complimentary drink to welcome guests. Jacob Obrechtstraat 33, 1071 KG, tel. 020/664–5182, fax 020/664–0809. 32 rooms. Bar, air-conditioning (some), in-room data ports, in-room safes, minibars, no-smoking rooms, room service, dry cleaning, laundry service, business services. AE, DC, MC, V. CP. www.omegahotel.nl

$$ TORO HOTEL. In a magnificent villa on the border of Vondelpark, the hotel offers a relaxing atmosphere. The views of the park, antiques, oil paintings, and chandeliers provide a special homelike environment that is rare in Amsterdam. Rooms are spacious and some have balconies. Although slightly out of the center in a chic residential area, the hotel is convenient to tram lines and a lovely stroll through the park from the center of Amsterdam. Koningslaan

64, 1075 AG, tel. 020/673–7223, fax 020/675–0031. 22 rooms. Breakfast room, lounge, in-room safes, minibars, laundry service, parking (fee). AE, DC, MC, V. CP.

$–$$ HOTEL HESTIA. Hotel Hestia is located on a street of extraordinary 19th-century houses, parallel to Vondelpark and close to the Leidseplein. The hotel's breakfast room has a view of the garden, and a large "family" room has a charming sitting area in a bay window with stained glass also overlooking the garden. Four rooms, two singles and two doubles, are very small, but also quite inexpensive. The hotel is family run, with a helpful and courteous staff. *Roemer Visscherstraat 7, 1054 EV, tel. 020/618–0801, fax 020/685–1382. 18 rooms. Breakfast room, in-room safes, minibars. AE, DC, MC, V. CP. www.hestia.demon.nl*

$–$$ HOTEL OWL. This is another friendly family-run hotel on the architecturally charming Roemer Visscherstraat. In the entrance there is a drawing from the turn of the 20th century with an architect's elevation drawings of the original facade of what is now the Hotel Owl and two adjoining houses. A '50s-style entrance does not detract from the charm of the lobby, lounge, and tiny bar. The lounge has a glass showcase filled with a collection of owls, all sent as gifts to the family from satisfied guests. *Roemer Visscherstraat 1, 1054 EV, tel. 020/618–9484, fax 020/618–9441. 34 rooms. Bar, breakfast room, lounge, baby-sitting, laundry service. AE, DC, MC, V. CP. www.owl-hotel.demon.nl*

$ ATLAS HOTEL. Just a block from Amsterdam's city-center Vondelpark, this hotel, renowned for its personal and friendly atmosphere, blends into a well-to-do residential area. The moderately sized rooms are decorated in art nouveau style. It's within easy walking distance of the museums. *Van Eeghenstraat 64, 1071 GK, tel. 020/676–6336, fax 020/671–7633. 23 rooms. Restaurant, bar, dry cleaning, laundry service, parking (fee). AE, DC, MC, V. CP.*

$ HOTEL AALDERS. This busy little hotel has reasonable-size rooms with large windows on a very quiet street. All rooms have shower or bath and computers can be connected to the telephone lines with the necessary adaptor that the hotel does not provide. All the doubles have twin beds. Breakfast (not included in the rate) is served in a large and beautiful second-floor room. *Jan Luykenstraat 13-15, 1071 CJ, tel. 020/ 673–4027, fax 020/673–4027. 28 rooms. Bar, breakfast room. AE, DC, MC, V. EP. www.hotelaalders.nl*

$ **HOTEL ACRO.** This is a simple, clean, and pleasant tourist hotel, with a friendly staff. The hotel is geared to the leisure traveler and can accommodate up to four in a room. There is a breakfast room and an informal bar with game machines that serves snacks, and you can buy post cards and newspapers at the desk. *Jan Luykenstraat 44, 1071 CR, tel. 020/662–5538, fax 020/675–0811. 57 rooms. Bar, breakfast room. AE, DC, MC, V. www.acro-hotel.nl*

$ **HOTEL DE FILOSOOF.** This hotel, on a quiet street near the Vondelpark, attracts artists, thinkers, and people looking for something a little different; bona fide Amsterdam philosophers are regularly to be found in the salon's comfy armchairs. The hotel hosts lecture and discussion evenings for the locals and guests. Each room is decorated with a different cultural motif or ideology, from Zen to feminism and, of course, including philosophers. There's an Aristotle room furnished in Greek style, with passages from the works of Greek philosophers hung on the walls, and a Goethe room adorned with Faustian texts. *Anna van den Vondelstraat 6, 1054 GZ, tel. 020/683–3013, fax 020/685–3750. 29 rooms. Bar, lounge, in-room safes, library. AE, MC, V. CP. www.xs4all.nl/ ~filosoof*

$ **HOTEL SANDER.** Inexpensive, with a great location for museum-going, the Hotel Sander is comfortable but the rooms are simple. Seating areas in window bays give some rooms additional charm. The bar and breakfast room open out on a garden. The hotel is gay friendly. *Jacob Obrechtstraat 69, 1071 KJ, tel. 020/662–7574, fax 020/679–6067. 20 rooms. Bar, breakfast room, in-room safes. AE, DC, MC, V. CP. www.xs4all.nl/ ~htlsandr*

Hip Hotels

New York, London, and Berlin may have had them first, but "hip hotels" (boutique or designer hotels with aesthetic or funky themes or special interests) are beginning to take off in Amsterdam. The veteran hip hotels in Amsterdam are the small Hotel de Filosoof, with rooms designed with serious thinkers in mind, and the larger, but still small Hotel Winston, with rooms and public spaces devoted to contemporary artists. The newest are the ultra-small and ultra-expensive Seven one Seven, the elegant East-meets-West Blake's and the minimalist Arena, a transformed 19th-century orphanage.

The **Black Tulip** (Geldersekade 16, 1012BH, 020/427-0933, 020/624-4281, www.blacktulip.nl) opened in time for the Gay Games in the Summer of 1998 and claims to be completely unique in the world: an exclusive and exclusively gay hotel for men only—men who are into a heavy leather scene. The rooms are equipped with fetish-specific sex furniture (bring or buy your own toys) as well as the amenities common to multi-star hotels; some have rubber floors and soundproof walls.

The **Tulip Inn Arthotel** (Spaarendammerdijk 302, 1013 ZX, 020/681-1110, 020/681-0802)—part of the Golden Tulip/Tulip Inn chain, with no connection to the Black Tulip—is aimed at a hip clientele, but had not opened at press time, so its success can't be determined. The hotel is located in a unique neighborhood (Spaarndammer) built between 1917 and 1920 by the visionary architect Michel de Klerck. The buildings at his Eigen Haard (Our Hearth) housing project are expressionist fantasies, with swoops and curves highlighted by brickwork details.

Other hip accommodation options include renting a houseboat permanently moored on a canal in Amsterdam. These homes are completely furnished with kitchens, toilets, and bathrooms and much larger and more stable than they look; some have floating terraces. Apartment rental agents (☞ Lodging in Practical Information) can help with booking.

$ HOTEL WASHINGTON. This small hotel is just a stone's throw from the Museumplein and often attracts international musicians performing at the nearby Concertgebouw. The owners are helpful and will lend from their collection of guide books. The breakfast room and lounge are filled with antiques and marvelous brass chandeliers, and the hotel is meticulously polished and sparkling clean. The rooms are simply and charmingly decorated in white and pastel shades, with modern prints on the walls. Large windows let in a flood of light. Four rooms have balconies. *F. van Mierisstraat 10, 1071 RS, tel. 020/679–6754, fax 020/673–4435. 21 rooms, 17 with shower. AE, DC, MC, V. CP.*

$ MUSEUMZICHT. When they call themselves "Museum View," they mean it: the hotel is directly across the street from the Rijksmuseum. The owner formerly had an antiques shop, so the house is filled with wonderful objects. The breakfast room–lounge is special, with a Murano glass chandelier and art deco pottery on the chimney walls. The rooms are simple but delightful, with pastel striped wallpaper and little etchings. The hotel is on the top floors of the building and guests must climb a narrow and steep stair with their luggage to the reception desk and to the rooms— the owners highly recommend traveling light. Artists who have stayed here have drawn thank you notes that emphasize the narrow halls and stairways. *Jan Luykenstraat 22, 1071 CN, tel. 020/ 671–2954, fax 020/671–3597. 14 rooms, 3 with shower. Breakfast room/lounge. CP.*

$ QUENTIN ENGLAND HOTEL. The very intimate Quentin England hotel is one of a series of adjoining buildings from 1884. Each of the houses is built in an architectural style of the country whose name it bears. The Quentin occupies the England and Netherlands buildings. Rooms are simple and vary greatly in size, but are cozy and clean. The tiny breakfast room is particularly enchanting, with flower boxes on the window sills, dark wood tables, and fin-de-siecle decorations (breakfast is not included in the room price). Behind the reception desk is a small bar and espresso machine. The hotel offers tremendous character and attention in place of space and facilities. There is an additional 5% fee for using a credit card. *Roemer Visscherstraat 30, 1054 EZ, tel. 020/689–2323, fax 020/ 685–3148. 40 rooms, 37 with bath. Breakfast room. AE, DC, MC, V. EP.*

$ SMIT HOTEL. Despite its location, at the foot of the exclusive P. C. Hooftstraat and south entrance to the Rijksmuseum, this hotel is anything but refined. It's a lively and friendly place and a good choice for those who want to enjoy the lively Leidseplein nightlife. There is a computer in the breakfast room on which guests can surf the Internet or check their e-mail with a card purchasable at the desk. The neighboring restaurant is open for lunch and snacks but closes at 6 PM. The rooms are very plain, but have a kitsch appeal; the bathrooms are relatively spacious and marbled. Some of the rooms facing the tram lines are noisy. *P. C. Hooftstraat 24– 28, 1071 BX, tel. 020/671–4785, fax 020/662–9161. 63 rooms. Restaurant, breakfast room. AE, DC, MC, V. CP.*

NIEUWEZIJDE AND THE DAM

$$$$ GRAND HOTEL KRASNAPOLSKY. Dominating the Dam Square, opposite the Royal Palace, this hotel, dating from 1866, is something of a landmark. The rooms vary greatly in size and tend towards serviceable functionality—somewhat of a disappointment after such a grand entrance. The business facilities (including 22 conference rooms) are some of the best in the city. Furnished apartments are available. The restaurants and café have fine reputations. Prices are wildly variable and bargains can be had. *Dam 9, 1018 JS, tel. 020/554–9111, fax 020/622–6807. 430 rooms. 5 restaurants, bar, brasserie, beauty salon, conference center, parking (fee). AE, DC, MC, V. EP. www.krasnapolsky.nl*

$$ HOTEL AMSTERDAM. Located at the hub of the city's business and shopping areas and close to the Centraal Station, on the corner of Dam Square and across from the leading department store, De Bijenkorf, the Hotel Amsterdam is a cut above other hotels on the Damrak. Rooms have soundproof windows to buffer the outside world, and rooms at the back are a safe bet. Triple rooms and extra beds are available, and the hotel boasts an award-winning restaurant serving Dutch haute cuisine. *Damrak 93–94, 1012 LP, tel. 020/555–0666, fax 020/620–4716. 80 rooms. Restaurant, brasserie, air-conditioning, in-room data ports, minibars, room service, business services.. AE, DC, MC, V. EP. www.hotelamsterdam.nl*

$–$$ AVENUE HOTEL. The older sister to the Hotel de Compagnie (☞ Rembrandtplein, *below*) is in a building that used to be a warehouse for the United East India Company. The hotel interior underwent renovation in 2000. The modernization brings bright and cheerful contemporary style to rooms that are small but comfortable. *Nieuwezijds Voorburgwal 27, 1012 RD, tel. 020/530–9530, fax 020/530– 9599. 60 rooms. Room service, laundry service. AE, DC, MC, V. CP. www.embhotels.nl*

$ AMSTEL BOTEL. This floating hotel, moored near Centraal Station, is an appropriate lodging in watery Amsterdam. The rooms are cabinlike, but the portholes have been replaced by windows that provide fine views of the city across the water. Make sure you don't get a room on the land side of the vessel, or you'll end up staring at an ugly postal sorting office. *Oosterdokskade 2, 1011 AE, tel. 020/ 626–4247, fax 020/639–1952. 175 rooms. AE, DC, MC, V. EP.*

OUDEZIJDS AND DE WALLEN

$$$$ THE GRAND SOFITEL DEMEURE AMSTERDAM. The hotel's city-
★ center site has long been associated with stately lodging: it started in the 14th century as a convent, becoming a *Princenhof* (Prince's Courtyard) in 1578. William of Orange stayed here in 1580 and, a little later, Maria de Medici. The buildings served as the city hall of Amsterdam from 1808 to 1988, and Queen Beatrix's civil wedding took place here in 1966. Today's incarnation, opened in 1992, is a deluxe hotel; contemporary guests have included Michael Jackson, Mick Jagger, President Chirac of France, and Prime Minister Blair of the United Kingdom. There are Gobelin tapestries, Jugendstil stained-glass windows, and in the café, a mural that

Karel Appel created early in his career to repay a debt to the city. The kitchen of the brasserie-style restaurant, Café Roux, is supervised by the incomparable Albert Roux. *Oudezijds Voorburgwal 197, 1012 EX, tel. 020/555–3111, fax 020/555–3222. 138 rooms, 28 suites, 16 apartments. Restaurant, bar, in-room data ports, in-room safes, minibars, room service, indoor pool, massage, sauna, Turkish bath, baby-sitting, dry cleaning, laundry service, meeting rooms, car rental, parking (fee). AE, DC, MC, V. EP. www.sofitel.com*

$$$$ HOTEL DE L'EUROPE. Quiet, gracious, and understated in both decor and service, this hotel (with a history extending back to 1638) overlooks the Amstel River, the Muntplein, and the flower market. The current owner is Freddy Heineken of beer fame. Guest rooms are furnished with reserved, classical elegance: the city-side rooms are full of warm, rich colors; riverside rooms are in brilliant whites and French windows to let in floods of light. All rooms have luscious swags of Victorian-style draperies as canopies over the beds. The Excelsior restaurant (☞ Eating Out) matches splendid river views with sublime French food. *Nieuwe Doelenstraat 2–8, 1012 CP, tel. 020/531–1777, fax 020/531–1778. 80 rooms, 20 suites. 2 restaurants, bar, air-conditioning, in-room data ports, in-room safes, minibars, room service, indoor pool, barbershop, beauty salon, hot tub, massage, sauna, exercise room, business services, meeting rooms, free parking. AE, DC, MC, V. EP. www.leurope.nl*

$–$$ HOTEL RÉSIDENCE LE COIN. Having hosted only visiting academics to the University of Amsterdam since its opening in 1997, Le Coin began offering rooms publicly in 1999. The hotel can provide guests with business cards and stationery and your own private door bell. The units, housed in seven historic buildings, are like small apartments, each with its own kitchenette. Guests have 24-hour access to the laundry room, which is offered at no additional charge. Additional beds are available, or some apartments can be joined to accommodate additional guests and there is one family-size room. Monthly rates are available. *Nieuwe Doelenstraat 5, 1012 CP, tel. 020/524–6800, fax 020/524–*

6801. 42 rooms. Air-conditioning, kitchenettes, in-room data ports, laundry service. AE, DC, MC, V. EP.

$ HOTEL WINSTON. Once a crash pad above a notorious bar, the hotel was transformed in 1996 to a venue for the young and the young-at-heart. There are paintings and decor by contemporary artists in hallways and guest rooms, many of which are re-created periodically with sponsorship from some forward-thinking corporations that target an artsy crowd. The less expensive rooms are not "Art Rooms" and many don't have private bath or toilet, but all the rooms are clean and cleverly done and some can accommodate six people. It's right in the center of town, so ask for a quiet room overlooking the inner courtyard if you want to sleep before the early hours. The downstairs bar has quickly regained its reputation as a vibrant venue for live performance and late-night music. *Warmoesstraat 123, 1012 JA, tel. 020/ 623–1380, fax 020/639–2308. 66 rooms. Bar. AE, DC, MC, V. CP. www.winston.nl*

REMBRANDTPLEIN

$$$ GOLDEN TULIP SCHILLER. Frits Schiller built the hotel in 1912 in the Dutch art deco style known as *Jugendstil*. He may have been an artist of varying ability, but he created a huge number of paintings that are proudly displayed in the hotel. His friends, bohemian painters and sculptors, came to the Schiller Café, which became a famous meeting place and is still an informal and popular bar with Amsterdammers. From the lobby lounge you can check your e-mail to the hum of the espresso machine from the Brasserie Schiller. A winter film series is held on Sunday afternoons in the restaurant, with cocktails and dinner included. Rooms are conveniently stocked with coffeemakers, trouser presses, and hair dryers, and six are large enough, with two double beds, to suit families. *Rembrandtplein 26–36, 1017 CV, tel. 020/554–0700, fax 020/624–0098. 98 rooms, 2 suites. Restaurant, bar, minibars, meeting rooms. AE, DC, MC, V. EP. www.goldentulip.com*

$$ HOTEL DE COMPAGNIE. One of the newest hotels in Amsterdam is located at the bustling center overlooking the Munt tower and flower market, with the Rembrandtplein to the back. All rooms are of a comfortable size, and even the street-side rooms are remarkably quiet due to their double-paned windows. The hotel lobby and rooms are tastefully decorated with wicker chairs and contemporary paintings from the owners' collection. The buffet in the light and cheerful breakfast room has the usual fare plus Dutch specialties. *Vijzelstraat 49, 1017 HE, tel. 020/530–6200, fax 020/530–6299. 75 rooms. Brasserie, breakfast room. AE, DC, MC, V. CP. www.embhotels.nl*

$$ SEVEN BRIDGES HOTEL. This homey hotel has idyllic views of the seven canal bridges from which it took its name, but it is also within a stone's throw of Rembrandtplein. All rooms are meticulously decorated with Oriental rugs, art deco lamps, and marble sinks. The proud owner scouts the antiques stores and auction houses for furnishings and all have thorough documentation. Handcrafted and inlaid bed frames and tables supplement the antique decorations for a whimsical atmosphere. In 1999, each room was equipped with television and bath or shower. Top-floor rooms are the smallest and priced accordingly; the first-floor room is practically palatial. Breakfast is delivered to your room. Reserve well in advance. *Reguliersgracht 31, 1017 LK, tel. 020/623–1329. 10 rooms. AE, MC, V. CP.*

PRACTICAL INFORMATION

Addresses

There are a number of address endings that indicate the form of thoroughfare: a *straat* is a street; a *laan* is a lane; a *gracht* or *sloot* is a canal, though some of these have been filled in to provide more room for road traffic; a *kade* is a canalside quay; and a *dijk* is a dike, though in the urban environment this is not always obvious. House numbers are counted from nearest the center of the city, with the Dam as epicenter. Unfortunately postcodes do not adhere to a system that will help you navigate from one neighborhood to another.

Air Travel to and from Amsterdam

BOOKING YOUR FLIGHT

Price is just one factor to consider when booking a flight: frequency of service and even a carrier's safety record are often just as important. Major airlines offer the greatest number of departures. Smaller airlines—including regional and no-frills airlines—usually have a limited number of flights daily. On the other hand, so-called low-cost airlines usually are cheaper, and their fares impose fewer restrictions, such as advance-purchase requirements. Safety-wise, low-cost carriers as a group have a good history—about equal to that of major carriers.

When you book **look for nonstop flights** and **remember that "direct" flights stop at least once.** Try to avoid connecting flights, which require a change of plane. Two airlines may jointly operate a connecting flight, so ask if your airline operates every segment—you may find that your preferred carrier flies you only part of the way. International flights on a country's flag carrier are almost always nonstop; U.S. airlines often fly direct.

Ask your airline if it offers electronic ticketing, which eliminates all paperwork. There's no ticket to pick up or misplace. You go directly to the gate and give the agent your confirmation number instead of waiting in line at the counter while precious minutes tick by.

CARRIERS

When flying internationally, you must usually choose between a domestic carrier, the national flag carrier of the country you're visiting, and a foreign carrier from a third country. National flag carriers have the greatest number of nonstops. Domestic carriers may have better connections to your home town and serve a greater number of gateway cities. Third-party carriers may have a price advantage.

KLM Royal Dutch Airlines is the national flag carrier of the Netherlands. The KLM City Hopper provides regular service between Amsterdam Schiphol Airport and Rotterdam, Eindhoven, and Maastricht, although air travel in a country this small is really unnecessary.

➤ FROM THE U.K. & IRELAND: **Aer Lingus** (tel. 0208/899–4747 in the U.K., 01/844–4747 in Ireland). **British Airways** (tel. 0345/222–111). **British Midland** (tel. 0870/607–0555). **EasyJet** (tel. 0870/600–0000). **KLM** and **KLMuk** (tel. 0870/507–4074 in the U.K., 01/844–4747 in Ireland).

➤ MAJOR U.S. AIRLINES: **Delta** (tel. 800/221–1212). **Northwest** (tel. 800/225–2525).**TWA** (tel. 800/892–4141). **United** (tel. 800/241–6522).

➤ NATIONAL CARRIERS: **KLM Royal Dutch Airlines** (tel. 020/474–7747 in the Netherlands, 800/474–4747 in the U.S.).

➤ REGIONAL CARRIERS: **KLM City Hopper** (tel. 020/474–7747).

CHECK-IN & BOARDING

Assuming that not everyone with a ticket will show up, airlines routinely overbook planes. When everyone does, airlines ask for volunteers to give up their seats. In return, these volunteers usually get a certificate for a free flight and are rebooked on the next flight out. If there are not enough volunteers, the airline must choose who will be denied boarding. The first to get bumped are passengers who checked in late and those flying on discounted tickets, so **get to the gate and check in as early as possible,** especially during peak periods.

Amsterdam's Schiphol Airport, a short ride from the city center, is slickly designed, and clearing check-in queues is less daunting than it can be during busy periods at major hubs in the United States or the United Kingdom. Bumping is much less common than in the U.S. If you do arrive on time, on the other side of passport control you can enjoy a wealth of facilities from the duty-free shops, reputed to be the best in the world, a big selection of bars and restaurants, or even fritter away your last Euros at the Holland Casino.

Always **bring a valid passport to the airport.** You will have to show it before you are allowed to check in.

FLYING TIMES
Flying time to Amsterdam from New York is just over 7 hours; from Chicago, closer to 8 hours; from Los Angeles, 10½ hours; from London, 1 hour.

RECONFIRMING
Although the trend on international flights is to drop reconfirmation requirements, many airlines still ask you to reconfirm each leg of your international itinerary. Failure to do so may result in your reservations being canceled.

Airports & Transfers

Amsterdam Schiphol Airport is 25 km (15 mi) southeast of the city and has efficient road and rail links. The comprehensive "Schiphol Information and Services" telephone service (Fl 1 [€0.45] per minute) provides information about arrivals, departures, transportation, and parking facilities.

➤ **Airport Information: Schiphol Airport** (tel. 0900–0141 in the Netherlands).

TRANSFERS

KLM Shuttle operates a half-hour shuttle bus service between Schiphol Airport and major city hotels (costs Fl 17.50 [€7.95] one-way). The Schiphol Rail Link operates between the airport and the city 24 hours a day, with service to the central railway station or to stations in the south of the city. The trip takes about 15 minutes and costs Fl 6.50 (€2.95). There is a taxi stand in front of the arrival hall at Schiphol Airport. All taxis are metered, and the fare is approximately Fl 60 (€27.25) to central Amsterdam. Service is included, but small additional tips are not unwelcome.

➤ Taxis & Shuttles: **KLM Shuttle** (tel. 020/649–5651). **Schiphol Rail Link** (tel. 0900/9292, costs Fl 0.75 [€0.35] per minute).

Bike Travel

Bicycling is the most convenient way to see Amsterdam. There are bike lanes on all major streets, bike racks in key locations, and special bike parking indentations in the pavement. To rent a bicycle, you'll pay from Fl 10 (€4.55) per day, plus a deposit of Fl 50–Fl 200 (€22.70–€90.75) per bike, and need a passport or other identification to rent. If you rent from Take-a-Bike under Centraal Station, there are cheaper rates if you buy a *huurfietskaart* (bike rental ticket) in combination with a train ticket.

➤ Bike Rentals: **Take-a-Bike at Centraal Station** (Stationsplein 12, 1012 AB, tel. 020/624–8391). **MacBike** (Marnixstraat 220, tel. 020/626–6964; Mr. Visserplein 2, tel. 020/620–0985).

Boat & Ferry Travel

Apart from the romance, sea travel can also mean you arrive well-rested at your destination. From the United Kingdom, there are short crossings from Dover to Calais or Oostende, and from Harwich to Hook of Holland, and these are now very inexpensive because of competition from the Eurotunnel (aka, Channel Tunnel, ☞ Car Travel, *below*).

There are two ferry services from northern England, from Hull to Rotterdam Europoort and from Newcastle-upon-Tyne to IJmuiden. These overnight services offer various classes of cabin accommodation or reclining seats, as well as various restaurants. In the winter the frequency of crossings is reduced, and weather conditions can make it a daunting voyage.

DFDS Seaways operates an overnight ferry service daily, every other day from January to March, between Newcastle-upon-Tyne and IJmuiden. Hoverspeed has services from Dover to Calais and Oostende, Folkestone and Boulogne, and Newhaven and Dieppe, with up to eight daily round trips. P&O North Sea Ferries operates overnight ferry services from Hull to Zeebrugge and Rotterdam Europoort. P&O Stena Line operates the Dover to Calais ferry. Stena Line operates HSS hydrofoils twice daily between Harwich in Essex and Hook of Holland.

➤ **FROM THE U.K.: DFDS Seaways** (Parkeston Quay, Scandinavia House, Harwich, Essex CO12 4QG UK, tel. 01233/647047 in the U.K., 0255/534–546 in the Netherlands, 800/533–3755, 112, in the U.S., www.dfdsseaways.com). **Hoverspeed** (International Hoverport, Marine Parade, Dover, Kent CT17 9TG UK, tel. 0870/240–8070 or 0990/240–241, www.hoverspeed.com). **P&O North Sea Ferries** (King George Dock, Hedon Rd., Hull, Humberside HU9 5QA, UK, tel. 01482/377177). **P&O Stena Line** (Channel House, Channel View Rd., Dover, Kent CT17 9TJ UK, tel. 0870/600–0600 or 0130/486–4003, www.posl.com). **Stena Line** (Charter House, Park St., Ashford, Kent TN24 BEX UK, tel. 01233/647047 in the U.K., 0174/315–811 in the Netherlands, www.stenaline.co.uk).

Bus & Tram Travel within Amsterdam

Many tram and bus routes start from the hub at Centraal Station. Trams and buses run from about 6 AM to midnight daily. The tram routes, with a network of 80 mi (130 km) of track, make this characteristic form of transport more useful than the bus for most tourists. Night owls can make use of the hourly nightbus services, with double frequency on Friday and Saturday night, but routes are restricted. All public transport is smoke-free.

The transit map published by GVB (Gemeentelijk Vervoer Bedrijf/Municipal Transport Company) is very useful. It's available at the GVB ticket office across from Centraal Station, or at the VVV (☞ Visitor Information, *below*) office next door. It is also reprinted as the center spread in *Day by Day, What's On in Amsterdam*, the monthly guide to activities and shopping published by the tourist office. The map shows the locations of all major museums, monuments, theaters, and markets, and it tells you which trams to take to reach them.

FARES & SCHEDULES

Single-ride tickets valid for one hour within two zones can be purchased from tram and bus drivers for Fl 3.25 (€1.50), but it is far more practical and economical to buy a *strippenkaart* (strip ticket) that includes 15 or 45 "strips," or ticket units. These can be used by people traveling together, and cost Fl 12 (€5.45) or Fl 32 (€14.50) respectively. You can purchase them from ticket booths or machines at the railway station, from newsagents or tobacconists, or from the GVB office opposite Centraal Station. The city is divided into zones, which are indicated on the transit map, and it is important to punch the correct number of zones on your ticket (one for the basic tariff and one for each additional zone traveled). By tradition, Dutch trams and buses work on the honor system: upon boarding, punch your ticket at one of the machines situated in the rear or center section of the tram or bus. Occasional ticket inspections can be expected: A fine of Fl 60 (€27.25) is the price for "forgetting" to stamp your ticket.

A service especially for visitors is the Circle Tram 20, which rides both ways around a loop that passes close to most of the main sights and offers a hop-on, hop-off ticket for one–three days. The ticket costs Fl 10 (€4.55) for one day, Fl 15 (€6.80) for two days, and Fl 19 (€8.60) for three days.

➤ Bus Information: **GVB information and ticket office** (opposite Centraal Station, tel. 0900/9292, costs 75¢ a minute).

Bus Travel to and from Amsterdam

Bus and coach travel is rarely the most comfortable or rapid mode of transport, but it can be cheap, and companies now offer reclining seats, air-conditioning, and video entertainment as standard. There are direct services to many other European capitals and cities, all non-smoking. The coaches make use of Le Shuttle service through the Eurotunnel (Channel Tunnel), and ferries. Check-in time is usually one hour before departure.

FARES & SCHEDULES

Eurolines comprises 30 motor-coach operators of international scheduled services, serving more than 500 destinations with services ranging from twice weekly to five times daily. Eurolines has its own office at Amsterdam Amstel bus station, a transport hub with quick and easy rail, tram, and metro links to the city center, and there is a ticket office in the city center itself.

➤ Bus Information: **Eurolines** (52 Grosvenor Gardens, near Victoria Coach Station, London SW1 WOAU, tel. 0870/5143–219 or 020/7730–8235, fax 01582/400–694). **Eurolines (Nederland)** (Julianaplein 5, Amstel Station, Amsterdam 1097 DN, tel. 020/560–8788). **Eurolines central ticket office** (Rokin 10, Amsterdam, tel. 020/560–8788) during normal business hours.

RESERVATIONS

Advance reservations are advisable especially during the summer and other vacation periods. The Eurolines Pass allows unlimited travel between 40 European cities on scheduled bus services. A 30-day summer pass costs $379 ($329 for those under 26 or over 60); a 60-day pass costs $449 ($409). Passes can be bought from Eurolines offices and travel agents in the Netherlands or the United Kingdom. For brochures, timetables, and sales agents in the U.S. and Canada contact the Eurolines

Pass Organization. In the United States, Eurolines Passes can be purchased from DER Travel Services and from most Hostelling International and all student travel associations (☞ Hostels *under* Lodging, *below*) offices.

➤ **INFORMATION: DER Travel Services** (9501 W. Devon Ave., Rosemont, IL 60018, tel. 847/692–6300 in IL; 800/782–2424). **Eurolines Pass Organization** (Keizersgracht 317, 1016 EE Amsterdam, The Netherlands, tel. 020/625–3010, fax 020/420–6904).

Business Hours

Banks are open weekdays from 9 to 5; post offices are open weekdays from 8:30 to 5 and often on Saturday from 8:30 to noon. Pharmacies are open weekdays from 8 or 9 to 5:30, with a rotating schedule in each city to cover nights and weekends. Gas stations on major highways are open 24 hours a day. Shops are open weekdays and Saturday from 10 to 6. Department stores and most shops do not open on Monday until 1 PM. In Amsterdam there is late-night shopping until 9 PM on Thursday, and Sunday shopping hours from noon to 5 is commonplace.

Car Rental

The major car rental firms have convenient booths at Schiphol Airport, but the airport charges rental companies a fee that is passed on to customers, so you'll get a better deal at downtown locations (☞ Cutting Costs, *below*).

Rates in Amsterdam vary from company to company; daily rates start at approximately $50 for a one-day rental, $140 for a three-day rental, and $190 for a week's rental. This does not include collision insurance, airport fee, or 19% V.A.T. tax. Weekly rates often include unlimited mileage. As standard, cars in Europe are stick shift. An automatic transmission will cost a little extra.

➤ **MAJOR AGENCIES: Alamo** (tel. 800/522–9696; 020/8759–6200 in the U.K.). **Avis** (tel. 800/331–1084; 800/331–1084 in Canada; 02/

9353–9000 in Australia; 09/525–1982 in New Zealand). **Budget** (tel. 800/527–0700; 0870/607–5000 in the U.K., through affiliate Europcar). **Dollar** (tel. 800/800–6000; 0124/622–0111 in the U.K., through affiliate Sixt Kenning; 02/9223–1444 in Australia). **Hertz** (tel. 800/654–3001; 800/263–0600 in Canada;020/8897–2072 in the U.K.; 02/9669–2444 in Australia; 09/256–8690 in New Zealand). **National Car Rental** (tel. 800/227–7368; 020/8680–4800 in the U.K., where it is known as National Europe).

CUTTING COSTS

To get the best deal, **book through a travel agent who will shop around.** Also **ask your travel agent about a company's customer-service record.** How has the company responded to late plane arrivals and vehicle mishaps? Are there often lines at the rental counter? If you're traveling during a holiday period, does a confirmed reservation guarantee you a car?

➤ **LOCAL AGENCIES: Avis** (Nassaukade 380, tel. 020/683–6061). **Budget** (Overtoom 121, tel. 020/612–6066). **Hertz** (Overtoom 333, tel. 020/612–2441).

INSURANCE

When driving a rented car you are generally responsible for any damage to or loss of the vehicle. Before you rent, see what coverage your personal auto-insurance policy and credit cards already provide.

Before you buy collision coverage, check your existing policies—you may already be covered. However, collision policies that car-rental companies sell for European rentals usually do not include stolen-vehicle coverage.

REQUIREMENTS & RESTRICTIONS

In the Netherlands your own national driver's license is acceptable. An International Driver's Permit is a good idea; it's available from the American or Canadian Automobile Associations, and, in the United Kingdom, from the Automobile Association or Royal Automobile Club. These international permits are universally recognized, and having one in your wallet may save you a problem with the local authorities.

SURCHARGES

Before you pick up a car in one city and leave it in another, **ask about drop-off charges or one-way service fees,** which can be substantial. Note, too, that some rental agencies charge extra if you return the car before the time specified in your contract. To avoid a hefty refueling fee, **fill the tank just before you turn in the car,** but be aware that gas stations near the rental outlet may overcharge.

Car Travel

A network of well-maintained superhighways and other roads covers the Netherlands, making car travel convenient. Major European highways leading into Amsterdam from the borders are E19 from western Belgium; E25 from eastern Belgium; and E22, E30, and E35 from Germany. Follow the signs for Centrum to reach center city. Traffic is heavy but not stationary at rush hour.

FROM THE UNITED KINGDOM

The Eurotunnel provides the fastest route across the English Channel—35 minutes from Folkestone to Calais, or 60 minutes from motorway to motorway. The company runs a rail shuttle for cars, buses, and trucks that departs frequently throughout the day and night. No reservations are necessary, although advance booking can result in lower ticket costs.

Five-day round-trip for a small car with passengers starts at £140 (low-season, night travel); high-season day travel is £219.

➤ CONTACTS: **Eurotunnel** (tel. 0870/535–3535 in the U.K., 03/2100–6100 in France, www.eurotunnel.com).

EMERGENCY SERVICES

In the event of a breakdown you can rely on the experienced, uniformed mechanics of the Wegenwacht, who patrol the highways in yellow cars 24 hours a day. The service is operated by the Royal Dutch Touring Club (ANWB), which also maintains direct-call phones, in bright yellow, where you can call for assistance on major roads. The ANWB collaborates closely with most other national automobile associations, so in a breakdown situation you will be helped as if you were at home, and for free, providing you can display a valid membership card for your own national automobile association.

➤ CONTACTS: **Wegenwacht** (tel. 0800/0888).

GASOLINE

There are 24-hour gas stations, known as *benzinestations*, on major city access roads and highways, usually self-service and accepting all major credit cards. They are, however, rare in the city center. Gas is known as *benzine* in Dutch, and costs around Fl 2.50 (€1.20) per liter for regular, Fl 2.60 (€1.15) for super unleaded, and Fl 1.75 (€0.80) for diesel. If you need a receipt ask for a *bon*.

PARKING

Parking on the street in pedestrian- and cyclist-friendly Amsterdam city center is an expensive and difficult battle, even for locals. Freeing your car of the wheel clamp for parking illegally or paying inadequate fees is equally time-consuming and expensive. Parking lots are indicated with a blue "P" sign on approach roads to the city, often with electronic indicators showing where spaces are free.

ROAD MAPS

Michelin maps are regularly updated and are the best Netherlands maps. They are available at newsdealers and bookshops. Free city maps are generally available at tourist offices, and more complete city guides can be bought in bookshops. Gas stations near borders generally sell a variety of more detailed maps.

RULES OF THE ROAD

Be sure to observe speed limits. In the Netherlands, the speed limit is 120 kph (74 mph) on superhighways, 100 kph (60 mph) on urban-area highways, and 50 kph (30 mph) on suburban roads. Driving is on the right.

For safe driving, go with the flow, stay in the slow lane unless you want to overtake, and make way for faster cars wanting to pass you. In cities and towns, approach crossings with care; local drivers may exercise the principle of priority for traffic from the right with some abandon.

Children in Amsterdam

Be sure to plan ahead and **involve your youngsters** as you outline your trip. When packing, include things to keep them busy en route. On sightseeing days try to schedule activities of special interest to your children.

If you are renting a car, don't forget to **arrange for a car seat** when you reserve.

BABYSITTING

Hopefully your hotel will be able to arrange babysitting. There is a massive demand for babysitting services, and there are long waiting lists, so there is only an off-chance that an agency will be able to help you. Reputable agencies will check references, hold copies of employees' passports, and ensure that the babysitter is experienced with children as young as infants. Expect to pay a base rate of Fl 40 (€18.15) for up to 4 hours, plus an hourly rate of Fl 10 (€4.55) thereafter.

➤ AGENCIES: **De Amsterdamse Babysitcenter** (Box 23536, 1100 EA, Amsterdam Zuid-Oost, tel. 020/697–2320).

LODGING

Many hotels in Amsterdam allow children under a certain age to stay in their parents' room at no extra charge, but others charge for them as extra adults; be sure to **find out the cutoff age for children's discounts**. Best Western hotels in Amsterdam allow children under 12 to stay free when sharing a room with two paying adults. A maximum of five persons is allowed per room.

The Intercontinental hotels and the Hilton hotels (☞ Lodging, *below*) in Amsterdam allow one child of any age to stay free in his or her parents' room. Many hotels have family rooms.

➤ **BEST CHOICES: Golden Tulip Schiller** (Rembrandtplein 26-36, 1017 CV, tel. 020/554–0700, fax 020/624–0098). **Hotel Rembrandt** (Plantage Middenlaan 17, 1018 DA, tel. 020/627–2714, fax 020/638–0293). **Weichmann Hotel** (Prinsengracht 328-330, 1016 HX, tel. 020/626–3321, fax 020/626–8962).

Computers on the Road

Always keep **computer disks out of the sun.** Carry an extra supply of batteries, and **be prepared to turn on your laptop** to prove to security personnel that the device is real. **Keep computer disks away from metal detectors.** Modern laptops have dual-voltage transformers, so you'll need only a plug adapter with two round prongs to use the Continental-type plugs in the Netherlands. More and more hotels are offering modem sockets for computer users to catch up on their e-mail.

Consulates & Embassies

Although Amsterdam is the capital of the Netherlands, the seat of government and diplomacy is in The Hague. If there is no consulate in Amsterdam, then you will have to travel to The Hague to solve problems such as lost passports.

➤ **CONTACTS: Australian Embassy** (Carnegielaan 4, The Hague, tel. 070/310–8200). **British Consulate** (Koningslaan 44, Amsterdam, tel. 020/676–4343). **Canadian Embassy** (Sophialaan 7, The Hague, tel. 070/311–1600). **Eire/Republic of Ireland Embassy** (Dr Kuyperstraat 9, The Hague, tel. 070/363–0993). **New Zealand Embassy** (Carnegielaan 10, The Hague, tel. 070/346–9324). **U.S. Consulate** (Museumplein 19, Amsterdam, tel. 020/664–5661).

Disabilities & Accessibility

The Netherlands leads the world in providing facilities for people with disabilities. Train and bus stations are equipped with special telephones, elevators, and toilets. Visitors can obtain special passes to ensure free escort service on Dutch trains. For general assistance at railway stations, contact the NS/Nederlandse Spoorwegen before 2 PM at least one day in advance, or by 2 PM Friday for travel on Saturday, Sunday, Monday, or public holidays. Modern intercity train carriages have wheelchair-accessible compartments, and many have a free Red Cross wheelchair available. Train timetables are available in Braille, and some restaurants have menus in Braille. Some tourist sites also have special gardens for visitors with vision impairments. For information on accessibility in Amsterdam, contact the national organization, De Gehandicaptenraad (Dutch Council of the Disabled).

Each year the **Netherlands Board of Tourism** (☞ Visitor Information, *below*) publishes a booklet listing hotels, restaurants, hostels and campsites, museums, and tourist attractions, as well as gas/petrol stations with 24-hour services and boat firms, with adapted facilities. For travelers with visual impairments, all Dutch paper currency is embossed with different symbols for each denomination. For information on tours and exchanges for travelers with disabilities, contact Mobility International Nederland.

➤ **LOCAL RESOURCES: De Gehandicaptenraad** (Postbus 19152, 3501 DD Utrecht, tel. 030/291–6666, for voice and text calls, fax 030/297–0111, www.gehandicaptenraad.nl). **NS/Nederlandse Spoorwegen** (Dutch Railways, tel. 030/230–5566, weekdays 8–4).

RESERVATIONS

When discussing accessibility with an operator or reservations agent, **ask hard questions.** Are there any stairs, inside *or* out? Are there grab bars next to the toilet *and* in the shower/tub? How wide is the doorway to the room? To the bathroom? For the most extensive facilities meeting the latest legal specifications, **opt for newer accommodations.**

Electricity

To use your U.S.-purchased electric-powered equipment, **bring a converter and adapter.** The electrical current in the Netherlands is 220 volts, 50 cycles alternating current (AC); wall outlets take Continental-type plugs, with two round prongs.

If your appliances are dual-voltage, you'll need only an adapter. Don't use 110-volt outlets marked FOR SHAVERS ONLY for high-wattage appliances such as blow-dryers. Most laptops operate equally well on 110 and 220 volts and so require only an adapter.

Emergencies

The Central Medical Service offers 24-hour medical assistance, including names and hours of pharmacists and dentists.

➤ EMERGENCY SERVICES: **Central Medical Service** (tel. 020/592–3434). **Nationwide emergency number** tel. 112 for police, ambulance, fire. **Police** tel. 0900/8844; nonemergency help; costs 30¢ a minute.

➤ HOSPITALS: **Academisch Medisch Centrum** (Meibergdreef 9, tel. 020/566–9111). **Onze Lieve Vrouwe Gasthuis** (1e Oosterparkstraat 279, tel. 020/599–9111). **VU Ziekenhuis** (De Boelelaan 1117, tel. 020/444–4444).

➤ 24-HOUR PHARMACIES: **Central Medical Service** (tel. 020/592–3434).

English-Language Media

BOOKS

There are a number of English-language bookstores in Amsterdam, and most local bookshops stock a small selection of English books. Prices are comparable to those in the English-speaking world.

➤ **Bookstores: American Book Center** (Kalverstraat 185, tel. 020/625–5537). **Athenaeum Boekhandel** (Spui 14, tel. 020/623–3933). **English Bookshop** (Lauriergracht 71, tel. 020/626–4230). **Waterstone's** (Kalverstraat 152, tel. 020/638–3821).

NEWSPAPERS & MAGAZINES

Except for quarterly publications distributed in hotels and filled with advertising, there are no local English-language publications. The back page *Het Financieele Dagblad* (The Financial Daily) summarizes the Dutch financial news in English. However, newsstands are filled with foreign-language dailies and weeklies, including European editions of the *International Herald Tribune, USA Today,* and the *Financial Times,* as well as all major British dailies.

The only regular English-language cultural and social listings—pop, alternative, and highbrow—is *Shark–Underwater Amsterdam,* published fortnightly and distributed free at selected bars, restaurants, and cafés. *Shark* is also available by subscription.

➤ **Resources:** *Shark–Underwater Amsterdam* (Krom Boomsloot 37, 1011 GR, Amsterdam, www.underwateramsterdam.com).

RADIO & TELEVISION

The cable television available throughout the Netherlands, and at most hotels, includes CNN, MSNBC, and BBC24 news stations. BBC1 and BBC2 are also standard. In addition, the Dutch must be one of the biggest purchasers of U.S.-produced soaps and chat shows, so as long as you don't mind watching Jerry Springer a couple of weeks after it was broadcast in the United States, you'll be able to keep abreast.

Gay & Lesbian Travel

The Netherlands is one of the most liberal countries in the world in its social and legal attitude toward gays and lesbians. The age of consent for everyone is 16, there are stringent anti-discrimination laws, and in autumn 2000 the Dutch parliament passed laws allowing same-sex marriage, with essentially the same partner and adoption rights as intersex marriages, with the exception of the right to adopt foreign children.

There are many helpful gay and lesbian organizations in Amsterdam. The COC (pronounced say-o-say) is the acronym for the *Cultuur- en Ontspanningscentrum* (Cultural and Social Center) of the N.V.I.H. (*Nederlandse Vereniging tot Integratie van Homosexualiteit*, or Dutch Association for the Integration of Homosexuality). The Amsterdam COC also operates a daytime coffee shop and weekend discos. There is a switchboard providing advice and information about events, and the SAD Schorerstichting is a health organization offering advice and support specific to lesbian and gay needs.

➤ RESOURCES & CONTACTS: **COC Amsterdam** (Rozenstraat 14, tel. 020/6263087). **Gay & Lesbian Switchboard** (tel. 020/623–6565). **SAD Schorerstichting** (P. C. Hooftstraat 5, 1071 BL Amsterdam, Netherlands, tel. 020/662–4206).

➤ GAY- & LESBIAN-FRIENDLY TRAVEL AGENCIES: **Different Roads Travel** (8383 Wilshire Blvd., Suite 902, Beverly Hills, CA 90211, tel. 323/651–5557 or 800/429–8747, fax 323/651–3678). **Kennedy Travel** (314 Jericho Turnpike, Floral Park, NY 11001, tel. 516/352–4888 or 800/237–7433, fax 516/354–8849, www.kennedytravel.com). **Now Voyager** (4406 18th St., San Francisco, CA 94114, tel. 415/626–1169 or 800/255–6951, fax 415/626–8626, www.nowvoyager.com). **Skylink Travel and Tour** (1006 Mendocino Ave., Santa Rosa, CA 95401, tel. 707/546–9888 or 800/225–5759, fax 707/546–9891, www.skylinktravel.com), serving lesbian travelers.

Holidays

National holidays are January 1, Easter, Queen's Day (April 30, unless it falls on a Sunday), Ascension Day, Pentecost/Whitsunday and the following Monday, and December 25–26. Banks and shops are closed, and many Dutch people take extended weekends or a full week off to travel. Amsterdam is busiest when there are holidays in neighboring countries, when hordes of tourists flock to the city for a short break.

Language

In the Netherlands, Dutch is the official language, but almost everybody knows at least some English and many speak it very well. If you take a side trip to a rural area you may need a phrase book, at least until the residents overcome their shyness about using the English they know.

Lodging

APARTMENT RENTALS

If you want a home base that's roomy enough for a family and comes with cooking facilities, **consider a furnished rental.** These can save you money, especially if you're traveling with a group. Home-exchange directories sometimes list rentals as well as exchanges.

➤ INTERNATIONAL AGENTS: **Villas International** (950 Northgate Dr., Suite 206, San Rafael, CA 94903, tel. 415/499–9490 or 800/221–2260, fax 415/499–9491, www.villasintl.com).

➤ LOCAL AGENTS: **Amsterdam House** (Amstel 176a, Amsterdam, 1017 AE, Amsterdam, tel. 020/626–2577; 800/618 1008 in the U.S., fax 020/626–2987, www.amsterdamhouse.com).

B&BS

The private booking service Bed & Breakfast Holland publishes a nationwide directory including about 30 properties in or around Amsterdam.

➤ ACCOMMODATION SERVICES: **Bed & Breakfast Holland** (Theophile de Bockstraat 3, 1058 TV, Amsterdam, tel. 020/615–7527, fax 020/669–1573).

HOSTELS

Opting for a youth hostel can save you a lot of money, but you must book well in advance for a destination popular with young people, like Amsterdam. There are a number of hostels in the city, two of which are affiliated with Hostelling International, and are centrally located. The Stadsdoelen youth hostel offers basic dormitory accommodations, while the top-notch, 493-bed youth hostel in the Vondelpark enjoys an idyllic setting and the most modern of facilities, including smaller dormitories and private family rooms. Rooms or beds are bookable via the International Booking Network, accessible via national organizations and websites.

Membership in any national hostel association, open to travelers of all ages, allows you to stay in Hostelling International-affiliated hostels at member rates; one-year membership is $25 for adults (C$25 in Canada, £12 in the U.K., $52 in Australia, and $40 in New Zealand). For dormitory beds expect to pay from $10 to $25 per night, more for private rooms. Members have priority if the hostel is full; they're also eligible for discounts around the world, even on rail and bus travel in some countries.

➤ BEST OPTIONS: **City Hostel Stadsdoelen** (Kloveniersburgwal 97, 1011 KB, Amsterdam, tel. 020/624–6832, fax 020/639–1035, www.njhc.nl). **City Hostel Vondelpark** (Zandpad 5, 1054 GA, Amsterdam, tel. 020/589–8996, fax 020/589–8955, www.njhc.nl).

➤ ORGANIZATIONS: **Hostelling International—American Youth Hostels** (733 15th St. NW, Suite 840, Washington, DC 20005, tel. 202/783–6161, fax 202/783–6171, www.hiayh.org). **Hostelling International—Canada** (205–400 Catherine St., Ottawa, Ontario K2P 1C3, Canada, tel. 613/237–7884 or 800/633–5777, fax 613/237–7868, www.hostellingintl.ca). **Youth Hostel Association of England and Wales** (Trevelyan House, 8 St. Stephen's Hill, St. Albans, Hertfordshire AL1 2DY, U.K., tel. 0870/870–8808, fax 01727/844–126, www.yha.org.uk). **Australian Youth Hostel Association** (10 Mallett St., Camperdown, NSW 2050, Australia, tel. 02/9565–1699, fax 02/9565–1325, www.yha.com.au). **Youth**

Hostels Association of New Zealand (Box 436, Christchurch, New Zealand, tel. 03/379–9970, fax 03/365–4476, www.yha.org.nz).

HOTELS

Netherlands Reservation Center handles bookings for Amsterdam, as well as other cities in the Netherlands.

➤ RESERVATIONS: **Netherlands Reservation Center** (Postbus 404, 2260 AK, Leidschendam, tel. 070/419–5500, fax 070/419–5519 www.hotelres.nl).

➤ TOLL-FREE NUMBERS: **Best Western** (tel. 800/528–1234, www.bestwestern.com). **Choice** (tel. 800/221–2222, www. hotelchoice.com). **Hilton** (tel. 800/445–8667, www.hilton.com). **Holiday Inn** (tel. 800/465–4329, www.basshotels.com). **Inter-Continental** (tel. 800/327–0200, www.interconti.com). **Marriott** (tel. 800/228–9290, www.marriott.com). **Le Meridien** (tel. 800/543–4300, www.forte-hotels.com). **Radisson** (tel. 800/333–3333, www.radisson.com). **Renaissance Hotels & Resorts** (tel. 800/468–3571, www.renaissancehotels.com).

Mail & Shipping

➤ POST OFFICES: **Hoofd Postkantoor** (main post office; Singel 250, 1016 AB, Amsterdam, tel. 020/556–3381, fax 020/556–3382).

➤ MAJOR SERVICES: **DHL** (tel. 0800/0552, www.dhl.com). **Federal Express** (tel. 0800/022–2333, www.fedex.com). **TNT** (tel. 0800/1234, www.tnt.com). **United Parcel Service** (tel. 0800/099–1330, www.upc.com).

POSTAL RATES

Airmail letters up to 20 grams (⅔ ounce) cost Fl 1.60 (€0.75) to the United States or Canada, Fl 1.10 (€0.50) to the United Kingdom; postcards to the United States or Canada cost Fl 1 (€0.45), to the United Kingdom 80¢. Aerograms cost Fl 1.30 (€0.60).

SHIPPING PARCELS

Post offices have a large selection of pre-formed packages to send smaller items home, from protective bubble bags to boxes in various sizes. For larger packages it is probably more economical and practical to use the freight services of companies such as the post office arm TNT, or international services such as DHL, FedEx, and UPS.

Money Matters

Compared with other European capitals the cost of living in Amsterdam is fairly low, certainly cheaper than London or New York. Some sample prices will help you to gauge the expense: Half bottle of wine, Fl 25 (€11.35); glass of beer, Fl 3.50 (€1.50); cup of coffee, Fl 3 (€1.35); ham and cheese sandwich, Fl 5 (€2.70); 2-km (1-mi) taxi ride, Fl 12 (€5.45).

Prices throughout this guide are given for adults. Substantially reduced fees are almost always available for children, students, and senior citizens. For information on taxes, *see* Taxes, *below*.

ATMS

The *pinautomaat* (ATM) is as ubiquitous as at home, with 24-hour machines at almost every bank, as well as at strategic spots like train stations. Ask your bank or credit card company to provide you with a four-figure pincode for your checking account card and credit card. All major banks are members of the Cirrus and Plus networks, so you can also withdraw cash direct from your checking account at the "hole in the wall" for a small fee.

CREDIT & DEBIT CARDS

The two types of plastic are virtually the same. Both offer excellent, wholesale exchange rates. And both protect you against unauthorized use if the card is lost or stolen. Your liability is limited to $50, as long as you report the card missing. When you want to rent a car, though, you may still need a credit card. Although you can always *pay for your car with a debit card*, some agencies will not allow you to *reserve a car with one*.

Throughout this guide, the following abbreviations are used: **AE,** American Express; **DC,** Diners Club; **MC,** MasterCard; and **V,** Visa.

➤ REPORTING LOST CARDS: **American Express** (tel. 800/327–2177, 020/504–8666 in the Netherlands); **Diners Club** (tel. 800/234–6377, 020/654–5511 in the Netherlands); **MasterCard** (tel. 800/307–7309, 030/283–5555 in the Netherlands); and **Visa** (tel. 800/847–2911, 020/660–0611 in the Netherlands).

CURRENCY

The official monetary unit of the Netherlands is the guilder, which may be abbreviated as Dfl, Fl, F, Hfl, and occasionally as NLG. There are 100 cents in a guilder, and coins are minted in denominations of 5, 10, and 25 cents, and 1, 2½, and 5 guilders. Banknotes are printed in amounts of 10, 25, 50, 100, 250, and 1,000 guilders. Banknotes in denominations of more than Fl 100 are seldom seen, and some shops refuse to accept Fl 1,000 notes. Don't confuse the 1- and 2.5-guilder coins and the 5-guilder and 5-cent coins. The brightly colored bills have a code of raised dots that can be identified by touch.

In early 2001, the exchange rate for the guilder was Fl 2.20 to the Euro, Fl 1.28 to the Australian dollar, Fl 3.47 to the pound sterling, Fl 1.57 to the Canadian dollar, Fl 2.80 to the Irish punt, Fl 1.04 to the New Zealand dollar, Fl 0.30 to the South African rand, Fl 2.40 to the U.S. dollar. These rates fluctuate daily, so check them at the time of your departure.

The euro, or single European currency, was launched on January 1, 1999. The rates of conversion between the euro (which uses the symbol) and local currencies were irrevocably fixed at that time. At the moment the euro is mainly used for trade transactions. National bank notes and coins won't disappear until 2002, but in the meantime, dual pricing of goods and services will accustom people to the new currency before its eventual introduction as a physical entity. January 1, 2002, new euro banknotes and coins will be put into circulation, and the

196

old national currencies will be withdrawn. In some countries this will be a gradual process over a period of three months, while in others it will be a swifter transition, after which euro banknotes and coins alone will have legal tender status.

CURRENCY EXCHANGE

Foreign currency is not usually accepted. At most hotels you can exchange major foreign currencies for Dutch guilders, but for the most favorable rates **change money through banks.** Although ATM transaction fees may be higher abroad than at home, ATM rates are excellent because they are based on wholesale rates offered only by major banks. You won't do as well at exchange booths in airports or rail and bus stations, in hotels, in restaurants, or in stores. To avoid lines at airport exchange booths, **get a bit of local currency before you leave home.**

➤ Exchange Services: **International Currency Express** (tel. 888/ 278–6628 for orders, www.foreignmoney.com). **Thomas Cook Currency Services** (tel. 800/287–7362 for telephone orders and retail locations, www.us.thomascook.com).

➤ In Amsterdam: **GWK/Grenswisselkantoren** (Centraal Station, tel. 020/627–2731).

TRAVELER'S CHECKS

Do you need traveler's checks? It depends on where you're headed. If you're going to rural areas and small towns, go with cash; traveler's checks are best used in cities. Lost or stolen checks can usually be replaced within 24 hours. To ensure a speedy refund, buy your own traveler's checks—don't let someone else pay for them: irregularities like this can cause delays. The person who bought the checks should make the call to request a refund.

Packing

The best advice for a trip to Amsterdam in any season is to pack light, be flexible, bring an umbrella (and trench coat with a liner in winter), and always have a sweater or jacket available. For daytime wear and casual evenings, turtlenecks and flannel shirts are ideal for winter, alone or under a sweater, and cotton shirts with sleeves are perfect in summer. Blue jeans are popular and are even sometimes worn to the office; sweat suits, however, are never seen outside fitness centers. For women, high heels are nothing but trouble on the cobblestone streets of Amsterdam, and sneakers or running shoes are a dead giveaway that you are an American tourist; a better choice is a pair of dark-color walking shoes or low-heel pumps.

In your carry-on luggage, **pack an extra pair of eyeglasses or contact lenses** and **enough of any medication you take** to last the entire trip. You may also ask your doctor to write a spare prescription using the drug's generic name, since brand names may vary from country to country. In luggage to be checked, **never pack prescription drugs or valuables.** To avoid customs delays, carry medications in their original packaging. And don't forget to carry with you the addresses of offices that handle refunds of lost traveler's checks.

CHECKING LUGGAGE

How many carry-on bags you can bring with you is up to the airline. Most allow two, but not always, so make sure that everything you carry aboard will fit under your seat or in the overhead bin, and get to the gate early. Note that if you have a seat at the back of the plane, you'll probably board first, while the overhead bins are still empty.

If you are flying internationally, note that baggage allowances may be determined not by piece but by weight—generally 88 pounds (40 kilograms) in first class, 66 pounds (30 kilograms) in business class, and 44 pounds (20 kilograms) in economy.

Airline liability for baggage is limited to $1,250 per person on flights within the United States. On international flights it amounts to $9.07 per pound or $20 per kilogram for checked baggage (roughly $640 per 70-pound bag) and $400 per passenger for unchecked baggage. You can buy additional coverage at check-in for about $10 per $1,000 of coverage, but it excludes a rather extensive list of items, shown on your airline ticket.

Before departure, **itemize your bags' contents** and their worth, and label the bags with your name, address, and phone number. (If you use your home address, cover it so potential thieves can't see it readily.) Inside each bag, **pack a copy of your itinerary.** At check-in, **make sure that each bag is correctly tagged** with the destination airport's three-letter code. If your bags arrive damaged or fail to arrive at all, file a written report with the airline before leaving the airport.

Passports & Visas

The best time to apply for a passport or to renew is in fall and winter. Before any trip, check your passport's expiration date, and, if necessary, renew it as soon as possible. When traveling internationally, **carry your passport** even if you don't need one (it's always the best form of I.D.) and **make two photocopies of the data page** (one for someone at home and another for you, carried separately from your passport). If you lose your passport, promptly call the nearest embassy or consulate and the local police.

➤ PASSPORT OFFICES: **Australian Passport Office** (tel. 131–232, www.dfat.gov.au/passports). **Canadian Passport Office** (tel. 819/994–3500; 800/567–6868 in Canada, www.dfait-maeci.gc.ca/passport). **New Zealand Passport Office** (tel. 04/494–0700, www.passports.govt.nz). **London Passport Office** (tel. 0870/521–0410, www.ukpa.gov.uk) for fees and documentation requirements and to request an emergency passport. **U.S. National Passport Information Center** (tel. 900/225–5674; calls are 35¢ per minute for automated service, $1.05 per minute for operator service; www.travel.state.gov/npicinfo.html).

Rest Rooms

Public toilets are a rare commodity. At main railway stations there are usually facilities with attendants for a charge of Fl 0.50 (€0.25). There are *krullen* (curly canalside urinals) for men throughout the city, but women will have to head for a café or bar, where a kind employee may allow you to use the facilities, or they may demand that you buy a drink first.

Safety

Street violence is rare in Amsterdam, and handguns are illegal, so firearms are much less commonplace than in the United States. Most parts of the city are safe, night and day, but no matter how confidently streetwise you think you are, be wary of pickpockets and panhandlers of illicit drugs in the Red Light District.

Senior-Citizen Travel

To qualify for age-related discounts, **mention your senior-citizen status up front** when booking hotel reservations (not when checking out) and before you're seated in restaurants (not when paying the bill). When renting a car, ask about promotional car-rental discounts, which can be cheaper than senior-citizen rates.

The Radisson SAS hotel in Amsterdam offers a 25% reduction off the rack rate to senior citizens 65 and over. For other hotels, check on the availability of senior rates when you book.

➤ EDUCATIONAL PROGRAMS: **Elderhostel** (75 Federal St., 3rd floor, Boston, MA 02110, tel. 877/426–8056, fax 877/426–2166, www.elderhostel.org). **Interhostel** (University of New Hampshire, 6 Garrison Ave., Durham, NH 03824, tel. 603/862–1147 or 800/733–9753, fax 603/862–1113, www.learn.unh.edu).

➤ HOTEL INFORMATION: **Radisson SAS Hotels** (tel. 800/333–3333).

Sightseeing Tours

BY BIKE

From April through October, guided three-hour bike trips through the central area of Amsterdam are available from Yellow Bike. **Let's Go** tours (☞ Contact the VVV in Visitor Information, *below*) takes you out of the city-center by train before introducing you to the safer cycling of the surrounding countryside. Their tours include, in season, a Tulip Tour.

➤ BIKE TOUR OPERATORS: **Yellow Bike** (Nieuwezijds Kolk 29, tel. 020/620–6940).

BOAT TOURS

Canalbus, which makes six stops along two different routes between Centraal Station and the Rijksmuseum, costs Fl 27.75 (€12.60), including a ticket for the Rijksmuseum and reductions for other museums. Museumboot Rederij Lovers makes seven stops near 20 different museums. The cost is Fl 22 (€10) for a day ticket that entitles you to a 50% discount on admission to the museums.

The quickest, easiest way to get your bearings in Amsterdam is to take a 1–1½-hour canal-boat cruise, covering the harbor as well as the main canal district. There is a taped or live commentary available in four languages. There are also dinner and candlelight cruises. Excursion boats leave from piers in various locations in the city every 15 minutes from March to October, and every 30 minutes in winter. Most launches are moored in the inner harbor in front of Centraal Station. Fares are about Fl 12–Fl 15 (€5.45–€6.80).

➤ BOAT TOUR OPERATORS: **Canalbus** (Nieuwe Weteringschans 24, tel. 020/623–9886). **Museumboot Rederij Lovers** (Stationsplein 8, tel. 020/530–1090).

➤ CANAL CRUISE OPERATORS: **Holland International** (Prins Hendrikkade, opposite Centraal Station, tel. 020/622–7788). **Meyers Rondvaarten** (Damrak, quays 4–5, tel. 020/623–4208). **Rederij D'Amstel** (Nicolaas Witsenkade, opposite the Heineken

Brewery, tel. 020/626–5636). **Rederij Lovers** (Prins Hendrikkade 26, opposite Centraal Station, tel. 020/530–1090). **Rederij P. Kooij** (Rokin, near Spui, tel. 020/623–3810). **Rederij Noord/Zuid** (Stadhouderskade 25, opposite Parkhotel, tel. 020/679–1370). **Rederij Plas** (Damrak, quays 1–3, tel. 020/624–5406).

BUS TOURS

Afternoon bus tours of the city operate daily. Itineraries and prices vary: Fl 25–Fl 35 (€11.35–€15.90). Key Tours (☞ Travel Agencies, *below*) offers a three-hour city tour that includes a drive through the suburbs, and Lindbergh Excursions (☞ Travel Agencies, *below*) offers a 3½-hour tour, focusing on the central city and including a canal-boat cruise. However, it must be said that this city of narrow alleys and canals is not best appreciated from the window of a coach. Also, a number of visitors feel unhappy that part of some tours involves a visit to a diamond factory, where they feel pressured into listening to a sales pitch. The same bus companies operate scenic trips to attractions outside the city.

WALKING TOURS

The VVV (☞ Visitor Information, *below*) maintains lists of personal guides and guided walking tours for groups in and around Amsterdam and can advise you on making arrangements. The costs are from Fl 208 (€94.40) for a half day and Fl 333 (€151.10) for a full day. The tourist office also sells brochures outlining easy-to-follow self-guided theme tours of the central city.

Audio Tours allows you to wander at your own pace with their 2–3 hour cassette-tape tours (with a map just in case you lose track) for Fl 15 (€6.80) per tour, plus a Fl 100 (€45.40) returnable deposit. There are three different tours available.

➤ RESOURCES: **Audio Tours** (Oude Spiegelstraat 9, behind Dam Palace, tel. 020/421–5580).

Taxes

In the Netherlands a Value Added Tax (BTW/V.A.T.) of 19% is added to most purchases, such as clothing, souvenirs, and car fuel. Certain items (books among them) fall into a 6% band, as do restaurant meals. All hotels in the Netherlands charge the 6% tax, which is usually included in the quoted room price; in addition, city authorities impose a 1% "tourist tax."

VALUE-ADDED TAX

To get a V.A.T. refund you need to be a resident of a country outside the European Union (EU) and to have spent Fl 300 (€136.15) or more in the same shop on the same day. Provided that you personally carry the goods out of the EU within three months after the month of purchase, you may claim a refund as you leave the final EU country on your itinerary. The easiest way to do this is to **ask for a Global Refund Cheque** at the place of purchase. The service is available Europe-wide at 125,000 affiliated stores, which display a Tax Free Shopping sticker.

If you are leaving the EU via Schiphol Airport, you must present the goods and the Global Refund Cheque at customs for validation, as with all exports. After you have passed through passport control, you can get a cash refund directly at the ABN AMRO Bank in Terminal Lounges 2 and 3, or at any International Cash Refund Office worldwide. There is a commission for the service. Alternatively, you can mail your validated Global Refund Cheque to Global Refund Holland and your credit card account will be credited.

➤ **V.A.T. REFUNDS: Global Refund Holland** (Leidsevaartweg 99, 2106 AS, Heemstede, tel. 023/524–1909, fax 023/524–6164, www.globalrefund.com). In the U.S., **Global Refund** (707 Summer St., Stamford, CT 06901, tel. 800/566–9828, fax 203/674–8709, www.globalrefund.com).

Taxis

Taxi stands are at major squares and in front of large hotels, or call Taxicentrale, the central taxi dispatching office, or their sole competitor Taxi Direkt. Fares are Fl 5.60 (€2.55), plus Fl 2.80

(€1.25) per kilometer. A 5-km (3-mi) ride will cost about Fl 20 (€9.10).

▶ Taxi Companies: **Taxicentrale** (tel. 0900/677–7777, Fl 0.50 [€0.25] per minute). **Taxi Direkt** (tel. 0900–0724, Fl 0.22 [€0.10] per minute).

WATER TAXIS

A Water taxi provides a novel, if pricey, means of getting about. Water taxis can be hailed anytime you see one cruising the canals of the city, or called by telephone. The boats are miniature versions of the large sightseeing canal boats, and each carries up to eight passengers. The cost is Fl 90 for a half hour, including pick-up charge, with a charge of Fl 30 (€13.60) per 15-minute period thereafter. The rate is per ride, regardless of the number of passengers.

▶ Water Taxis: **Water Taxi** (tel. 020/530–1090).

Telephones

The **country code** for the Netherlands is 31. Numbers with 0800 or 0900 codes are generally information numbers; the former free, the latter a charged service. When dialing a Dutch number from abroad, drop the initial 0 from the local area code.

Dial 0900/8008 for **directory inquiries** within the Netherlands, 0900/8418 for numbers elsewhere. Both services cost about Fl 1.50 (€0.70) per minute. Operators speak English. The **area code for Amsterdam** is 020 (or 20 if you are calling from outside the Netherlands), and it is used only when you call from other parts of the Netherlands to Amsterdam. Within the immediate environs of any municipality you do not need to use an area code. To make a long-distance call within the Netherlands simply dial the area code and number. It is usually much cheaper to call direct, instead of using your international calling card, which will normally connect you via your home country.

To call outside the Netherlands, dial 00 followed by the country code, area code, and number. The country code is 1 for the

United States and Canada, 61 for Australia, 64 for New Zealand, and 44 for the United Kingdom.

LONG-DISTANCE SERVICES

AT&T, MCI, and Sprint access codes make calling long distance and internationally relatively convenient, but you may find the local access number blocked in many hotel rooms. First ask the hotel operator to connect you. If the hotel operator balks, ask for an international operator, or dial the international operator yourself. One way to improve your odds of getting connected to your long-distance carrier is to travel with more than one company's calling card (a hotel may block Sprint, for example, but not MCI). If all else fails, call from a pay phone.

➤ ACCESS CODES: **AT&T Direct** (tel. 0800/022–9111). **MCI WorldPhone** (tel. 0800/022–9122). **Sprint International Access** (tel. 0800/022–9119).

PUBLIC PHONES

Coin-operated telephones are becoming a rarity in the Netherlands, except in bars and cafés; public phones take credit cards and KPN (Dutch telephone company) phone cards, available from outlets including newsagents, tobacconists, and post offices for Fl 10 (€4.55) and up. Phones in railway stations require a Telfort phone card, available from ticket offices.

Time

The Netherlands is in the Central European Time (CET) zone, which is Greenwich Mean Time (GMT) plus one hour. CET moves forward one hour for summer time (the equivalent of daylight savings time in the United States) on the night of Saturday to Sunday on the last weekend in March, and goes back one hour on the last weekend in October.

Amsterdam is one hour ahead of London, nine hours ahead of Los Angeles, seven hours ahead of Chicago, and six hours ahead of New York. Going the other way, Amsterdam is nine hours behind Sydney.

Tipping

Service is included in the prices, though it is customary to round up to the nearest guilder or two on small bills, and add about 10% to restaurant and bar bills for good service. Give a doorman or concierge Fl 3 (€1.35) for calling a cab. Bellhops in first-class hotels should be tipped Fl 2 (€0.90) for each bag they carry. Hat-check attendants expect at least Fl 1 (€0.45), and washroom attendants get 50¢. Round up your taxi fare to the nearest Fl 5 (€2.25).

Train Travel to and from Amsterdam

The city has several substations, but all major Dutch national, as well as European international, trains arrive at and depart from Centraal Station. The station also houses the travel information office of NS/Nederlandse Spoorwegen (Dutch Railways) and their international rail office.

The modern, clean trains have first- and second-class coaches and no-smoking and smoking cars. Rail fares are based upon distance; there are one-way fares, day-return fares for same-day round-trip travel, and weekend return fares; bicycles may be carried aboard for a nominal fee. Children under 3 travel free, and up to three children under 11 can travel for just Fl 2.50 if they are accompanied by an adult.

➤ TRAIN INFORMATION: NS/Nederlandse Spoorwagen (Dutch Railways; tel. 0900/9292, Fl 0.75 (€0.35) per minute, for local and national service information; 0900/9296, Fl 0.50 (€0.25) per minute, for international).

TO AND FROM THE U.K.

The Eurostar high-speed train service whisks riders and their cars through the Eurotunnel ((☞ Car Travel, *above*) between London (Waterloo) and Brussels (Midi) in three and a quarter hours, and London (Waterloo) and Paris (Gare du Nord) in three hours. There are connecting services to Amsterdam running every hour, 6:30 am–8:30 pm, with a journey time of about three hours. For a higher price you can take the high-speed Thalys, reducing travel time to two and a half hours from Amsterdam Centraal Station to the Eurostar terminal in Brussels, and vice versa. Tickets for these services are available from NS Internationaal ticket counters at Dutch railway stations. Eurostar and Thalys tickets are available in the United Kingdom through Eurostar and Rail Europe respectively, and in North America through both Rail Europe and BritRail Travel. British Rail International runs two trains a day from London (Liverpool Street) to Amsterdam, and vice versa, with a journey time of seven and three quarters hours, transferring to the high-speed Stena HSS ferry from Harwich to Hook of Holland.

➤ SCHEDULE AND TICKET INFORMATION: **BritRail Travel** (tel. 800/677–8585 in the U.S., 800/555–2748 in Canada). **Eurostar** (tel. 0990/186–186 in the U.K., 0900/9296 in the Netherlands, 800/942–4866 in the U.S., 800/361–7245 in Canada). **Rail Europe** (tel. 800/942–4866 in the U.S. and Canada, 0990/848–848 in the U.K.). **Thalys** (tel. 0900/9228 in the Netherlands, costs Fl 0.50 [€0.25] per minute).

Travel Agencies

A good travel agent puts your needs first. Look for an agency that has been in business at least five years, emphasizes customer service, and has someone on staff who specializes in your destination. In addition, **make sure the agency belongs to a professional trade organization.** The American Society of Travel Agents (ASTA), with 27,000 agents in some 170 countries, is the largest and most influential in the field. Operating under the motto "Integrity in Travel," it maintains and enforces a strict code of ethics and will step in to help mediate any agent-client disputes if necessary. ASTA also maintains a Web site that includes a directory of agents.

➤ LOCAL AGENT REFERRALS: **American Society of Travel Agents** (ASTA; tel. 800/965–2782 24-hr hot line, fax 703/684–8319, www.astanet.com). **Association of British Travel Agents** (68–71 Newman St., London W1P 4AH, U.K., tel. 020/7637–2444, fax 020/7637–0713, www.abtanet.com). **Association of Canadian Travel Agents** (1729 Bank St., Suite 201, Ottawa, Ontario K1V 7Z5, Canada, tel. 613/237–3657, fax 613/521–0805). **Australian Federation of Travel Agents** (Level 3, 309 Pitt St., Sydney 2000, Australia, tel. 02/9264–3299, fax 02/9264–1085, www.afta.com.au). **Travel Agents' Association of New Zealand** (Box 1888, Wellington 10033, New Zealand, tel. 04/499–0104, fax 04/499–0827).

➤ AMSTERDAM AGENCIES: **American Express International** (Damrak 66, tel. 020/520–7777). **Thomas Cook** (Damrak 1, tel. 020/620–3236). **Holland International Travel Group** (Dam 6, tel. 020/622–2550). **Key Tours** (Dam 19, tel. 020/623–5051). **Lindbergh Excursions** (Damrak 26, tel. 020/622–2766). For student travel, **NBBS** (Rokin 38, tel. 020/624–0989).

Visitor Information

The VVV (Vereniging voor Vreemdelingenverkeer) offers tourist information and reservations services to travelers within Amsterdam. The Netherlands Board of Tourism offices outside the Netherlands have access to a data bank for special-interest travel, including specialized tours for senior citizens, gay and lesbian travelers, and travelers with disabilities.

➤ IN AMSTERDAM: The **VVV** (Spoor 2/Platform 2, Centraal Station; Stationsplein 10, opposite Centraal Station; Leidsestraat 106, near Leidseplein; Stadionplein; Schiphol Airport; tel. 0900/400–4040, Fl 1.05 per minute, weekdays 9–5, fax 020/625–2869).

➤ IN THE U.S.: The **Netherlands Board of Tourism** (355 Lexington Ave., 21st floor, New York, NY 10017, tel. 212/370–7360, fax 212/370–9507, www.goholland.com; P.O. Box 220079, Chicago, IL 60622, tel. 312/455–1601, fax 312/455–1602; 11101 Aviation Blvd., Suite 200, Los Angeles, CA 90045, tel. 310/348–9339, fax 310/348–9344. Nationwide brochure line tel. 888/464–6552).

➤ IN CANADA: The **Netherlands Board of Tourism** (25 Adelaide St. E, Suite 710, Toronto, Ontario M5C 1Y2, tel. 416/363–1577, fax 416/363–1470).

➤ IN THE U.K.: The **Netherlands Board of Tourism** (18 Buckingham Gate, London SW1E 6LD, tel. 020/7828–7900; 0906/871–7777 for 24-hour brochure line, costs 60p per minute, fax 020/7828–7941).

➤ U.S. GOVERNMENT ADVISORIES: **U.S. Department of State** (Overseas Citizens Services Office, Room 4811 N.S., 2201 C St. NW, Washington, DC 20520, tel. 202/647–5225 for interactive hot line, 301/946–4400 for computer bulletin board, fax 202/647–3000 for interactive hot line); enclose a self-addressed, stamped, business-size envelope.

Web Sites

Do check out the World Wide Web when you're planning your trip. You'll find everything from current weather forecasts to virtual tours of famous cities. Fodor's Web site, www.fodors.com, is a great place to start your on-line travels.

When to Go

The best times to visit Amsterdam are late spring—when the northern European days are long and the summer crowds have not yet filled the beaches, the highways, or the museums—and in fall.

Amsterdam's high season begins in late March to late April, when the tulips come up, and runs through October, when the Dutch celebrate their Autumn Holiday. June, July, and August are the most popular months with both international visitors and the Dutch themselves. The cultural season lasts from September to June, but there are special cultural festivals and events scheduled in summer months.

CLIMATE

Amsterdam has a mild maritime climate, with bright, clear summers and damp, overcast winters. The driest months are from February through May; the sunniest, May through August.

► FORECASTS: **Weather Channel Connection** (tel. 900/932–8437), 95¢ per minute from a Touch-Tone phone.

What follows are average daily maximum and minimum temperatures for Amsterdam.

AMSTERDAM

Jan.	40F	4C	May	61F	16C	Sept.	65F	18C
	34	1		50	10		56	13
Feb.	41F	5C	June	65F	18C	Oct.	56F	13C
	34	1		56	13		49	9
Mar.	47F	8C	July	70F	21C	Nov.	47F	8C
	38	3		59	15		41	5
Apr.	52F	11C	Aug.	68F	20C	Dec.	41F	5C
	43	6		59	15		36	2

INDEX

A

Akhnaton club, 139

Albert Cuypmarkt, 67

Allard Pierson Museum, 80, 84

Almshouses, 109

Al's Place, 45

Alto jazz club, 138

Ambassade, 160

American, 162

Amstel Botel, 170

Amstel Inter-Continental Hotel, 156

Amstel Taveerne, 136

Amsterdam, 99

Amsterdam School, 103

Amsterdams Historisch Museum, 80, 84

Amsterdams Marionetten Theater, 148

Amsterdamse Bos, 85

Anne Frankhuis, 105, 106

Annet Gelink Gallery, 144

April, 136

April's Exit, 136

Arena, 135

Arti en Amicitiae, 144

Artis Zoo, 93, 94–95

Atlas Hotel, 165

Avenue Hotel, 170

B

Balraj, 49

Bamboo Bar, 138

Beddington's, 52–53

Begijnhof, 80, 84, 86, 109

Bellevue Cinerama and Calypso, 145

Bep, 139

Beurs van Berlage, 105, 106–107, 146

Bierbrouwerij 't IJ, 132

Bimhuis club, 138

Bird, 59

Black Tulip, 167

Blake's, 157

Blauw aan de Wal, 56

Bloemenmarkt, 67

Bloemenveiling Aalsmeer, 115, 117

Bodega Keyzer, 53–54

Boekenmarkt, 67

Boerderij Meerzicht, 85

Bollenstreek Route (Bulb District Route), 115, 117

Boom Chicago cabaret, 133

Bosmuseum, 85

Bourbon Street Jazz & Blues Club, 138

Brasserie van Baerle, 54

Breitner, 46

Broodje van Kootje, 86

Brouwersgracht Canal, 105, 107

C

C&A department store, 64

Café Americain, 51

Café de Jaren, 134

Café de Reiger, 48–49, 133

Café Meander, 138

Café Restaurant Brinkman, 118

Caffe Esprit, 41, 86

Canal House, 160

Casablanca club, 138

Cash club, 135

Centraal Station, 105, 107–108

Christophe, 45–46

Ciel Bleu Bar, 134

Claes Claeszhofje, 109

Club Havana, 136

Cockring, 136

Collection D'Art, 144

Concertgebouw, 81, 86, 146

Conservatorium van Amsterdam, 146

D

D' Theeboom, 46–47

D'Vijff Vlieghen, 42

Dam Square, 80, 87

Damrak, 105, 108

Dantzig, 134

De Admiraal café, 132

De Appel, 144

De Balie, 145

De Belhamel, 42

De Bijenkorf, 64, 66

De Brakke Grond, 149

De Hoge Berg, 124

De Kersentuin, 54

De Klankspeeltuin, 149

De Koog, 126

De Kooning van Siam, 59

De Kroon, 134

De Melkweg club, 139

De Muy nature reserve, 126

De Oesterbar, 52

De Oude Kerk, 148

De Poort, 56

De Reiger café, 133

De Rode Kerk, 148

De Silvern Spieghel, 46

De Slufter nature reserve, 126

De Twee Zwaantjes café, 133

De Uitkijk, 145

De Waag, 121

Den Burg, 124–125

Dikker and Thijs Fenice Hotel, 162

Dim Sum Court, 55

Downtown, 136

Dynasty, 41

E

Ecomare nature center, 124

Eerste Klas, 60

Engelse Kirk, 86

Enkhuizen, 121–122

Escape club, 135

Espressobar "Puccini," 102

Excelsior, 58

F

Felix Meritis, 146

F. G. S. He Hwa Buddhist
Temple, 104

Fons Welters, 144

Fort De Schans, 125

Frans Hals Museum, 119

Frascati Theater, 149

Freddy's, 134

Friday Night Skate, 91

G

Gables and gable stones, 97

Galerie Espace and Metis, 144

Galerie Rob Jurka, 144

Goethe Institute, 145

Golden Palm Bar, 134

Golden Tulip Schiller, 172

Goodies, 47–48

Gouden Bocht, 81, 87

Grand Hotel Krasnapolsky, 169

Grand Sofitel Demeure
Amsterdam, 170–171

Greenhouse, 135

Grote Kerk, 118

Grote Markt, 118

Grote Vijver, 85

H

Hemelse Modder, 60–61

Hennes & Mauritz (H & M), 66

Het Gasthuys, 58

Het Koninklijk Paleis te
Amsterdam, 104, 108, 110

Hof en Huyser, 144

Holland Casino Amsterdam,
133–134

Hollandsche Schouwburg,
92–93, 95

Hoorn, 120–122

Hortus Botanicus, 92, 95

Hotel Aalders, 165–166

Hotel Acro, 166

Hotel Amsterdam, 169–170

Hotel Arena, 156–157

Hotel Armada, 161

Hotel Concert Inn, 164

Hotel de Compagnie, 173

Hotel de Filosoof, 166

Hotel de l'Europe, 171

Hotel De Lindeboom, 125

Hotel De Stadhouder, 153, 156

Hotel Estheréa, 159–160

Hotel Hestia, 165

Hotel New York, 161

Hotel Owl, 165

Hotel Rembrandt, 157

Hotel Sander, 166

Hotel Résidence Le Coin,
171–172

Hotel-Restaurant De Zeven
Provinciën, 125

Hotel Toren, 160–161

Hotel Vondel, 162–163

Hotel Washington, 168

Hotel Winston, 172

Humphreys, 44

213

I

In de Waag, 58
In de Wildeman café, 133
In 't Aepjen, 104
iT club, 135

J

Jan Luyken, 163
Japan Inn, 52
Jeugdtheater de Krakeling, 149
Joods Historisch Museum,
92, 96
Joseph Lam club, 138

K

Kalverstraat, 64
Kalvertoren, 66
Kamyin, 55
Kandinsky, 135
Kantjil en de Tijger, 47
Karthuizerhof, 109
Katwijk, 115
Kayaking, 123
Ketelhuis, 145
Keukenhof, 114–115, 117
Kindermuseum, 101–102
Kint & Co, 61
Kleine Komedie cabaret, 133
Koninklijk Theater Carré, 149
Koninklijke Wachtkamer,
107–108
Kriterion, 145
Kunsthandel M.L. De Boer, 144
KunstRAI, 142, 144

L

La Rive, 37, 40
La Vallade, 40
Land Van Walem, 45
Lanskroon, 86
Le Garage, 53
Le Montmartre club, 136, 138
Leidsestraat, 64
Lido Dinner Show, 133
L'Indochine, 41–42
Loerakker's, 144
Lonny's, 49
Lorreinen, 49
Lucius, 42, 44
Lux, 139
Luxembourg, 134

M

Maoz falafel, 99
Madame Tussaud Scenerama,
80, 87–88
Magna Plaza, 66
Maison de Bonneterie en
Pander, 66
Maison Descartes, 145
Maritiem en Jutters Museum, 125
Marks & Spencer, 66
Max Euweplein, 66
Mazzo, 135
Memphis Hotel, 163–164
Metz & Company, 66
Montelbaanstoren, 93, 96
Mozes en Aa[u]ronkerk, 93, 96
Museum Amstelkring, 94, 96

Museum het Rembrandthuis, 93, 96, 98

Museum van Loon, 81, 88

Museumwerf 't Kromhout, 93, 98

Museumzicht, 168

Muziekcentrum De IJsbreker, 146

Muziektheater/Stadhuis, 92, 98–99

N

Nederlands Filmmuseum, 90

Nederlands Instituut voor Mediakunst Montevideo, 144

Nederlands Scheepvaartmuseum, 93, 99

Nederlands Theatermuseum, 105, 110–111

Nemo Science & Technology Center, 93, 99–100

Niewe Kerk, 104, 111

Nieuwendijk mall, 64

Nieuwmarkt, 67, 93, 100

Nol café, 133

Noorderkerk, 148

Noordermarkt, 67

Noordwijk, 115

NZ Lounge, 139

O

Odeon club, 135

Okura Amsterdam, 153

Omega Hotel, 164

Oosterdok, 101

Other Side, 135

Oude Kerk, 94, 100–101

Oudeschild, 125

Oudheidkamer, 124–125

P

P. C. Hooftstraat, 64

Pancake Bakery, 106

Paradiso club, 136

Paradox, 135

Parks and gardens
Hortus Botanicus, 92, 95
Vondelpark, 81, 90

Pathé City Theatre, 145

Paul Andriesse, 144

Peek & Cloppenburg, 66

Pianeta Terra, 47

Plancius, 37

Portugees Israelitische Synagoge, 92, 101

Postzegelmarkt, 67

Pulitzer, 159

Q

Quentin England Hotel, 168–169

R

Rembrandthuis, 93, 96, 98

Rijksmuseum, 81, 88–89

Rokin, 64

Rooie Nelis café, 133

Rose's Cantina, 59–60

Round Blue Tea House, 90

S

Saarein (club), 138

Sama Sebo, 54–55

Sassenheim, 115

Sauna Deco, 131

Schreierstoren, 93, 101

Seven Bridges Hotel, 173

Seven One Seven, 159
Seymour Likely, 139
Seymour Likely Too, 136
Sint Andrieshofje, 109
Slewe, 144
Sluizer, 44
Small World Catering, 107
Smit Hotel, 169
Song Kwae, 59
Soup En Zo, 40–41
Stadhuis, 92, 98–99
Stadsschouwburg theater, 149
Stedelijk Museum, 81, 89
Stedelijk Museum Bureau
Amsterdam, 144–145
Supper Club, 139

T
't Smalle café, 133
't Swarte Schaep, 51–52
Teylers Museum, 119
Theatre Cosmic, 149
Theatre De Engelbak, 149
Tibet Restaurant, 55–56
Toro Hotel, 164–165
Toscanini, 51
Traanroier molen (windmill), 125
Tropeninstituut, 139, 146
Tropenmuseum, 93, 101–102
Tulip Inn Arthotel, 167
Turquoise, 48
Tuschinski theater, 145
Tweede Kamer, 135

U
Uilenberger Synagoge, 148
Utrechtsestraat, 64

V
Van Baerlestraat, 64
Van Brienenhofje, 109
Van Gogh Museum, 81, 89–90
Van Puffelen, 44
Vandemarkt, 40
Verzetsmuseum, 92, 102
Vive-la-Vie, 138
Vleeshal (meat market), 118
Vondelpark, 81, 90
Vroom & Dreesmann, 66

W
Waag (Weigh House), 100
Waalse Kerk, 148
Warner en Consorten, 147
Waterlooplein flea market, 67,
92, 102
Weichmann Hotel, 161–162
West Pacific, 136
Westergasfabriek, 145
Westerkerk, 105, 111
Westfries Museum, 121
Wildschut, 134
Wilhelmina-Dok, 61

Z
Zaanse Schans, 120–121, 122
Zeedijk, 94, 102, 104
Zevenkeurvorstenhofje, 109
Zuiderkerk, 93, 104
Zuiderzee Museum, 121–122

FODOR'S POCKET AMSTERDAM

EDITOR: Langdon Faust

Editorial Contributors: Barbara S. Krulik, Andrew May, Olivia Mollet

Editorial Production: Kristin Milavec

Maps: David Lindroth, *cartographer;* Bob Blake and Rebecca Baer, *map editors*

Design: Fabrizio La Rocca, *creative director;* Tigist Getachew, *art director;* Melanie Marin, *photo editor*

Production/Manufacturing: Yexenia Markland

Cover Photograph: © Fotostock b. v.

Second Edition

ISBN 0–679–00772–5

ISSN 1532–6837

IMPORTANT TIP

Although all prices, opening times, and other details in this book are based on information supplied to us at press time, changes occur all the time in the travel world, and Fodor's cannot accept responsibility for facts that become outdated or for inadvertent errors or omissions. So **always confirm information when it matters,** especially if you're making a detour to visit a specific place.

SPECIAL SALES

Fodor's Travel Publications are available at special discounts for bulk purchases for sales promotions or premiums. Special editions, including personalized covers, excerpts of existing guides, and corporate imprints, can be created in large quantities for special needs. For more information, contact your local bookseller or write to Special Markets, Fodor's Travel Publications, 280 Park Avenue, New York, NY 10017. Inquiries from Canada should be directed to your local Canadian bookseller or sent to Random House of Canada, Ltd., Marketing Department, 2775 Matheson Boulevard East, Mississauga, Ontario L4W 4P7. Inquiries from the United Kingdom should be sent to Fodor's Travel Publications, 20 Vauxhall Bridge Road, London SW1V 2SA, England.

PRINTED IN THE UNITED STATES OF AMERICA

10 9 8 7 6 5 4 3 2 1